The Enigma of Capital

The Enigma of Capital
and the Crises of Capitalism

DAVID HARVEY

OXFORD
UNIVERSITY PRESS

OXFORD
UNIVERSITY PRESS

Oxford University Press, Inc., publishes works that further
Oxford University's objective of excellence
in research, scholarship, and education.

Oxford   New York
Auckland   Cape Town   Dar es Salaam   Hong Kong   Karachi
Kuala Lumpur   Madrid   Melbourne   Mexico City   Nairobi
New Delhi   Shanghai   Taipei   Toronto

With offices in
Argentina   Austria   Brazil   Chile   Czech Republic   France   Greece
Guatemala   Hungary   Italy   Japan   Poland   Portugal   Singapore
South Korea   Switzerland   Thailand   Turkey   Ukraine   Vietnam

Published in North America in 2010
by Oxford University Press, Inc.
198 Madison Avenue, New York, NY 10016
www.oup.com

Published in the United Kingdom in 2010
by Profile Books Ltd.

First issued as an Oxford University Press paperback, 2011

Oxford is a registered trademark of Oxford University Press

Library of Congress Cataloging-in-Publication data is available

ISBN: 978-0-19-975871-5 (hardcover); 978-0-19-983684-0 (paperback)

9 8 7 6 5 4 3 2 1
Printed in the United States of America
on acid-free paper

Contents

Preamble

This book is about capital flow.

Capital is the lifeblood that flows through the body politic of all those societies we call capitalist, spreading out, sometimes as a trickle and other times as a flood, into every nook and cranny of the inhabited world. It is thanks to this flow that we, who live under capitalism, acquire our daily bread as well as our houses, cars, cell phones, shirts, shoes and all the other goods we need to support our daily life. By way of these flows the wealth is created from which the many services that support, entertain, educate, resuscitate or cleanse us are provided. By taxing this flow states augment their power, their military might and their capacity to ensure an adequate standard of life for their citizens. Interrupt, slow down or, even worse, suspend the flow and we encounter a crisis of capitalism in which daily life can no longer go on in the style to which we have become accustomed.

Understanding capital flow, its winding pathways and the strange logic of its behaviour is therefore crucial to our understanding of the conditions under which we live. In the early years of capitalism, political economists of all stripes struggled to understand these flows and a critical appreciation of how capitalism worked began to emerge. But in recent times we have veered away from the pursuit of such critical understanding. Instead, we build sophisticated mathematical models, endlessly analyse data, scrutinise spread sheets, dissect the detail and bury any conception of the systemic character of capital flow in a mass of papers, reports and predictions.

When Her Majesty Queen Elizabeth II asked the economists at

the London School of Economics in November 2008 how come they had not seen the current crisis coming (a question which was surely on everyone's lips but which only a feudal monarch could so simply pose and expect some answer), the economists had no ready response. Assembled together under the aegis of the British Academy, they could only confess in a collective letter to Her Majesty, after six months of study, rumination and deep consultation with key policy makers, that they had somehow lost sight of what they called 'systemic risks', that they, like everyone else, had been lost in a 'politics of denial'. But what was it that they were denying?

My early seventeenth-century namesake William Harvey (like me, born a 'Man of Kent') is generally credited with being the first person to show correctly and systemically how blood circulated through the human body. It was on this basis that medical research went on to establish how heart attacks and other ailments could seriously impair, if not terminate, the life force within the human body. When the blood flow stops the body dies. Our current medical understandings are, of course, far more sophisticated than Harvey could have imagined. Nevertheless, our knowledge still rests on the solid findings that he first laid out.

In trying to deal with serious tremors in the heart of the body politic, our economists, business leaders and political policy makers have, in the absence of any conception of the systemic nature of capital flow, either revived ancient practices or applied postmodern conceptions. On the one hand the international institutions and pedlars of credit continue to suck, leech-like, as much of the lifeblood as they can out of all the peoples of the world – no matter how impoverished – through so-called 'structural adjustment' programmes and all manner of other stratagems (such as suddenly doubling fees on our credit cards). On the other, the central bankers are flooding their economies and inflating the global body politic with excess liquidity in the hope that such emergency transfusions will cure a malady that calls for far more radical diagnosis and interventions.

In this book I attempt to restore some understanding of what the flow of capital is all about. If we can achieve a better understanding of the disruptions and destruction to which we are all now exposed, we might begin to know what to do about it.

David Harvey
New York, October 2009

1

The Disruption

Something ominous began to happen in the United States in 2006. The rate of foreclosures on housing in low income areas of older cities like Cleveland and Detroit suddenly leapt upwards. But officialdom and the media took no notice because the people affected were low income, mainly African-American, immigrant (Hispanics) or women single-headed households. African-Americans in particular had actually been experiencing difficulties with housing finance from the late 1990s onwards. Between 1998 and 2006, before the foreclosure crisis struck in earnest, they were estimated to have lost somewhere between $71 billion and $93 billion in asset values from engaging with so-called subprime loans on their housing. But nothing was done. Once again, as happened during the HIV/ AIDS pandemic that surged during the Reagan administration, the ultimate human and financial cost to society of not heeding clear warning signs because of collective lack of concern for, and prejudice against, those first in the firing line was to be incalculable.

It was only in mid-2007, when the foreclosure wave hit the white middle class in hitherto booming and significantly Republican urban and suburban areas in the US south (particularly Florida) and west (California, Arizona and Nevada), that officialdom started to take note and the mainstream press began to comment. New condominium and housing tract development (often in 'bedroom communities' or across peripheral urban zones) began to be affected. By the end of 2007, nearly 2 million people had lost their homes and 4 million more were thought to be in danger of foreclosure. Housing values plummeted almost everywhere across the US and many households found themselves owing more on their houses than they were worth. This set in motion a downward spiral of foreclosures that depressed housing values even further.

In Cleveland, it looked like a 'financial Katrina' had hit the city. Abandoned and boarded-up houses dominated the landscape in poor, mainly black neighbourhoods. In California, the streets of whole towns, like Stockton, were likewise lined with empty and abandoned houses, while in Florida and Las Vegas condominiums stood empty. Those who had been foreclosed upon had to find accommodation elsewhere: tent cities began to form in California and Florida. Elsewhere, families either doubled up with friends and relatives or turned cramped motel rooms into instant homes.

Those who stood behind the financing of this mortgage catastrophe initially appeared strangely unaffected. In January 2008, Wall Street bonuses added up to $32 billion, just a fraction less than the total in 2007. This was a remarkable reward for crashing the world's financial system. The losses of those at the bottom of the social pyramid roughly matched the extraordinary gains of the financiers at the top.

But by the autumn of 2008 the 'subprime mortgage crisis', as it came to be called, had led to the demise of all the major Wall Street investment banks, through change of status, forced mergers or bankruptcy. The day the investment bank Lehman Brothers went under – 15 September 2008 – was a defining moment. Global credit markets froze, as did most lending worldwide. As the venerable ex-chair of the Federal Reserve, Paul Volcker (who five years earlier, along with several other knowledgeable commentators, had predicted financial calamity if the US government did not force the banking system to reform its ways) noted, never before had things gone downhill 'quite so fast and quite so uniformly around the world'. The rest of the world, hitherto relatively immune (with the exception of the United Kingdom, where analogous problems in the housing market had earlier surfaced such that the government had been forced to nationalise a major lender, Northern Rock, early on), was dragged precipitously into the mire

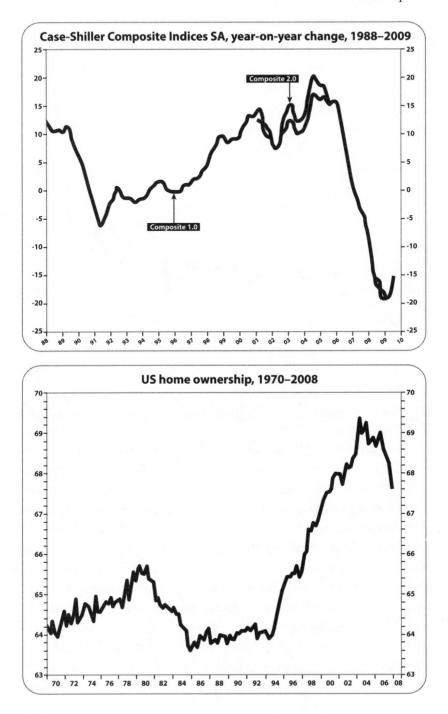

Case-Shiller Composite Indices SA, year-on-year change, 1988–2009

Composite 2.0

Composite 1.0

US home ownership, 1970–2008

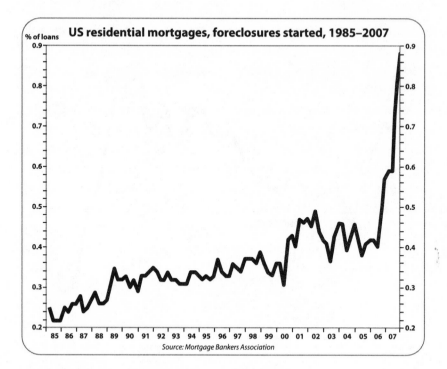

US residential mortgages, foreclosures started, 1985–2007
% of loans
Source: Mortgage Bankers Association

generated primarily by the US financial collapse. At the epicentre of the problem was the mountain of 'toxic' mortgage-backed securities held by banks or marketed to unsuspecting investors all around the world. Everyone had acted as if property prices could rise for ever.

By autumn 2008, near-fatal tremors had already spread outwards from banking to the major holders of mortgage debt. United States government-chartered mortgage institutions Fannie Mae and Freddie Mac had to be nationalised. Their shareholders were destroyed but the bondholders, including the Chinese Central Bank, remained protected. Unsuspecting investors across the world, from pension funds, small regional European banks and municipal governments from Norway to Florida, who had been lured into investing in pools of 'highly rated' securitised mortgages, found themselves holding worthless pieces of paper and unable to meet their obligations or pay their employees. To make matters worse, insurance giants like

4

AIG, which had insured the risky bets of US and international banks alike, had to be bailed out because of the huge claims they faced. Stock markets swooned as bank shares in particular became almost worthless; pension funds cracked under the strain; municipal budgets shrank; and panic spread throughout the financial system.

It became clearer and clearer that only a massive government bail-out could work to restore confidence in the financial system. The Federal Reserve reduced interest rates almost to zero. Shortly after Lehman's bankruptcy, a few Treasury officials and bankers including the Treasury Secretary, who was a past president of Goldman Sachs, and the present CEO of Goldman, emerged from a conference room with a three-page document demanding a $700 billion bail-out of the banking system while threatening Armageddon in the markets. It seemed like Wall Street had launched a financial coup against the government and the people of the United States. A few weeks later, with caveats here and there and a lot of rhetoric, Congress and then President George Bush caved in and the money was sent flooding off, without any controls whatsoever, to all those financial institutions deemed 'too big to fail'.

But credit markets remained frozen. A world that had earlier appeared to be 'awash with surplus liquidity' (as the IMF frequently reported) suddenly found itself short on cash and awash with surplus houses, surplus offices and shopping malls, surplus productive capacity and even more surplus labour than before.

By the end of 2008, all segments of the US economy were in deep trouble. Consumer confidence sagged, housing construction ceased, effective demand imploded, retail sales plunged, unemployment surged and stores and manufacturing plants closed down. Many traditional icons of US industry, such as General Motors, moved closer to bankruptcy, and a temporary bail-out of the Detroit auto companies had to be organised. The British economy was in equally serious difficulty, and the European Union was impacted, though unevenly, with Spain and Ireland along with several of the eastern European states which had recently joined the Union most seriously affected. Iceland, whose banks had speculated in these financial markets, went totally bankrupt.

By early 2009 the export-led industrialisation model that had generated such spectacular growth in east and south-east Asia was contracting at an alarming rate (many countries like Taiwan, China, South Korea and Japan saw their exports falling by 20 per cent or more in just two months). Global international trade fell by a third in a few months creating stresses in export-dominated economies such as those of Germany and Brazil. Raw material producers, who rode high in the summer of 2008, suddenly found prices plunging, bringing serious difficulties for oil-producing countries like Russia and Venezuela, as well as the Gulf States. Unemployment began to increase at a startling rate. Some 20 million people were suddenly unemployed in China and troubling reports of unrest surfaced. In the United States the ranks of the unemployed increased by over 5 million in a few months (again, heavily concentrated in African-American and Hispanic communities). In Spain the unemployment rate leapt to over 17 per cent.

By the spring of 2009, the International Monetary Fund was estimating that over $50 trillion in asset values worldwide (roughly equal to the value of one year's total global output of goods and services) had been destroyed. The US Federal Reserve estimated an $11 trillion loss of asset values for US households in 2008 alone. By then, also, the World Bank was predicting the first year of negative growth in the global economy since 1945.

This was, undoubtedly, the mother of all crises. Yet it must also be seen as the culmination of a pattern of financial crises that had become both more frequent and deeper over the years since the last big crisis of capitalism in the 1970s and early 1980s. The financial crisis that rocked east and south-east Asia in 1997–8 was huge and spin-offs into Russia (which defaulted on its debt in 1998) and then Argentina in 2001 (precipitating a total collapse that led to political instability, factory occupations and take-overs, spontaneous highway blockades and the formation of neighbourhood collectives) were local catastrophes. In

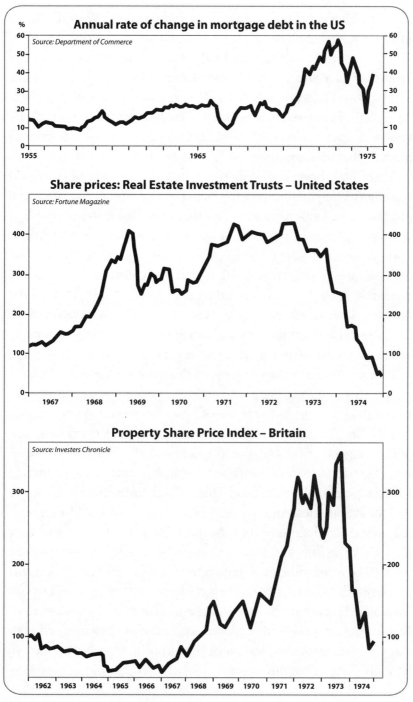

% **Annual rate of change in mortgage debt in the US**

Source: Department of Commerce

Share prices: Real Estate Investment Trusts – United States

Source: Fortune Magazine

Property Share Price Index – Britain

Source: Investers Chronicle

the United States the fall in 2001 of star companies like WorldCom and Enron, which were basically trading in financial instruments called derivatives, imitated the huge bankruptcy of the hedge fund Long Term Capital Management (whose management included two Nobel Prize winners in economics) in 1998. There were plenty of signs early on that all was not well in what became known as the 'shadow banking system' of over-the-counter financial trading and hence unregulated markets that had sprung up as if by magic after 1990.

There have been hundreds of financial crises around the world since 1973, compared to very few between 1945 and 1973; and several of these have been property- or urban-development-led. The first full-scale global crisis of capitalism in the post-Second World War era began in spring 1973, a full six months before the Arab oil embargo spiked oil prices. It originated in a global property market crash that brought down several banks and drastically affected not only the finances of municipal governments (like that of New York City, which went technically bankrupt in 1975 before ultimately being bailed out) but also state finances more generally. The Japanese boom of the 1980s ended with a collapse of the stock market and plunging land prices (still ongoing). The Swedish banking system had to be nationalised in 1992 in the midst of a Nordic crisis that also affected Norway and Finland, caused by excesses in the property markets. One of the triggers for the collapse in east and south-east Asia in 1997–8 was excessive urban development, fuelled by an inflow of foreign speculative capital, in Thailand, Hong Kong, Indonesia, South Korea and the Philippines. And the long-drawn-out commercial-property-led savings and loan crisis of 1984–92 in the United States saw more than 1,400 savings and loans companies and 1,860 banks go belly up at the cost of some $200 billion to US taxpayers (a situation that so exercised William Isaacs, then chairman of the Federal Deposit Insurance Corporation, that in 1987 he threatened the American Bankers Association with nationalisation unless they mended their ways). Crises associated with problems in property markets tend to be more long-lasting than the short sharp crises that occasionally

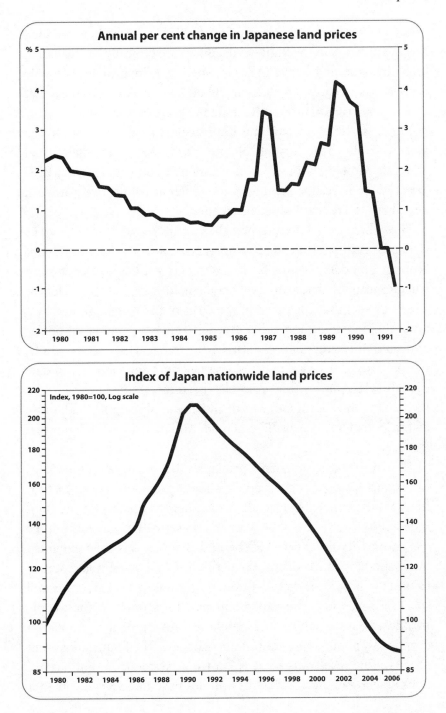

Annual per cent change in Japanese land prices

Index of Japan nationwide land prices

Index, 1980=100, Log scale

rock stock markets and banking directly. This is because, as we shall see, investments in the built environment are typically credit-based, high-risk and long in the making: when over-investment is finally revealed (as recently happened in Dubai) then the financial mess that takes many years to produce takes many years to unwind.

There is, therefore, nothing unprecedented, apart from its size and scope, about the current collapse. Nor is there anything unusual about its rootedness in urban development and property markets. There is, we have to conclude, some inherent connectivity at work here that requires careful reconstruction.

How, then, are we to interpret the current mess? Does this crisis signal, for example, the end of free market neoliberalism as a dominant economic model for capitalist development? The answer depends on what is meant by that word neoliberalism. My view is that it refers to a class project that coalesced in the crisis of the 1970s. Masked by a lot of rhetoric about individual freedom, liberty, personal responsibility and the virtues of privatisation, the free market and free trade, it legitimised draconian policies designed to restore and consolidate capitalist class power. This project has been successful, judging by the incredible centralisation of wealth and power observable in all those countries that took the neoliberal road. And there is no evidence that it is dead.

One of the basic pragmatic principles that emerged in the 1980s, for example, was that state power should protect financial institutions at all costs. This principle, which flew in the face of the non-interventionism that neoliberal theory prescribed, emerged from the New York City fiscal crisis of the mid-1970s. It was then extended internationally to Mexico in the debt crisis that shook that country to the core in 1982. Put crudely, the policy was: privatise profits and socialise risks; save the banks and put the screws on the people (in Mexico, for example, the standard of living of the population dropped by about a quarter in four years after the financial bail-out of 1982). The result was what is known as systemic 'moral hazard'. Banks behave badly because they do not have to be responsible for the negative consequences of high-risk behaviour. The current bank bail-out is this same old story, only bigger and this time centred in the United States.

In the same way that neoliberalism emerged as a response to the crisis of the 1970s, so the path being chosen today will define the character of capitalism's further evolution. Current policies propose to exit this crisis with a further consolidation and centralisation of capitalist class power. There are only four or five major banking institutions left in the United States, yet many on Wall Street are thriving right now. Lazard's, for example, which specialises in mergers and acquisitions, is making money hand over fist and Goldman Sachs (which many now jokingly refer to as 'Government Sachs', to mark its influence over Treasury policy) has been doing very well, thank you. Some rich folk are going to lose out, to be sure, but as Andrew Mellon (US banker, Secretary of the Treasury 1921–32) once famously remarked, 'In a crisis, assets return to their rightful owners' (i.e. him). And so it will be this time around unless an alternative political movement arises to stop it.

Financial crises serve to rationalise the irrationalities of capitalism. They typically lead to reconfigurations, new models of development, new spheres of investment and new forms of class power. This could all go wrong, politically. But the US political class has so far caved in to financial pragmatism and not touched the roots of the problem. President Obama's economic advisers are of the old school – Larry Summers, director of his National Economic Council, was Secretary of the Treasury in the Clinton administration when the fervour for deregulation of finance crested. Tim Geithner, Obama's Treasury Secretary, formerly head of the New York Federal Reserve, has intimate contacts with Wall Street. What might be called 'the Party of Wall Street' has immense influence within the Democratic Party as well as with the Republicans (Charles Schumer, the powerful Democratic senator from New York, has raised millions from Wall Street over the years, not only for his own political campaigns but for the Democratic Party as a whole).

Those who did the bidding of finance capital back in the Clinton years are now back at the helm. This does not mean they are not going to redesign the financial architecture, because they must. But who are they going to redesign it for? Will they nationalise the banks and turn them into instruments to serve the people? Will banks simply become, as influential voices even in the *Financial Times* now propose, regulated public utilities? I doubt it. Will the powers that currently hold sway seek merely to clean up the problem at popular expense and then give the banks back to the class interests that got us into the mess? This is almost certainly where we are headed unless a surge of political opposition dictates otherwise. Already what are called 'boutique investment banks' are rapidly forming on the margins of Wall Street, ready to step into the shoes of Lehman and Merrill Lynch. Meanwhile, the big banks that remain are stashing away funds to resume payment of the huge bonuses they paid before the crash.

———

Whether we can get out of this crisis in a different way depends very much upon the balance of class forces. It depends upon the degree to which the mass of the population rises up and says, 'Enough is enough, let's change this system.' The average Joe and Jean (even if he or she is a plumber) has good reason to say that. In the United States, for example, household incomes since the 1970s have generally stagnated in the midst of an immense accumulation of wealth by capitalist class interests. For the first time in US history, working people have failed to share in any of the gains from rising productivity. We have experienced thirty years of wage repression. Why and how did this come about?

One of the major barriers to sustained capital accumulation and the consolidation of capitalist class power back in the 1960s was labour. There were scarcities of labour in both Europe and the US. Labour was well organised, reasonably well paid and had political

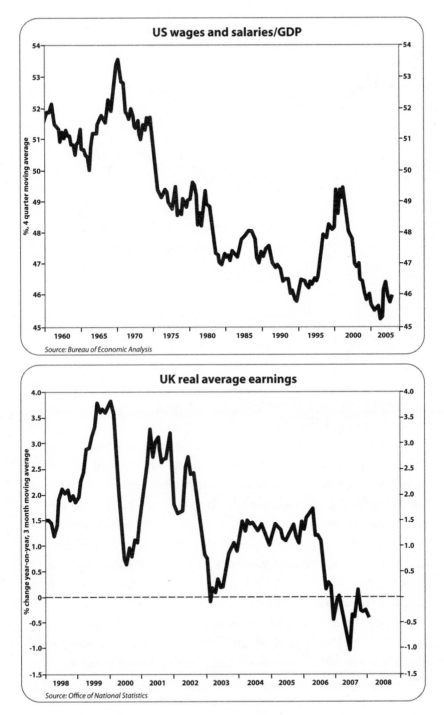

US wages and salaries/GDP

Source: Bureau of Economic Analysis

UK real average earnings

Source: Office of National Statistics

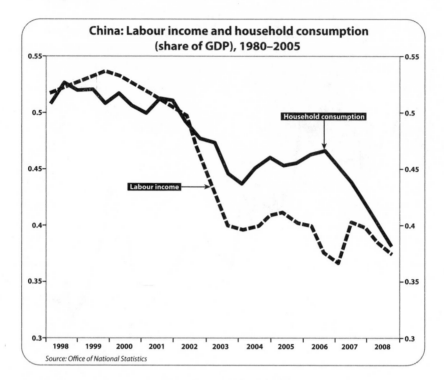

China: Labour income and household consumption (share of GDP), 1980–2005

Source: Office of National Statistics

clout. However, capital needed access to cheaper and more docile labour supplies. There were a number of ways to do that. One was to encourage immigration. The Immigration and Nationality Act of 1965, which abolished national-origin quotas, allowed US capital access to the global surplus population (before that only Europeans and Caucasians were privileged). In the late 1960s the French government was subsidising the import of labour from North Africa, the Germans were hauling in the Turks, the Swedes were bringing in the Yugoslavs, and the British were drawing upon inhabitants of their past empire.

Another way was to seek out labour-saving technologies, such as robotisation in automobile manufacture, which created unemployment. Some of that happened, but there was a lot of resistance from labour, who insisted upon productivity agreements. The consolidation of monopoly corporate power also weakened the drive to deploy new technologies because higher labour costs could be passed on to the consumer as higher prices (resulting in steady inflation). The 'Big Three' auto companies in Detroit typically did this. Their monopoly power was eventually broken when the Japanese and Germans invaded the US auto market in the 1980s. The return to conditions of greater competition, which became a vital policy objective in the 1970s, then forced labour-saving technologies. But this came fairly late in the game.

If all of that failed then there were people like Ronald Reagan, Margaret Thatcher and General Augusto Pinochet waiting in the wings, armed with neoliberal doctrine, prepared to use state power to crush organised labour. Pinochet and the Brazilian and Argentinian generals did so with military might, while both Reagan and Thatcher orchestrated confrontations with big labour, either directly in the case of Reagan's showdown with the air traffic controllers and Thatcher's fierce fight with the miners and the print unions, or indirectly through the creation of unemployment. Alan Budd, Thatcher's chief economic adviser, later admitted that 'the 1980s policies of attacking inflation by squeezing the economy and public spending were a cover to bash the workers', and so create an 'industrial reserve army' which would undermine the power of labour and permit capitalists to make easy profits ever after. In the US, unemployment surged, in the name of controlling inflation, to over 10 per cent by 1982. The result: wages stagnated. This was accompanied in the US by a politics of criminalisation and incarceration of the poor that had put more than 2 million behind bars by 2000.

Capital also had the option to go to where the surplus labour was. Rural women of the global south were incorporated into the workforce everywhere, from Barbados to Bangladesh, from Ciudad Juarez to Dongguan. The result was an increasing feminisation of the proletariat, the destruction of 'traditional' peasant systems of self-sufficient production and the feminisation of poverty worldwide. International trafficking of women into domestic slavery and prostitution surged as more than 2 billion people, increasingly crammed into the slums, favelas and ghettos of insalubrious cities, tried to get by on less than $2 a day.

Awash with surplus capital, US-based corporations actually began to offshore production in the mid-1960s, but this movement only gathered steam a decade later. Thereafter parts made almost anywhere in the world – preferably where labour and raw materials were cheaper – could be brought to the US and assembled for final sale close to the market. The 'global car' and the 'global television set' became a standard item by the 1980s. Capital now had access to the whole world's low-cost labour supplies. To top it all, the collapse of communism, dramatically in the ex-Soviet Bloc and gradually in China, then added some 2 billion people to the global wage labour force.

'Going global' was facilitated by a radical reorganisation of transport systems that reduced costs of movement. Containerisation – a key innovation – allowed parts made in Brazil to be assembled in cars made in Detroit. The new communications systems allowed the tight organisation of commodity chain production across the global space (knock-offs of Paris fashions could almost immediately be sent to Manhattan via the sweatshops of Hong Kong). Artificial barriers to trade such as tariffs and quotas were reduced. Above all, a new global financial architecture was created to facilitate the easy international flow of liquid money capital to wherever it could be used most profitably. The deregulation of finance that began in the late 1970s accelerated after 1986 and became unstoppable in the 1990s.

Labour availability is no problem now for capital, and it has not been so for the last twenty-five years. But disempowered labour means low wages, and impoverished workers do not constitute a vibrant market. Persistent wage repression therefore poses the problem of lack of demand for the expanding output of capitalist corporations. One barrier to capital accumulation – the labour question – is overcome at the expense of creating another – lack of a market. So how could this second barrier be circumvented?

———

The gap between what labour was earning and what it could spend was covered by the rise of the credit card industry and increasing indebtedness. In the US in 1980 the average household owed around $40,000 (in constant dollars) but now it's about $130,000 for every household, including mortgages. Household debt sky-rocketed, but this required that financial institutions both support and promote the debts of working people whose earnings were not increasing. This started with the steadily employed population, but by the late 1990s it had to go further because that market was exhausted. The market had to be extended to those with lower incomes. Political pressure was put on financial institutions like Fannie Mae and Freddie Mac to loosen the credit strings for everyone. Financial institutions, awash with credit, began to debt-finance people who had no steady income. If that had not happened, then who would have bought all the new houses and condominiums the debt-financed property developers were building? The demand problem was temporarily bridged with respect to housing by debt-financing the developers as well as the buyers. The financial institutions collectively controlled both the supply of, and demand for, housing!

The same story occurred with all forms of consumer credit on everything from automobiles and lawnmowers to loading down with Christmas gifts at Toys 'R' Us and Wal-Mart. All this indebtedness was obviously risky, but that could be taken care of by the wondrous financial innovations of securitisation that supposedly spread the risk around and even created the illusion that risk had disappeared. Fictitious financial capital took control and nobody wanted to stop it because everyone who mattered seemed to be making lots of money. In the US, political contributions from Wall Street soared. Remember Bill Clinton's famous rhetorical question as he took office? 'You mean to tell me that the success of the economic program and my re-election hinges on the Federal Reserve and a bunch of fucking bond traders?' Clinton was nothing if not a quick learner.

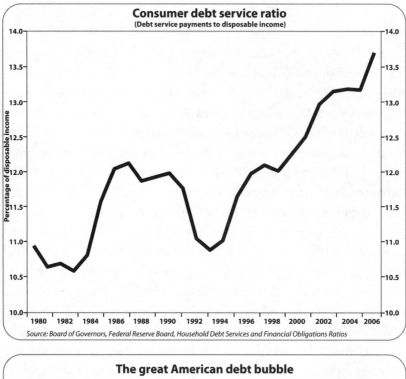

Consumer debt service ratio
(Debt service payments to disposable income)

Source: Board of Governors, Federal Reserve Board, Household Debt Services and Financial Obligations Ratios

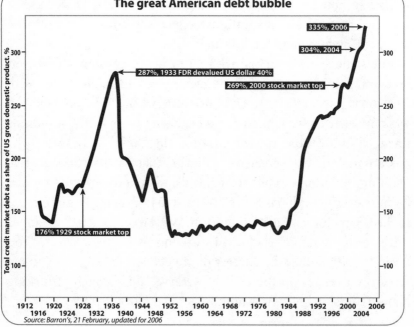

The great American debt bubble

176% 1929 stock market top
287%, 1933 FDR devalued US dollar 40%
269%, 2000 stock market top
304%, 2004
335%, 2006

Source: Barron's, 21 February, updated for 2006

But there was another way to solve the demand problem: the export of capital and the cultivation of new markets around the world. This solution, as old as capitalism itself, was pursued with added vigour from the 1970s onwards. The New York investment banks, then flush with surplus petrodollars from the Gulf States and desperate for new investment opportunities at a time when the potential for profitable investment within the United States was exhausted, took to lending massively to developing countries like Mexico, Brazil, Chile and even Poland. This happened because, as Walter Wriston, head of Citibank, put it, countries can't disappear – you always know where to find them in the event of difficulties.

Difficulties soon did arise, with the developing country debt crisis of the 1980s. More than forty countries, mainly in Latin America and Africa, had trouble repaying their debts when interest rates suddenly rose after 1979. Mexico threatened bankruptcy in 1982. The United States promptly reinvigorated the International Monetary Fund (IMF) (which the Reagan administration had sought to de-fund in 1981 in accordance with strict neoliberal principle) as the global disciplinarian that would ensure that the banks would get their money back and that the people would be forced to pay up. IMF 'structural adjustment programs', which mandated austerity in order to pay back the banks, thereafter proliferated around the world. The result was a rising tide of 'moral hazard' in international bank lending practices. For a while, this practice was hugely successful. On the twentieth anniversary of the Mexican bail-out the chief economists from Morgan Stanley hailed it as 'a factor that set the stage of increasing investor confidence worldwide and helped to ignite the growth market of the late 1990s, along with a strong US economic expansion'. Save the banks and screw the people worked wonders – for the bankers.

But for all of this to be truly effective, a globally interlinked system of financial markets needed to be constructed. Within the United States, the geographical constraints on banking were step by step removed from the late 1970s onwards. Hitherto, all banks, except for the investment banks – which were legally separated from deposit institutions – had been confined to operating within single states, while savings and loans companies financed mortgages which had been kept separate from deposit banks. But integrating global as well as national financial markets was also seen as vital and this led, in 1986, to the interlinking of global stock and financial trading markets. The 'Big Bang', as it was called at the time, linked London and New York and immediately thereafter all the world's major (and ultimately local) financial markets into one trading system. Thereafter, banks could operate freely across borders (by 2000 most of Mexico's banks were foreign-owned and HSBC was everywhere, fondly referring to itself as 'the people's local global bank'). This did not mean that there were no barriers to international capital flows, but technical and logistical barriers to global capital flow were certainly much diminished. Liquid money capital could more easily roam the world looking for locations where the rate of return was highest. The suspension in 1999 of the distinction between investment and deposit banking in the United States that had been in place since the Glass–Steagall Act of 1933 further integrated the banking system into one giant network of financial power.

But as the financial system went global, so competition between financial centres – chiefly London and New York – took its coercive toll. The branches of international banks such as Goldman Sachs, Deutsches Bank, UBS, RBS and HSBC internalised competition. If the regulatory regime in London was less strict than that of the US, then the branches in the City of London got the business rather than Wall Street. As lucrative business naturally flowed to wherever the regulatory regime was laxest, so the political pressure on the regulators to look the other way mounted. Michael Bloomberg, the mayor of New York City, commissioned a report in 2005 that concluded that excessive regulation in the US threatened his city's future financial industry. Everyone on Wall Street along with the 'Party of Wall Street' in Congress trumpeted these conclusions.

The successful politics of wage repression after 1980 allowed the rich to get much richer. We are told that this is good because the rich will invest in new activity (after first satisfying their competitive urge to indulge in conspicuous consumption, of course). Well, yes, they do invest, but not necessarily directly in production. Most of them prefer to invest in asset values. For example, they put money in the stock market and stock values go up, so they put even more money in the stock market, irrespective of how well the companies they invest in are actually doing. (Remember those predictions in the late 1990s of the Dow at 35,000?) The stock market has a Ponzi-like character even without the Bernie Madoffs of this world explicitly organising it so. The rich bid up all manner of asset values, including stocks, property, resources, oil and other commodity futures, as well as the art market. They also invest in cultural capital through sponsorship of museums and all manner of cultural activities (thus making the so-called 'cultural industries' a favoured strategy for urban economic development). When Lehman Brothers tanked, the Museum of Modern Art in New York lost a third of its sponsorship income.

Strange new markets arose, pioneered within what became known as the 'shadow banking' system, permitting investment in credit swaps, currency derivatives, and the like. The futures market embraced everything from trading in pollution rights to betting on the weather. These markets grew from almost nothing in 1990 to circulating nearly $250 trillion by 2005 (total global output was then only $45 trillion) and maybe as much as $600 trillion by 2008. Investors could now invest in derivatives of asset values and ultimately even in derivatives of insurance contracts on derivatives of asset values. This was the environment in which hedge funds flourished, with enormous profits for those who invested in them. Those who managed them amassed vast fortunes (more than $1 billion in personal remuneration a year for several of them in 2007 and 2008, and as much as $3 billion for the top earners).

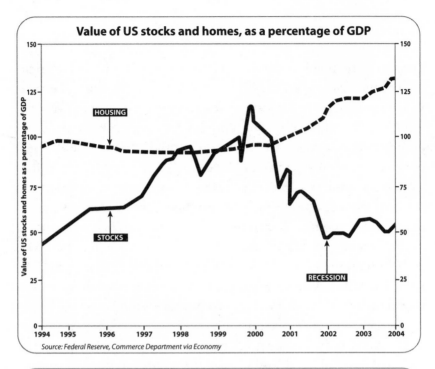

Value of US stocks and homes, as a percentage of GDP

HOUSING

STOCKS

RECESSION

Source: Federal Reserve, Commerce Department via Economy

The reversing origins of US corporate profits, 1950–2004

FINANCIALS

MANUFACTURING

Source: Ray Dalio, Bridgewater Associates

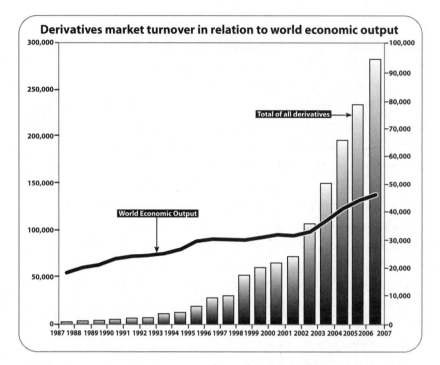

Derivatives market turnover in relation to world economic output

The trend towards investment in asset values became widespread. From the 1980s onwards reports have periodically surfaced suggesting that many large non-financial corporations were making more money out of their financial operations than they were out of making things. This was particularly true in the auto industry. These corporations were now run by accountants rather than by engineers and their financial divisions dealing in loans to consumers were highly profitable. General Motors Acceptance Corporation soon became one of the largest private holders of property mortgages, as well as a lucrative business financing car purchases. But even more importantly, the internal trading within a corporation producing auto parts all over the world allowed prices and profit statements to be manipulated across currencies in such a way as to both declare profits in those countries where the tax rates were lowest and to use currency fluctuations in themselves as a means to make monetary gains. But

23

to protect themselves, the corporations also had to hedge against potential losses from unexpected shifts in exchange rates.

The breakdown in 1973 of the fixed exchange rate system of the 1960s meant the rise of a more volatile currency exchange system. A new currency futures market formed in the 1970s in Chicago, but it was organised around strict rules of the game. Then, towards the end of the 1980s, to offset the volatility, the practice of hedging (placing two-way bets on currency futures) became more common. An 'over the counter' market arose outside of the regulatory framework and the rules of the exchanges. This was the kind of private initiative that led to an avalanche of new financial products in the 1990s – credit default swaps, currency derivatives, interest rate swaps, and all the rest of it – which constituted a totally unregulated shadow banking system in which many corporations became intense players. If this shadow system could operate in New York, then why not also in London, Frankfurt, Zurich and Singapore? And why confine the activity to banks? Enron was supposed to be about making and distributing energy but it increasingly merely traded in energy futures and when it went bankrupt in 2002 it was shown to be nothing but a derivatives trading company that had been caught out in high-risk markets.

Since what happened appears incredibly opaque, let me recount an anecdote to illustrate. Having had some success trading currency futures at investment bank Salomon Brothers, a 29-year-old, Andy Krieger, joined Bankers Trust in 1986 just in time for the 'Big Bang'. He found a neat mathematical way to price currency options to make a profit. He also managed to manipulate the market by placing an option to buy a large quantity of currency at some future date, which lured other traders into buying up the currency as fast as they could. Krieger would then sell them the currency he held at the rising price before cancelling his option. He lost the deposit on the option, of course, but made a mint on selling the currency at a profit. This could happen because the trades were 'over the counter' (i.e. privately contracted and outside of the framework of the Chicago currency futures exchange). Krieger placed huge bets – on one occasion betting the whole value of the New Zealand kiwi (which sent the New Zealand government into a panic) – and came off making around $250 million in 1987, a financial crisis year in which the rest of Bankers Trust made losses. He had, it appeared, single-handedly kept Bankers Trust afloat. He had been promised a 5 per cent bonus, which at that time would have been enormous, so when he received a mere $3 million he resigned 'on principle'. Meanwhile, Bankers Trust, without checking his figures, put out reassuring statements on its profitability to prop up its share value. Krieger's figures turned out to be faulty by $80 million but, rather than admit its profitability had disappeared, the bank tried all manner of 'creative' accounting practices to cover over the discrepancy before finally having to admit that it had been wrong.

Notice the elements in this tale. First, unregulated over-the-counter trading permits all sorts of financial innovation and shady practices which nevertheless make a lot of money. Secondly, the bank supports such practices, even though they don't understand them (the mathematics in particular), because they are often so profitable relative to their core business and hence improve share value. Third, creative accounting enters the picture, and fourth, the valuation of assets for accounting practices is extremely uncertain in volatile markets. Lastly, it was driven by a young trader who had skills that seemed to put him in a league of his own. Frank Partnoy, in his account of all this, *Infectious Greed* (published, it should be noted, in 2003), writes:

> In just a few years, regulators had lost what limited control they had over market intermediaries, market intermediaries had lost what limited control they had over corporate managers, and corporate managers had lost what limited control they had over employees. This loss-of-control daisy chain had led to exponential risk-taking at many companies, largely hidden from public view. Simply put, the appearance of control in financial markets was a fiction.

As asset values were bid up, so this carried over to the whole economy. Stocks were one thing but property was another. To buy or even live in Manhattan became all but impossible unless you went incredibly into debt. Everyone was caught up in this inflation of asset values, including the working classes whose incomes were not rising. If the super rich could do it, why not a working person who could buy into a house on easy credit terms and treat that house as a rising value ATM machine to cover health care emergencies, send the kids to college or take a Caribbean cruise?

But inflation in asset values cannot go on for ever. Now it is the turn of the United States to experience the pain of falling asset values, even as US policy makers do their level best to export their perverse version of capitalism to the rest of the world.

––––––

The relationship between representation and reality under capitalism has always been problematic. Debt relates to the future value of goods and services. This always involves a guess, which is then set by the interest rate, discounting into the future. The growth of debt since the 1970s relates to a key underlying problem which I call 'the capital surplus absorption problem'. Capitalists are always producing surpluses in the form of profit. They are then forced by competition to recapitalise and reinvest a part of that surplus in expansion. This requires that new profitable outlets be found.

The eminent British economist Angus Maddison has spent a lifetime trying to collate the data on the history of capital accumulation. In 1820, he calculates, the total output of goods and services in the capitalist world economy was worth $694 billion (in 1990 constant dollars). By 1913 it had risen to $2.7 trillion; by 1950, it was $5.3 trillion; in 1973 it stood at $16 trillion; and by 2003 nearly $41 trillion. The most recent World Bank Development Report of 2009 puts it (in current dollars) at $56.2 trillion, of which the US accounts for nearly $13.9 trillion. Throughout the history of capitalism, the

Growth of GDP: The world and major regions, 1950–2030						
	Levels in billion 1990 PPP dollars				Average annual rate of change	
	1950	1973	1990	2003	2030	1990–2003 2003–30
W. Europe	1,396	4,097	6,033	7,857	12,556	2.05 1.75
USA	1,456	3,537	5,803	8,431	16,662	2.91 2.56
Other W.O.	180	522	862	1,277	2,414	3.07 2.39
Japan	161	1,243	2,321	2,699	3,488	1.17 0.95
'RICH'	**3,193**	**9,399**	**15,019**	**20,264**	**35,120**	**2.33 2.06**
E. Europe	185	551	663	786	1,269	1.33 1.79
Russia	315	872	1,151	914	2,017	-1.76 2.98
Other f.USSR	199	641	837	638	1,222	-2.17 2.43
Latin America	416	1,389	2,240	3,132	6,074	2.61 2.48
China	245	739	2,124	6,188	22,983	8.56 4.98
India	222	495	1,098	2,267	10,074	5.73 5.68
Other Asia	363	1,387	3,099	5,401	14,884	4.36 3.83
Africa	203	550	905	1,322	2,937	2.96 3.00
'REST'	**2,148**	**6,624**	**12,117**	**20,648**	**61,460**	**4.19 4.12**
WORLD	**5,341**	**16,022**	**27,136**	**40,913**	**96,580**	**3.21 3.23**

actual compound rate of growth has been close to 2.25 per cent per annum (negative in the 1930s and much higher – nearly 5 per cent – in the period 1945–73). The current consensus among economists and within the financial press is that a 'healthy' capitalist economy, in which most capitalists make a reasonable profit, expands at 3 per cent per annum. Grow less than that and the economy is deemed sluggish. Get below 1 per cent and the language of recession and crisis erupts (many capitalists make no profit).

British Prime Minister Gordon Brown, in a fit of unwarranted optimism, argued in late autumn 2009 that we could look forward to a further doubling of the world economy over the next twenty years. Obama also hopes we will be back to 3 per cent 'normal' growth by 2011. If so, there will be over $100 trillion in the global economy by 2030. Profitable outlets would then have to be found for an extra $3 trillion investment. That is a very tall order.

Think of it this way. When capitalism was made up of activity within a fifty-mile radius around Manchester and Birmingham in England

and a few other hotspots in 1750, then seemingly endless capital accumulation at a compound rate of 3 per cent posed no big problem. But right now think of endless compound growth in relation not only to everything that is going on in North America, Oceania and Europe, but also east and south-east Asia as well as much of India and the Middle East, Latin America and significant areas of Africa. The task of keeping capitalism going at this compound rate is nothing if not daunting. But why does 3 per cent growth presuppose 3 per cent reinvestment? That is a conundrum that needs to be addressed. (Stay tuned!)

There has been a serious underlying problem, particularly since the crisis of 1973–82, about how to absorb greater and greater amounts of capital surplus in the production of goods and services. During these past years, monetary authorities such as the International Monetary Fund have frequently commented that 'the world is awash with surplus liquidity', that is, there is an increasing mass of money looking for something profitable to engage in. Back in the crisis of the 1970s vast surpluses of dollars piled up in the Gulf States as a result of the hike in oil prices. These were then recycled into the global economy via the New York investment banks which lent big time to developing countries, setting the stage for the developing world debt crisis of the 1980s.

Less and less of the surplus capital has been absorbed in production (in spite of everything that has happened in China) because global profit margins began to fall after a brief revival in the 1980s. In a desperate attempt to find more places to put the surplus capital, a vast wave of privatisation swept around the world carried on the backs of the dogma that state-run enterprises are by definition inefficient and lax and that the only way to improve their performance is to pass them over to the private sector. The dogma does not stand up to any detailed scrutiny. Some state-run enterprises are indeed inefficient, but some are not. Travel the French train network and compare it to the pathetically privatised US and British systems. And nothing could possibly be more inefficient and profligate than the privately insured health care system in the United States (Medicare, the state-run segment, has far lower overhead costs). No matter. Industries run by the state, so the mantra went, had to be opened up to private capital which had nowhere else to go, and public utilities like water, electricity, telecommunications and transportation – to say nothing of public housing and public education and health care – all had to be opened up to the blessings of private enterprise and market economics. In some instances there may have been gains in efficiency, but in others not. What did become obvious, however, was that the entrepreneurs who took over these public assets, usually at a discounted rate, quickly became billionaires. Mexican Carlos Slim Helú, rated the third richest man in the world by *Forbes* magazine in 2009, got his big boost with the privatisation of Mexico's telecommunications in the early 1990s. This wave of privatisation in a country riddled with poverty catapulted several Mexicans on to the *Forbes* wealthiest list in short order. Shock market therapy in Russia put seven oligarchs in control of nearly half the economy within a few years (Putin has been fighting with them ever since).

As more surplus capital went into production during the 1980s, particularly in China, heightened competition between producers started to put downward pressure on prices (as seen in the Wal-Mart phenomenon of ever-lower prices for US consumers). Profits began to fall after 1990 or so in spite of an abundance of low-wage labour. Low wages and low profits are a peculiar combination. As a result, more and more money went into speculation on asset values because that was where the profits were to be had. Why invest in low-profit production when you can borrow in Japan at a zero rate of interest and invest in London at 7 per cent while hedging your bets on a possible deleterious shift in the yen–sterling exchange rate? And in any case, it was right around this time that the debt explosion and the new derivatives markets took off, which, along with the infamous dot.com internet bubble, sucked up vast amounts of surplus capital. Who needed to bother with investing in production when all this was going on? This was the moment when the financialisation of capitalism's crisis tendencies truly began.

Three per cent growth for ever is running into serious constraints. There are environmental constraints, market constraints, profitability constraints, spatial constraints (only substantial zones of Africa, though thoroughly ravaged by exploitation of their natural resources, along with remote usually interior regions of Asia and Latin America, have yet to be fully colonised by capital accumulation).

The turn to financialisation since 1973 was one born of necessity. It offered a way of dealing with the surplus absorption problem. But where was the surplus cash, the surplus liquidity, to come from? By the 1990s the answer was clear: increased leverage. Banks typically lend, say, three times the value of their deposits on the theory that depositors will never all cash out at the same time. When a bank run does occur the bank will almost certainly have to close its doors because it will never have enough cash in hand to cover its obligations. From the 1990s on, the banks upped this debt–deposit ratio, often lending to each other. Banking became more indebted than any other sector of the economy. By 2005 the leveraging ratio went as high as 30 to 1. No wonder the world appeared to be awash with surplus liquidity. Surplus fictitious capital created within the banking system was absorbing the surplus! It was almost as if the banking community had retired into the penthouse of capitalism where they manufactured oodles of money by trading and leveraging among themselves without any mind whatsoever for what the working people living in the basement were doing.

But when a couple of banks got into trouble, trust between banks eroded and fictitious leveraged liquidity disappeared. De-leveraging began, sparking the massive losses and devaluations of bank capital. It then became clear to those in the basement what the inhabitants of the penthouse had been up to over the preceding twenty years.

Government policies have exacerbated rather than assuaged the problem. The term 'national bail-out' is inaccurate. Taxpayers are simply bailing out the banks, the capitalist class, forgiving them their debts, their transgressions, and only theirs. The money goes to the banks but so far in the US not to the homeowners who have been foreclosed upon or to the population at large. And the banks are using the money, not to lend to anybody but to reduce their leveraging and to buy other banks. They are busy consolidating their power. This unequal treatment has prompted a surge of populist political anger from those living in the basement against the financial institutions, even as the right wing and many in the media castigate irresponsible and feckless homeowners who bit off more than they could chew. Tepid measures to help the people, far too late, are then proposed to fend off what could be a serious legitimation crisis for the future of capitalist-class ruling power. Can we return to the credit-fuelled economy once the banks start lending again? If not, why not?

———

The last thirty years have seen a dramatic reconfiguration of the geography of production and the location of politico-economic power. At the end of the Second World War it was well understood that inter-capitalist competition and state protectionism had played an important role in the rivalries that had led to war. If peace and prosperity were to be achieved and maintained, then a more open and secure framework for international political negotiation and trade, a framework from which all could in principle benefit, had to be created. The leading capitalist power of the time, the United States, used its dominant position to help create, along with its main allies, a new framework for the global order. It sought decolonisation and the dismantling of former empires (British, French, Dutch, etc.) and brokered the birth of the United Nations and the Bretton Woods Agreement of 1944 which defined rules of international trade. When the Cold War broke out, the US used its military might to offer ('sell') protection to all those who chose to align themselves with the non-communist world.

The United States, in short, assumed the position of a hegemonic power within the non-communist world. It led a global alliance to keep as much of the world as possible open for capital surplus absorption. It pursued its own agenda while seeming to act for the universal good. The support the US offered to stimulate the capitalist recovery in Europe and Japan immediately after the Second World War was an example of such a strategy. It ruled by a mix of coercion and consent.

At the Bretton Woods conference of 1944, the British negotiator, the renowned economist John Maynard Keynes, had sought a global currency unit outside of any one nation's control. The US rejected this idea, insisting that the US dollar play that role, backed by a fixed exchange rate of the dollar against gold. All other currencies would then fix their exchange rate against the dollar to facilitate global trade. Obviously there was no need for any currency futures market because the exchange rate in six months' time was known, barring, of course, the occasional catastrophic devaluation. Financial crises – as opposed to crises of overproduction of the sort that produced severe downturns in 1958 and 1966 – were rare under this system. The powers of finance capital, though important, were circumscribed and reasonably transparent.

This system worked well, as long as the US refrained from using its power to print dollars in a self-serving way. However, the war in Vietnam and the 'Great Society' anti-poverty programmes of the 1960s (a strategy of 'guns *and* butter', as it was said at the time) led to a crisis of the dollar after 1968 or so. It was around this time also that US corporations began to take their surplus capital abroad. Surplus dollars, outside of US control, were accumulating within the European banking system. Belief in the fixed exchange rate of the dollar against gold began to erode. But what was to replace it?

Keynes' idea of a neutral global currency in the form of 'special drawing rights', based on the value of five major currencies and managed by the IMF, was revived in 1969. But this threatened US hegemony. A more acceptable solution to the US, worked out in a series of complicated international accords between 1968 and 1973, was for the fixed exchange rate with gold to be abandoned. All the major currencies of the world would then float against the dollar.

While this introduced both flexibility and volatility into the international trading system, the global reserve currency remained under US control.

The effect was to displace one challenge to US hegemony by another. If the dollar was to remain strong, the US productive economy had to perform as well as, if not better than, its rivals. By the 1980s it was clear that the economies of Japan and West Germany were way ahead of the US in terms of productivity and efficiency and that there were other competitive threats lurking in the wings. The US could not revert to protectionism. If anything, it had to take the lead in pushing for ever freer international trade as a means for capital surplus absorption. The US simply had to compete. Capitalism, which had developed earlier along monopolistic lines within nation state frameworks, became far more internationally competitive (witness the sudden invasion of the US auto market by Japanese and German car makers). Finance capital, both internally within the US and internationally, had to move to the fore to allocate surplus capital to wherever the profit rate was highest.

In many industries that turned out not to be in the United States, and especially not in the traditional centres of production in the north-east and the mid-west, but in the west and the south. The result was the wrenching and relentless reorganisation and relocation of production throughout the world. Deindustrialisation of older production centres occurred everywhere from Pittsburgh's, Sheffield's and Essen's steel industry to Mumbai's textile industry. This was paralleled by an astonishing spurt in the industrialisation of entirely new spaces in the global economy, particularly those with specific resource or organisational advantages – Taiwan, South Korea, Bangladesh and the special production zones such as Mexico's maquiladoras (tax-free assembly plants) or the export platforms created in China's Pearl River delta. Global shifts in production capacity accompanied by highly competitive technological innovations, many of which were labour-saving, contributed further to the disciplining of global labour.

The United States still retained immense financial power, even as it lost its earlier dominance (though not significance) in the realm of production. Increasingly, the US relied upon the extraction of rents, either on the basis of its advantages in technological and financial innovation or from intellectual property rights. But this meant that finance should not be burdened by excessive regulation.

The crash of the US financial sector in 2008–9 has jeopardised US hegemony. The ability of the US to launch a go-it-alone debt-financed recovery plan is limited politically by staunch conservative opposition at home as well as by the huge debt-overhang accumulated from the 1990s on. The US has been borrowing at the rate of around $2 billion a day for several years now and while the lenders – such as Chinese and other East Asian Central banks along with those of the Gulf States – have so far kept lending because the US economy is far too big to fail, the increasing power of the lenders over US policy is palpable. Meanwhile, the position of the dollar as the global reserve currency is threatened. The Chinese have resurrected Keynes' original suggestion and urged the creation of a global currency of special drawing rights to be managed by a presumably democratised IMF (in which the Chinese would have an important voice). This threatens US financial hegemony.

The end of the Cold War has also rendered military protection against the communist menace irrelevant, even as the ex-Soviet Bloc countries, along with China and Vietnam by very different paths, have become integrated into the global capitalist economic system. While this creates new opportunities for surplus absorption, it also poses the problem of accelerating surplus creation. Attempts to mobilise the rest of the world under the US military umbrella for protection against another enemy – the so-called War on Terror – have not succeeded.

It is in this context that we have to read the delphic estimates of the US National Intelligence Council, published shortly after Obama's election, on what the world will be like in 2025. Perhaps for the first time, an official US body has predicted that by then the United States, while still a powerful player in world affairs, will no longer be the dominant player. The world will be multi-polar and less centred, while the significance of non-state actors (from terrorist organisations to NGOs) will increase. Above all, 'the unprecedented shift in relative wealth and economic power roughly from west to east now under way will continue'.

This 'unprecedented shift' has reversed the long-standing drain of wealth from east, south-east and south Asia to Europe and North America that has been occurring since the eighteenth century – a drain that Adam Smith noted with regret in *The Wealth of Nations*. The rise of Japan in the 1960s, followed by South Korea, Taiwan, Singapore and Hong Kong in the 1970s, and then the rapid growth of China after 1980, later accompanied by industrialisation spurts in Indonesia, India, Vietnam, Thailand and Malaysia during the 1990s, has altered the centre of gravity of capitalist development, although it has not done so smoothly. The east and south-east Asian financial crisis of 1997–8 saw wealth flow briefly but strongly back towards Wall Street and the European and Japanese banks.

If crises are moments of radical reconfigurations in capitalist development, then the fact that the United States is having to deficit-finance its way out of its financial difficulties on such a huge scale and that the deficits are largely being covered by those countries with saved surpluses – Japan, China, South Korea, Taiwan and the Gulf States – suggests this may be the occasion for such a shift. It is even possible to interpret the current difficulties in the US and UK as payback for what Wall Street and the City of London did to east and south-east Asia in 1997–8.

Tectonic shifts of this sort have occurred before, as described at length in Giovanni Arrighi's 1994 book *The Long Twentieth Century*. There is, he notes, a clear pattern in which periods of financialisation precede a shift in hegemony. To accommodate endless accumulation, hegemony moves from smaller (e.g. Venice) to larger (e.g. the Netherlands, Britain and then the United States) political entities over time. Hegemony typically lies with that political entity within which much of the surplus is produced (or to which much of the surplus flows in the form of tribute or imperialist extractions). With total global output standing at $56.2 trillion in 2008, the US share of $13.9 trillion still made it the controlling shareholder in global capitalism, able to call the shots with respect to global policies (as it does in its role as the chief shareholder in international institutions such as the World Bank and the IMF).

But the map of the world's productive activity and wealth accumulation looks radically different today from the way it was in 1970. Asia has caught up fast. Small Chinese villages like Shenzhen and Dongguan, close to Hong Kong, have become multimillion cities and production powerhouses overnight. Much of the global surplus has been absorbed in the production of these new spaces of capitalist activity as well as in the infrastructures required to facilitate their increasing volume of international trade (e.g. airports and container ports). The specific spaces into which activity has moved were not given in advance, but determined by a whole host of contingent and local factors, depending in part on so-called 'natural' as well as human resources and locational advantages (such as northern Mexico's proximity to the US market). The specifics of state policies (such as investment in infrastructures, subsidies for investment, policies towards labour or the setting up of the 'maquila' zone legislation in Mexico and the 'special economic zones' designated after 1980 in China) have also played an important role.

The geography of this development and of the subsequent crisis has been uneven. Those countries that had been most profligate in promoting the housing bubble – the United States, Britain, Ireland and Spain – were the initial epicentres of the crisis but there were plenty of pockets elsewhere. The financial epicentres were New York and London, which had shared the lead in slicing, dicing and securitising housing mortgages and other forms of debt, and in constructing the financial instruments (chiefly collateralised debt obligations and special investment vehicles) for marketing and trading this debt along with the secondary mechanisms for insuring, hedging and swapping it. And the financial architecture that arose after the 'Big Bang' unification of global financial markets in 1986 meant that failures in London and New York were immediately felt everywhere else. This was, after all, the financial system that had allowed a back office trader in Singapore, Nicholas Leeson, to trade on the Tokyo market in such a way as to bankrupt the venerable London-based Barings Bank in 1995. This was why the shock delivered to the global financial system by the Lehman bankruptcy was so instantaneous and so deep.

The collapse of credit markets had, however, a differential impact according to the degree to which economic activity depended on them. Iceland, which had assumed the role of a speculative credit and banking entrepreneur, lost almost all of its asset wealth in a matter of weeks, leaving investors (many in Britain) with immense losses and its government in disarray. Many countries in eastern Europe that had recently joined the European Union and borrowed heavily could not roll over their debts and faced bankruptcy (the Latvian government collapsed).

On the other hand, those countries that had not fully integrated their financial system into the global network, like China and India, were better protected. And, as consumers drew back, those countries like the US and UK with huge household debt relative to income, were differentially hit, as were those countries, like the US again, that had the least generous social protections against rising unemployment. (European countries generally were much better off in this regard and therefore did not need to respond with extra stimulus packages). Those countries which relied heavily upon the US as a primary export market, particularly in east and south-east Asia, were ultimately pulled down, as were their stock markets, while raw material and commodity producers, which were riding high in early 2008 and considered themselves immune to the crisis, suddenly found themselves in serious difficulties as commodity and raw material prices plunged in the second half of 2008. Oil prices, which had risen to near $150 a barrel in the summer of 2008 (prompting a lot of chatter about 'peak oil'), were back down to $40 within a few months, causing all manner of problems for Russia, Venezuela and the Gulf States. The collapse of the oil-revenue based building boom in the Gulf saw thousands of migrant workers from India, Palestine and south-east Asia sent home.

Mexico, Ecuador, Haiti and Kerala in India, which depended heavily on remittances from those employed elsewhere, suddenly found household incomes drying up as overseas jobs in construction were lost and female domestic workers were cast off. Malnutrition and deaths from starvation surged in many of these poorer countries, giving the lie to the idea that marginalised populations are somehow unaffected by a financial crash in the advanced capitalist world.

The crisis cascaded from one sphere to another and from one geographical location to another, with all manner of knock-on and feedback effects that seemed almost impossible to bring under control, let alone halt and turn back. While populations appeared initially stunned by the turn of events, popular protests against the ways of international capital, which had surfaced and escalated after the Seattle protests of 1999 but diminished after 9/11, suddenly resurfaced, though this time with a sharpened target and again with a lot of geographical unevenness. Strikes erupted in France, along with protests in China, rural uprisings in India and student unrest in Greece. In the United States, a movement of the displaced to occupy foreclosed and abandoned housing began to take shape.

What was certain was that the Anglo-American model of world economic development that dominated in the post-Cold War period of free market triumphalism in the 1990s was discredited.

So why does capitalism periodically generate such crises? To answer this we need a far better understanding of how capitalism works than we currently possess. The problem is that the economic theories and orthodoxies which manifestly failed to predict the crisis continue to inform our debates, dominate our thinking and underpin political action. Without challenging these dominant mental conceptions there can be no alternative (as Margaret Thatcher liked to say) other than a botched return to the sort of capitalism that got us into this mess in the first place. How, then, can we best understand the crisis-prone character of capitalism and by what means might we identify an alternative? These are the questions that animate the analysis that follows.

2

Capital Assembled

How does capitalism survive and why is it so crisis prone? To answer these questions I first describe the conditions necessary for capital accumulation to flourish. I will then identify the potential barriers that exist to perpetual growth and examine how these have typically been transcended in the past, before going on to show what the principle blockages are this time around.

Capital is not a thing but a process in which money is perpetually sent in search of more money. Capitalists – those who set this process in motion – take on many different personae. Finance capitalists look to make more money by lending to others in return for interest. Merchant capitalists buy cheap and sell dear. Landlords collect rent because the land and properties they own are scarce resources. Rentiers make money from royalties and intellectual property rights. Asset traders swap titles (to stocks and shares for example), debts and contracts (including insurance) for a profit. Even the state can act like a capitalist, as, for example, when it uses tax revenues to invest in infrastructures that stimulate growth and generate even more tax revenues.

But the form of capital circulation that has come to dominate from the mid-eighteenth century onwards is that of industrial or production capital. In this case the capitalist starts the day with a certain amount of money, and, having selected a technology and organisational form, goes into the market place and buys the requisite amounts of labour power and means of production (raw materials, physical plant, intermediate products, machinery, energy and the like). The labour power is combined with the means of production through an active labour process conducted under the supervision of the capitalist. The result is a commodity that is sold by its owner, the capitalist, in the market place for a profit. The next day, the capitalist, for reasons that will shortly become apparent, takes a portion of yesterday's profit, converts it into fresh capital and begins the process anew on an expanded scale. If the technology and organisational forms do not change, then this entails buying more labour power and more means of production to create even more profit during the second day. And so it continues, ad infinitum.

In the service and entertainment industries this process looks a little different because the labour process (cutting the hair or entertaining the crowd) is in itself the commodity being sold, so there is no time lag between producing and selling the commodity (though there may be a lot of preparatory time involved). The necessity to reinvest in expansion, given the personal nature of the services often on offer, is not as strong, though there are plenty of examples of expanding service store and cinema chains, coffee shops and even private higher education centres.

Continuity of flow in the circulation of capital is very important. The process cannot be interrupted without incurring losses. There are also strong incentives to accelerate the speed of circulation. Those who can move faster through the various phases of capital circulation accrue higher profits than their competitors. Speed-up nearly always pays off in higher profits. Innovations which help speed things up are much sought after. Our computers, for instance, are becoming faster and faster.

Any interruption in the process threatens the loss or devaluation of the capital deployed. The 11 September 2001 attacks in the United States, for example, stopped the flows of goods, services and people into and out of New York City (and elsewhere) and closed down financial markets for a while. Within three days, though, it became clear that the flows had to be revived or the economy would be in deep trouble. Vigorous public appeals were made to everyone to go out and shop, travel, consume and return to business (particularly in the financial sector). It was patriotic to help the economy back on track by going shopping! President George W. Bush even took the extraordinary step of appearing in a collective airline commercial urging everyone to forget their fears and take to the skies again. While temporary disruptions of the 9/11 sort can be papered over, long-term lack of motion betokens a crisis for capitalism.

The circulation of capital also entails spatial movement. Money is assembled from somewhere and brought to a particular place to utilise labour resources that come from somewhere else. I deposit money in a savings account in my local bank in Baltimore and the money ends up in the hands of an entrepreneur in China who built a sock factory in Dongguan hiring migrant labourers (mainly young women) from the countryside. The means of production (including raw materials) have to be brought from yet another place to produce a commodity that has to be taken to market somewhere else. Frictions within or barriers to this spatial movement take time to negotiate and slow down circulation. Throughout the history of capitalism much effort has therefore been put into reducing the friction of distance and barriers to movement. Innovations in transport and communications have been crucial. Increasing the openness of state borders to commerce and finance, signing free trade agreements and securing proper legal frameworks for international trade are also seen as essential in the long term. Imagine if the customs barriers in Europe had never been abolished. To take another contemporary example, the securitisation of local mortgages and their sale to investors all over the world was viewed as a way of connecting areas of capital shortage with those in surplus in a way that supposedly minimised risk.

Throughout the history of capitalism there has been a trend towards the general reduction of spatial barriers and speed-up. The space and time configurations of social life are periodically revolutionised (witness what happened with the coming of the railroads in the nineteenth century and the current impact of the worldwide web). Movement becomes ever faster and space relations ever closer.

But this trend is neither smooth nor irreversible. Protectionism can return, barriers can be refortified, civil wars can disrupt flows. Furthermore, revolutions in spatial and temporal relations produce stresses and crises (witness the difficult adjustments forced on many cities by widespread deindustrialisation in the heartlands of capitalist production in the 1980s as production moved to east Asia). The geography this produces will be examined later.

Why do capitalists reinvest in expansion rather than consume away their profits in pleasures? This is where 'the coercive laws of competition' play a decisive role. If I, as a capitalist, do not reinvest in expansion and a rival does, then after a while I am likely to be driven out of business. I need to protect and expand my market share. I have to reinvest to stay a capitalist. This assumes, however, the existence of a competitive environment, which requires that we also explain how competition is perpetuated in the face of tendencies towards monopolisation or other social or customary barriers to competitive behaviour. I will return to this problem shortly.

There is, however, another motivation to reinvest. Money is a form of social power that can be appropriated by private persons. Furthermore, it is a form of social power that has no inherent limit. There is a limit to the amount of land I can possess, of the physical assets I can command. Imelda Marcos had 6,000 pairs of shoes, it was discovered, after the overthrow of her husband's dictatorship in the Philippines, but that still constituted a limit in the same way that the very rich cannot own billions of yachts or MacMansions. But there is no inherent limit to the billions of dollars an individual can command. The limitlessness of money, and the inevitable desire to command the social power it confers, provides an abundant range of social and political incentives to want more of it. And one of the key ways to get more of it is to reinvest a part of the surplus funds gained yesterday to generate more surplus tomorrow. There are, sad to say, many other ways to amass the social power that money commands: fraud, corruption, banditry, robbery and illegal trafficking. But I will mainly focus here on the legally sanctioned ways, even though a serious case can be made that the extra-legal forms are fundamental rather than peripheral to capitalism (the three largest sectors of global foreign trade are in drugs, illegal guns and human trafficking).

The importance of the limitless nature of money power cannot be overstressed. The leading hedge fund managers in New York pulled in personal remuneration of $250 million each in 2005, while in 2006 the top manager made $1.7 billion and in 2007, which was a disastrous year in global finance, five of them (including George Soros) earned around $3 billion apiece. This is what I mean about the limitlessness of money as a form of social power. What would George Soros do if he was paid in pairs of shoes?

Personal lust for gold is nothing new, of course. But social systems have long been constructed to try to constrain the excessive concentration of personal power that the possession of monetary wealth confers. What anthropologists refer to as the 'potlatch' in non-capitalist societies, for example, confers prestige on those who give away, renounce or in some instances even outright destroy, through elaborate ceremonies, the material possessions they have accumulated. Various forms of gift economies do likewise. Philanthropic generosity has a long tradition even within the history of capitalism – think of the Carnegie, Ford, Rockefeller, Gates, Leverhulme and Soros foundations. Non-capitalist institutions such as the Vatican may also soak up personal wealth (in medieval times, the Catholic Church sold indulgences – entry tickets into heaven – to wealthy merchants). For most of the last century, many of the advanced capitalist states embraced progressive taxation, redistributions in kind and strong inheritance taxes, thereby curbing excessive concentrations of personal wealth and power.

So why were the constraints to excessive concentration of money power loosened in the US and elsewhere after 1980? Explanations in terms of a sudden burst of 'infectious greed' (Alan Greenspan's term) simply do not wash, since the underlying desire for money power has always been around. Why did President Bill Clinton cave in so easily to the bondholders? Why did Larry Summers when he was Clinton's

Treasury Secretary violently oppose regulating finance, and why did Joseph Stiglitz, who now positions himself on the left of mainstream but who was Clinton's Chief Economic Adviser in the 1990s, find himself supporting moves that 'incidentally' ended up always making the rich richer? Did George W. Bush embrace taxation principles that immensely favoured the rich just because he liked them or needed their support for re-election? Was it simply that the 'Party of Wall Street' had taken power both in Congress and in the executive branch? If so, why did Gordon Brown, New Labour's Chancellor of the Exchequer in Britain, also so easily go along with it? (Did the City of London get to him, too?) And why was it that the wealthier grew immeasurably wealthier everywhere, from Russia and Mexico to India and Indonesia?

In the absence of any limits or barriers, the need to reinvest in order to remain a capitalist propels capitalism to expand at a compound rate. This then creates a perpetual need to find new fields of activity to absorb the reinvested capital: hence 'the capital surplus absorption problem'. Where are the new investment opportunities to come from? Are there limits? Clearly, there is no inherent limit to the monetary capacity to fuel growth (as became obvious in 2008–9, when states conjured up, seemingly out of nowhere, trillions of dollars to bail out a failing financial system).

But there are other potential barriers to the circulation of capital, any one of which, if it becomes insurmountable, can produce a crisis (defined as a condition in which surplus production and reinvestment are blocked). Growth then stops and there appears to be an excess or overaccumulation of capital relative to the opportunities to use that capital profitably. If growth does not resume, then the overaccumulated capital is devalued or destroyed. The historical geography of capitalism is littered with examples of such overaccumulation crises, some local and short-lived (such as the crash of the Swedish banking system in 1992), others on a somewhat larger scale (the long-standing depression that has afflicted the Japanese economy since about 1990) and at other times systemwide and, latterly, global (as in 1848, 1929,

45

1973 and 2008). In a general crisis, a lot of capital gets devalued (the $50 trillion or so loss in global asset values so far estimated for the current crisis is a case in point). Devalued capital can exist in many forms: deserted and abandoned factories; empty office and retail spaces; surplus commodities that cannot be sold; money that sits idle earning no rate of return; declining asset values in stocks and shares, land, properties, art objects, etc.

Both Karl Marx and Joseph Schumpeter wrote at length on the 'creative-destructive' tendencies inherent in capitalism. While Marx clearly admired capitalism's creativity he (followed by Lenin and the whole Marxist tradition) strongly emphasised its self-destructiveness. The Schumpeterians have all along gloried in capitalism's endless creativity while treating the destructiveness as mostly a matter of the normal costs of doing business (although they admit that occasionally the destructiveness regrettably gets out of hand). While the costs (particularly when measured in lives lost in two world wars which were, after all, inter-capitalist wars) have been larger than the Schumpeterians typically concede, it could be that they were basically right from the perspective of the *longue durée* at least up until recently. The world has, after all, been made and remade several times over since 1750 and the aggregate output as well as the standard of living measured in material goods and services for an expanding number of privileged people has risen significantly even as total population has soared from less than 2 billion to around 6.8 billion. The performance of capitalism over the last 200 years has been nothing short of astonishingly creative. But the situation today may be far closer then ever before to that which Marx described – and not only because social and class inequalities have deepened within a far more volatile global economy (it has done that before – most ominously in the 1920s before the last great depression).

Capitalism has so far survived in the face of many predictions of its imminent demise. This record suggests that it has sufficient fluidity and flexibility to overcome all limits, though not, as the history of periodic crises also demonstrates, without violent corrections. Marx advances a useful way of looking at this in his notebooks, eventually published as the *Grundrisse der Kritik des Politischen Ökonomie* in 1941. He contrasts the potential limitlessness of monetary accumulation on the one hand, with the potentially limiting aspects of material activity (production, exchange and consumption of commodities), on the other. Capital cannot abide, he suggests, such limits. 'Every limit appears,' he notes, 'as a barrier to be overcome.' There is, therefore, within the historical geography of capitalism a perpetual struggle to convert seemingly absolute limits into barriers that can be transcended or circumvented. How, then, does this happen and what are the principle limits?

Examination of the flow of capital through production reveals six potential barriers to accumulation that have to be negotiated for capital to be reproduced: i) insufficient initial money capital; ii) scarcities of, or political difficulties with, labour supply; iii) inadequate means of production, including so-called 'natural limits'; iv) inappropriate technologies and organisational forms; v) resistance or inefficiencies in the labour process; and vi) lack of demand backed by money to pay in the market. Blockage at any one of these points will disrupt the continuity of capital flow and, if prolonged, eventually produce a crisis of devaluation. Let us consider these potential barriers one by one.

———

The original accumulation of capital during late medieval times in Europe entailed violence, predation, thievery, fraud and robbery. Through these extra-legal means, pirates, priests and merchants, supplemented by the usurers, assembled enough initial 'money power' to begin to circulate money systematically as capital. The Spanish robbery of Inca gold was the paradigmatic example. In the early stages, however, capital did not circulate directly through production. It took a variety of other forms, such as agrarian, merchant, landed and sometimes state mercantilist capital. These forms were not adequate to absorb the vast inflows of gold. Too much gold pursued too few goods. The result was the 'grand inflation' of the sixteenth century in Europe. It was only when capitalists learned to circulate capital through production employing wage labour that compound growth could begin after 1750 or so.

A rising bourgeoisie gradually asserted their money power to influence and reconstitute state forms, ultimately assuming a commanding influence over military institutions and administrative and legal systems. It then could use legally sanctioned ways to assemble money power through dispossession and destruction of pre-capitalist forms of social provision. It did so both within the state – through, for example, the enclosure of the landed commons and the monetisation of rents in Britain – and externally, through colonial and imperialistic practices (imposing land taxes in India). A close tie then arose between finance and the state, particularly through the rise of national debt (usually to fight wars).

At the heart of the credit system lies a set of arrangements that constitute what I shall call the 'state–finance nexus'. This describes a confluence of state and financial power that confounds the analytic tendency to see state and capital as clearly separable from each other. This does not mean that state and capital constituted then or now an identity, but that there are structures of governance (such as power over the coinage of the realm in the past and central banks and treasury departments today) where the state management of capital creation and monetary flows becomes integral to, rather than separable from, the circulation of capital. The reverse relation also holds as taxes or borrowings flow into the coffers of the state and as state functions also become monetised, commodified and ultimately privatised.

As more and more of the surplus created yesterday is converted into fresh capital today, so more and more of the money invested today comes from the profits procured yesterday. This would seem to render redundant the violent accumulation practised in earlier times. But 'accumulation by dispossession' continues to play a role in assembling the initial money power. Both legal as well as illegal means – such as violence, criminality, fraud and predatory practices of the sort that have been uncovered in recent times in the subprime mortgage market, or even more significantly in the drug trade – are deployed. The legal means include privatisation of what were once considered common property resources (like water and education), the use of the power of eminent domain to seize assets, widespread practices of takeovers, mergers and the like that result in 'asset stripping', and reneging on, say, pension and health care obligations through bankruptcy proceedings. The asset losses many have experienced during the recent crisis can be viewed as a form of dispossession that can be turned into further accumulation as speculators buy up the assets cheaply today with an eye to selling them at a profit when the market improves. This is what the bankers and hedge funds did during the crash of 1997–8 in east and south-east Asia. Huge losses on the ground in that part of the world lined the coffers of major financial centres.

If it were only the accumulation from yesterday that could be capitalised into expansion today, then over time we would see a gradual increase in the concentration of money capital in individual hands. But the credit system permits large quantities of money power to be brought together very rapidly by different means. This becomes important because, as the eighteenth-century French utopian thinker Saint-Simon long ago argued, it takes the 'association of capitals' on a large scale to set in motion the kinds of massive works such as railroads that are required to sustain long-term capitalist development. This was what the nineteenth-century financiers the Péreire brothers, schooled in Saint-Simonian theory, effectively achieved through the new credit institutions they set up to help Baron Haussmann transform the built environment of Second Empire Paris in the 1850s. (The boulevards we see today date from this period.)

In the case of limited and joint stock companies and other corporate organisational forms that came into their own in the nineteenth century, enormous quantities of money power are amassed and centralised (often out of myriad small amounts of personal savings) under the control of a few directors and managers. Acquisitions (both friendly and hostile), mergers and leveraged buy-outs have also long been big business. Activity of this kind can entail new rounds of accumulation by dispossession. In recent times, private equity groups (such as Blackstone) typically take over public firms, reorganise them, asset strip them and lay off workers before selling them back into the public domain at a hefty profit. Furthermore, there are all sorts of tricks whereby big capital can drive out small (state regulation that is particularly burdensome for small businesses leads to further centralisation of capital). The dispossession of the small operators (neighbourhood stores or family farms) to make way for large enterprises (supermarket chains and agribusiness), frequently with the aid of credit mechanisms, has also been a long-standing practice.

The question of the organisation, configuration and mass of the money capital available at the starting point of circulation never goes away. Building a steel mill, a railroad or launching an airline requires an immense initial outlay of money capital before production can even begin and the time delays between initiation and completion can be substantial. Only relatively recently, for example, has it become possible for private consortia of associated capitals, rather than the state, to undertake massive infrastructural projects like the Channel Tunnel that links Britain to Europe. Such vast infrastructural projects become more and more necessary as capitalism grows in scale through compounding growth.

Geographical networks also have to be constructed to facilitate global capital financial flows connecting zones of capital surplus with regions of capital scarcity. Here, too, there is a long history of innovation in the financial services industry and in state and inter-state relations. The primary objective is to overcome any potential blockage to the free circulation of capital across the world market. This opens up the possibility of cascading 'spatial fixes' to the capital surplus absorption problem. Too much surplus capital in Britain in the late nineteenth century? Then send it to the United States, Argentina or South Africa where it can be profitably deployed. Surplus capital in Taiwan? Then send it to create sweatshops in China or Vietnam. Capital surpluses in the Gulf States in the 1970s? Then send them to Mexico via the New York investment banks.

For all of this to happen effectively ultimately requires the creation of state-like international institutions such as those set up under the Bretton Woods Agreement to facilitate and regulate the international flows of capital. The World Bank and the International Monetary Fund, along with the Bank of International Settlements in Basel, are central here, but other organisations, such as the Organisation for Economic Co-operation and Development (OECD) and the G7 (later the G8), now expanded to the G20, also play an influential role as the world's central banks and treasury departments seek to coordinate their actions to constitute an evolving global financial architecture for an international version of the state–finance nexus.

There are, however, two important points to be made about the role of this state–finance nexus. The first is that it extracts interest and taxes in return for its services. Furthermore, its power position in relation to the circulation of capital permits it to extract monopoly rents from those who need its services. On the other hand, in order to lure idle money back into circulation, it either has to offer security and transactional efficiency to its depositor clients or a rate of return to those savers with money surpluses. It then relies on the gap between the cost of its services and the interest rate offered to savers and the interest rate or fees it charges to users to sustain its own prof- itability. But banks can also lend out more than they borrow. It makes a difference if banks lend out three or thirty times what they have on deposit. Increased leveraging meant quite simply money creation within the banking system and rapidly rising profits. In the run-up to the present crisis, the profitability of the financial sector surged. The percentage of total profits in the US attributable to financial services rose from around 15 per cent in 1970 to 40 per cent by 2005.

———

The credit system and the institutions that specialise in the assemblage and dispensation of money power therefore become more rather than less significant over time. An inadequate configuration of the credit system or some crisis within it of the sort we are now witnessing forms a potential point of blockage for further capital accumulation.

This centralisation of money power by way of the credit system has all manner of implications for the trajectory of capitalist development. If nothing else, it endows a privileged class of financiers with immense potential social power over producers, merchants, landholders, developers, wage labourers and consumers. Increasing centralisation of capital poses the danger, furthermore, of ascendant monopoly power and diminished competition, which can lead to stagnation. Capitalist states have, therefore, sometimes found themselves obliged to foster competition by legislating against excessive monopoly power (e.g. anti-trust legislation in the United States or the Monopolies Commission in Europe). But it is just as likely that the state–finance nexus, overwhelmed by centralised credit power, will get constituted in a form best titled 'state–monopoly capitalism'. This was how many critical theorists in the United States described the situation in the 1960s. Paul Baran and Paul Sweezey, for example, published their influential text *Monopoly Capital* (1966). The official line of the influential French Communist Party in the 1960s was that they were struggling against 'state monopoly capitalism'.

The circulation of capital is inherently risky and always speculative. 'Speculation' popularly refers to a situation where an excess of capital is applied to activities where the underlying returns are negative but the ferment in the market allows this condition to be disguised. Enron, for example, effectively disguised its losses (as did the whole banking system thereafter) during the 1990s and continued to make fictitious profits even in the face of real losses. These are the special cases that we generally refer to as 'speculative binges'. But it is vital to remember that all capital circulation is speculative through and through. 'You must understand,' the French novelist Emile Zola once wrote, 'that speculation, gambling, is the central mechanism, the heart itself of a vast affair like ours. Yes, it attracts blood, takes it from every source in little streamlets, collects it, sends it back in rivers in all directions, and establishes an enormous circulation of money, which is the very life of great enterprises ...'

The money that is launched into circulation at the beginning of the day is not necessarily realised as profit at the end of the day. When the surplus is realised at the end of the day then we laud the prescience, imagination and creativity of the entrepreneur, but if it is not (often through no particular fault of the entrepreneur) we typically condemn the capitalist as a speculator! In the space of a year, Kenneth Lay, the CEO of Enron, went from being an entrepreneurial genius to a reviled speculator.

While everything possible must be done to make sure that capital generates (produces) and gets (realises) its surplus at the end of the day, things often go wrong. This means that expectations, faith, beliefs, anticipations, desires and 'animal spirits' (as the economist John Maynard Keynes called them in the 1930s) have an important role to play in the decision to launch capital into circulation. Investor psychology cannot be ignored any more than the state of trust in the integrity of the financial system that takes many small savings and lends them to the capitalist in return for an interest payment. If I can't trust the banks then I would rather store gold under my pillow, which would diminish the loan capital available to the capitalist. The saying 'as safe as the Bank of England' has always been a popular iconic way to register this faith. Credit is very Protestant, noted Marx – it rests on pure faith.

From time to time, however, the expectations become so excessive and the financing so profligate as to give rise to a distinctive financial crisis within the financial system itself. Marx provides a brief description in *Capital*. 'The bourgeois [read Wall Street], drunk with prosperity and arrogantly certain of himself, has just declared that money is a purely imaginary creation. Commodities [read as safe as houses] alone are money,' he said. 'But now the opposite cry resounds over the markets of the world: only money [read liquidity] is a commodity. As the hart pants after fresh water, so pants his soul after money, the only wealth. In a crisis the antithesis between commodities and their value form, money, is raised to the level of an absolute contradiction.' In the depth of that contradiction, expectations become riddled with fear (neither houses nor the Bank of England appear as safe as they were once presumed to be) and the financing becomes far too meagre to support further accumulation.

Financial and monetary crises have been long-standing features of the historical geography of capitalism. But their frequency and depth have increased markedly since 1970 or so, and we have to grapple with why this is happening and what might be done about it. The compounding rate of growth of global capital accumulation has put immense pressure upon the state–finance nexus to find new and innovative ways to assemble and distribute money capital in quantities, forms and locations where it is best positioned to exploit profitable opportunities. Many of the recent financial innovations were designed to overcome the barriers posed by pre-existing institutional and regulatory arrangements. The pressure to deregulate seemingly became irresistible. But moves of this kind invariably create a serious probability of unrestrained financing going wild and generating a crisis. This is what happened when the Péreire brothers' Crédit Mobilier and Crédit Immobilièr crashed, along with the Parisian municipal budget, in the crisis of 1868. And this is what has happened within the global financial system in 2008.

The state–finance nexus has long functioned as the 'central nervous system' for capital accumulation. When the signals internal to its functioning go haywire, then crises obviously result. Much of what happens within the central banks and treasury departments of contemporary states is hidden from view and wrapped in mystery. Not for nothing did William Greider call his exhaustive 1989 investigation of how the Federal Reserve works *Secrets of the Temple*. Marx depicted the world of high finance as the 'Vatican' of capitalism. In today's world it might be even more ironic to call it the 'Kremlin', since the world seems more likely to end up being ruled by the dictatorship of the world's central bankers than by that of the workers. The state–finance nexus has all the characteristics of a feudal institution, riddled with intrigues and secret passages, exercising a strange and totally undemocratic power over not only how capital circulates and accumulates but almost all aspects of social life. Blind belief in the corrective powers residing in this state–finance nexus underpins the confidence and the expectations that Keynes considered so crucial to sustaining capitalism.

Each state has a particular form of the state–finance nexus. The geographical variations in institutional arrangements are considerable and the mechanisms for inter-state coordination, such as the Bank of International Settlements in Basel and the International Monetary Fund, also have an influential role. The powers involved in the construction of arrangements such as those that assembled to make key international decisions on the future financial architecture of the world trading system, as at Bretton Woods in 1944, are typically élite, expert, highly technocratic and undemocratic. And so it continues in our own times. Only those initiated into the secret ways are being called upon to correct them.

Broad-based political struggles do take place, however, over and around the state–finance nexus. More often populist than class-based, these protests typically focus on the actions of that class faction that controls the state–finance nexus. The 'Fifty Years is Enough' campaign against the continuation of the IMF and the World Bank in the late 1990s drew upon a diverse alliance of interests bringing together, for example, labour as well as environmentalists to produce the 'Teamsters for Turtles' logo after the street protests against the WTO in Seattle in 1999. The focus was very much on the disciplinary, neocolonial and imperialist role of these institutions. Labour, for its part, often only relates to such struggles at one step removed. It can, however, easily be drawn into a politics of populist outrage (often led by petty bourgeois or even nationalist interests – recall when the then British Shadow Chancellor Harold Wilson back in 1956 railed at the powers of what he called 'the gnomes of Zurich' who held the British economy in check). More commonly, populism focuses on what the barons of high finance get up to, the immense fortunes and money power they frequently acquire and the overwhelming social power they often wield to dictate the terms of existence for everyone else. The furore over bankers' pay and bonuses in 2009 in both Europe and the United States is illustrative of this kind of populist movement and its limits. This parallels the outrage in the United States against the banks and financiers who were widely blamed for the ills of the 1930s. The popular sympathy with the 'Bonnie and Clyde' bank robbers is part of the legendary folklore of the period.

The social forces engaged in shaping how the state–finance nexus works – and no state is exactly like any other – therefore differ somewhat from the class struggle between capital and labour typically privileged in Marxian theory. I do not mean to suggest by this that political struggles against high finance are of no interest to the labour movement, because of course they are. But there are many issues, varying from tax, tariff, subsidy and both internal and external regulatory policies, where industrial capital and organised labour in specific geographical settings will be in alliance rather than opposition. This happened with the request for a bail-out for the US auto industry in 2008–9. Auto companies and unions sat side by side in the attempt to preserve jobs and save the companies from bankruptcy. On the other hand, there are plenty of interests other than labour that fight against the power of high finance. When the financiers become, as happened in the United States from the mid-1980s onwards, dominant over all other sectors and when those who should be regulated capture the state regulatory apparatus, then the state–finance nexus tilts to favour particular interests rather than those of the body politic at large. Sustained populist outrage is then essential to restore the balance.

However, when the financial system and the 'state–finance nexus fails, as it did in 1929 and 2008, then everyone recognises there is a threat to the survival of capitalism and no stone is left unturned and no compromise is left unexamined in our endeavours to resuscitate it. We can't, it seems, live without it even as we complain about it.

3

Capital Goes to Work

Once the money is assembled in the right hands and in the right place at the right time, then it has to be put to work to mobilise the raw materials, the plant and equipment, the energy flows and the labour power to produce a commodity. Let's consider, then, the various elements that must be procured for production to occur.

Perpetual accumulation at a compound rate depends on the permanent availability of sufficient accessible reserves of labour power. What Marx calls 'an industrial reserve army' is therefore a necessary condition for the reproduction and expansion of capital. This reserve army needs to be accessible, socialised, disciplined and of the requisite qualities (i.e. flexible, docile, manipulable and skilled when necessary). If these conditions are not met, then capital faces a serious barrier to continuous accumulation.

The dispossession of the mass of the population from direct access to the means of production (land in particular) releases labour power as a commodity into the market place. Marx's account of so-called 'primitive accumulation' may be overdramatised and oversimplified but its essential truth is undeniable. Somehow or other the mass of a population has been put in a position of having to work for capital in order to live. Primitive accumulation did not end with the rise of industrial capitalism in Britain in the late eighteenth century. In the last thirty years, for example, some 2 billion wage labourers have been added to the available global workforce, through the opening-up of China and the collapse of communism in central and eastern Europe. All around the world the integration of rural and hitherto independent peasant populations into the workforces has occurred.

Most dramatic of all has been the mobilisation of women, who now form the backbone of the global workforce. A massive pool of labour power for capitalist expansion is now available.

Labour markets are, however, geographically segmented. A daily commuting time of four hours comes close to defining an outer limit for workers to get to their jobs on a daily basis. How far away four hours gets you depends, of course, on the speed and cost of transportation, but the inevitable geographical segmentation of labour markets means that questions of labour supply boil down to a series of local problems embedded in regional and state strategies, mitigated by migratory movements (of both capital and labour). The state becomes involved, *inter alia*, when it comes to immigration and labour laws (minimum wages, hours of work and regulation of the conditions of labour), the provision of social infrastructures (such as education, training and health care) that affect the qualities of labour supply and policies designed to maintain the reserve army (social welfare provision).

Capitalists can manage and circumvent the potential limits of labour supply, even in local contexts, in a variety of ways. Some expansion can be had through population growth (and in some instances pro-natalist policies on the part of the state, such as subsidies to large families in France, have had a definite impact upon labour supply conditions to the advantage of capital). There is, in fact, a very general relation between compound population growth and compounding capital accumulation. The astonishing growth performance of capitalism in China after 1980 depended, for example, on the radical reduction of infant mortality in the Mao years that later resulted in a massive young labour force clamouring for employment.

In the absence of increasing productivity, accumulation leads to relatively full employment of local labour resources. Scarcity of labour means increasing wages. Either wages continue to rise in such a way as to not interfere with the increasing mass of accumulation (because more labourers are employed) or accumulation slows along with the demand for labour, thus pushing wages down. On occasion, capitalists in effect go on strike, refusing to reinvest because higher wages are cutting into profitability. The hope is that the resultant unemployment will rediscipline labour to accept a lower wage rate.

While such instances of 'capital strike' can be identified (the 'Reagan recession' of 1980–82, when unemployment rose to more than 10 per cent, had some of this quality to it), there are other more advantageous ways for capital to address problems of labour scarcity. Labour-saving technologies and organisational innovations can throw people out of work and into the industrial reserve. The result is a 'floating' army of laid-off workers whose very existence puts a downward pressure on wages. Capital simultaneously manipulates both the supply of and demand for labour.

Labour, knowing this full well, often fights against the deployment of new technologies (as happened in the case of the so-called Luddite movement in the early nineteenth century). 'Productivity agreements' that accept new technologies in return for job security became important in union bargaining after 1945 or so in the advanced capitalist countries. An alternative capitalist strategy is to mobilise elements within the population that have not yet been proletarianised. The most obvious target would be peasant and rural populations (as has happened in China in recent years). In the advanced capitalist countries, where such populations have largely disappeared, there has been a major turn towards the mobilisation of women into the labour force, along with the proletarianisation of elements in the population that have managed to live outside of the wage labour economy. In the United States, the family farm and small shopkeepers have been major targets for proletarianisation since the 1930s. In many respects the mobilisation of these reserves is preferable to increasing unemployment by lay-offs and technological change, which can be politically problematic as well as economically costly if the state is held responsible for unemployment benefits.

Since labour scarcities are always localised, geographical mobility of either capital or labour (or both) becomes vital in regulating the dynamics of local labour markets. Even short distance movements (such as the move of businesses from unionised central cities in the US to suburbs where there were abundant non-unionised latent reserves, particularly of women, from the 1950s onwards) can radically transform the balance of class power with respect to wage rates and conditions of labouring. Longer distance moves, as from the industrialised and unionised north-east and midwest of the United States to the south and west, or the long migration of surplus southern labour to northern cities from the 1920s onwards, also impinge upon the labour supply problem. In recent times global labour flows have become of added significance. While the foreign-born population of the US stood at around 5 per cent in 1970, it is over 12.5 per cent today. One negative consequence of such policies has been a rising tide of anti-immigrant fervour accompanied by surges of racism and ethnic discriminations within the working classes.

All along, capitalists have sought to control labour by putting individual workers in competition with each other for the jobs on offer. To the degree that the potential labour force is gendered, racialised, ethnicised, tribalised or divided by language, political and sexual orientation and religious beliefs, so these differences emerge as fundamental to the workings of the labour market. They become tools through which capitalists manage labour supplies in tandem with privileged sectors of the workforce who use racism and sexism to minimise competition. The history of primitive accumulation itself entailed the manufacture of claims of 'natural', and hence biologically based, superiorities that legitimised forms of hierarchical power and class domination in the face of religious or secular claims to equal status in the eyes of God or of the state (the US and French Revolutions). Throughout its history, capital has been in no way reluctant to exploit, if not promote, such fragmentations, even as workers themselves struggle to define collective means of action that all too often stop at the boundaries of ethnic, religious, racial or gender identities. Indeed, in the US in the 1950s and 1960s, labour organisations sought to curb competition in labour markets by imposing exclusions based on race and gender.

The ability to preserve such distinctions is illustrated by the fact that even after nearly a half century of campaigning for the principle of 'equal pay for equal work', the wage gap between men and women has not disappeared even in the United States where the pressures have probably been strongest. Elsewhere, for example in east Asia, the gender disparities are far worse and it is there, of course, that the bulk of the newly proletarianised populations are made up of women. The wage distinctions between blacks and whites as well as between Hispanics and Asiatics in the United States have similarly persisted, if not, in some instances, grown over the years. Elsewhere, as in India, caste distinctions have remained a formidable barrier in labour markets in spite of constitutional provisions for equal treatment. And to the degree that all labour markets are local, and more so for the workers than for the capitalists, so social and political solidarities, if they are to mean anything at all, have in the first instance to be constructed on a local geographical basis before any national or international movement can become possible. While capitalists are also often divided along ethnic and other lines (though they are usually much more homogeneous than their labour forces), workers find it hard to exploit such differences systematically to their own advantage, though the history of popular anti-Semitism towards the financiers of Wall Street often played a lamentable role.

From the mid-1960s onwards, also, innovations in transport technology made it far easier to offshore production to low wage locations with weak labour organisation. In the last few decades, as noted earlier, massive relocations of manufacturing activity have radically transformed the way labour markets work, compared to the circumstances that typically prevailed before about 1970.

There are, however, many contradictory aspects internalised within labour supply politics, not least arising out of the dynamics of class organisation and class politics as practised individually and collectively by workers within their distinctive labour markets. The real wage rate is set by the costs of supplying those goods and services required to reproduce labour power at a given and acceptable standard of living. What is 'acceptable' or 'given' is a product of class struggle, of customary standards and social compacts (more often than not tacit, but sometimes explicit as to the right to decent health care and education) achieved usually within some territorialised social organisation. (Hence, again, the significance of the state as one key institutional framework for defining some sort of rough consensus as to how social life shall be regulated.) Since labour markets are invariably local, so these other questions of costs and standards of living vary geographically even within fairly short distances (New York City is not Buffalo and neither of these cities, of course, is anything like Mumbai). The institutional framework within which wage bargaining occurs also varies from statewide (as in Sweden and until recently, the United Kingdom) to always local (the United States). In the latter case the result has been 'living wage campaigns', each with its own definition of what constitutes a living wage, proliferating from one locality to another, as happened from the mid-1990s onwards at a time when the federal government was politically opposed to raising the national minimum wage. The militancy, degree of organisation and level of aspiration within localised labour movements plainly vary from place to place and time to time, such that the potential barriers to continuous capital accumulation can proliferate here and fade away there. The ultimate power of the workforce – to withdraw its labour and strike – is always there, but here too there is all too often an asymmetry of power, since those with money reserves (typically the capitalists) can outwait those with little (the workers and their unions) even as the long-term threat to capitalism of widespread labour unrest remains a reserve power of great significance.

But within this sea of struggle there are usually enough calm spots where capital can have its way with relative ease and ensure that the supply of labour power is adequate for its purposes. I think it fair to say that since 1980, the combination of political repressions (including the collapse of communist regimes), technological changes, the heightened capacity for capital mobility and a massive wave of primitive accumulation in (and migration from) formerly peripheral zones have effectively solved the labour provision problem for capital. While local constraints exist here and there, the availability of massive labour reserves (including those with high level education, increasingly from India and east Asia) throughout the world is undeniable and weighs heavily upon the scales of class struggle so as to advantage capital mightily.

It is under these circumstances that enlightened capitalist class interests (as opposed to those of individual capitalists in intense competition with each other, who often practise the politics of *après moi le déluge*) can rally around a political project to subsidise the supply of cheaper wage goods to keep the value of labour power down (as happened when the industrial interest in Britain sought to reduce tariffs on imported wheat in order to cheapen the supply of bread in the mid-nineteenth century and, as has happened in the US with the advent of the Wal-Mart phenomenon, of cheap retail goods from China). They can also support investing in improvements to the qualities of labour supply through health care, education and housing and ultimately, as did Henry Ford when he moved to establish a $5 dollar 8-hour day in the 1920s, propose higher wages and rationalised worker consumption as a means to ensure a stronger effective demand in the market place.

The role of state power in relation to such struggles is by no means fixed. To be sure, if labour is too well organised and too powerful in a particular location, then the capitalist class will seek to command the state apparatus to do its bidding, as happened, noted earlier, with Pinochet, Reagan, Thatcher, Kohl et al. But labour organising through political parties of the left can push in the opposite direction, as has happened in various places (such as Scandinavia) and at certain times (viz. the 'social democratic' consensus of the 1960s in much of Europe). But the use of state power to transcend the barrier of strong labour organisation has been very effective since the mid-1970s in many parts of the world. Another method is to facilitate, if not subsidise, the mobility of capital so it can move to where business conditions, including those of labour supply and weak labour organisation (as, for example, in the anti-union so-called 'right to work' states of the US south), are most advantageous to capital. Inter-urban, inter-regional and international competition on the part of state apparatuses for capital investment here plays an important role. The state (local, regional or national) becomes responsible for guaranteeing the supply of labour power of adequate quantities and qualities (including skills, training and political docility) in relation to corporate labour demand. While, therefore, the state apparatus may shift to following the corporate rather than labour's agenda, there is still a vested interest in localities supporting high-quality educational opportunities (universities and community colleges) since this will help to attract the high-tech manufacturing which will contribute more to the tax base of the locality.

Some Marxists have built a distinctive theory of crisis formation on the basis of barriers to adequate labour supply. The so-called 'profit squeeze' theory of crisis hinges on the perpetually fraught problem of labour relations and class struggle, both in the labour process and in the labour market. When these relations pose a barrier to further capital accumulation then a crisis ensues, unless some way (or, more likely, mix of ways of the sort outlined above) can be found for capital to overcome or circumvent that barrier. Some analysts, such as Andrew Glyn (see his impressive account, written with others, in 'British Capitalism, Workers and the Profits Squeeze' (1972)) would interpret what happened in the late 1960s and early 1970s (particularly in Europe and North America) as an excellent example of a profit squeeze situation. Certainly, the management of labour resources and the politics of labour organisation and supply dominated the politics of the period. Working-class organisation throughout much of Europe and even in the United States was relatively strong and state apparatuses everywhere were either wary of the power of organised labour or, through political parties of the left, rendered partly subservient to the interests of organised labour. There is no question but that this constituted a serious barrier to continuous capital accumulation. How that barrier was circumvented by capital through the rise of neoliberalism during the 1970s and early 1980s defines in many respects the nature of the dilemmas we now face.

The survival of capitalism depends upon the perpetual overcoming or circumvention of this potential barrier to sustained accumulation. As I write at the end of 2009, there is very little sign of a profit squeeze. Labour reserves exist everywhere and there are few geographical barriers to capitalist access to them. The political attack upon working-class movements worldwide has reduced serious worker resistance to very modest levels almost everywhere. The crisis of 2008–9 cannot therefore be understood in profit squeeze terms. Wage repression because of superabundant labour supply and consequent lack of effective consumer demand is a much more serious problem.

The labour question never goes away, however. Labour unrest can well up as a serious problem, at any time and in any place. Contemporary evidence from China, for example, suggests a rising tide of unrest there as the worldwide economic downturn creating unwelcome and unaccustomed (in China) increases in unemployment (in early 2009 estimated to be close to 20 million unemployed) within a recently proletarianised population. The uneven geographical development of labour struggles is important to keep an eye on.

The capital–labour relation always plays a central role in the dynamics of capitalism and may lie at the root of crises. But these days the main problem lies in the fact that capital is too powerful and labour too weak, rather than the other way around.

——

When capitalists reinvest, they need to find extra means of production available in the market place. The inputs they require are of two sorts: intermediate products (already shaped by human labour) that can be used up in the production process (such as the energy and cloth needed to make a coat) and the machinery and fixed capital equipment, including factory buildings and the physical infra-structures such as transport systems, canals and ports that support the activity of production. The category of means of production is evidently very broad and complicated. But if any of these means of production turn out to be unavailable, then this constitutes a barrier to further capital accumulation. The auto industry cannot expand without more steel inputs, plastic and electronic components and rubber tyres, nor, incidentally, will its expansion make sense unless there are highways to drive on. Technological innovations in one part of what we now call a 'commodity' or 'supply chain' flowing into production invariably render necessary innovations elsewhere. Rising productivity in the nineteenth-century cotton industry with the advent of the power loom, Marx points out, required innovations in cotton production (the cotton gin), transport and communications, chemical and industrial dyeing techniques, and the like.

The conversion of a part of yesterday's profit into fresh capital depends, therefore, on the availability of an ever-increasing quantity of means of production, as well as an increasing quantity of wage goods to feed the extra workers to be employed. The problem is to organise the supply of material inputs so as to sustain the continuity of capital flow. Capital has, in other words, to produce the conditions for its own continued expansion in advance of that expansion! How does it do this in a smooth and trouble-free manner?

The answer is, as Marx quaintly put it, that 'the course of true love never does run smooth'. There are always shortages here and surpluses there and occasionally these shortages coalesce into formidable barriers to further expansion which disrupt the continuity of capital flow. But efficiently functioning markets with freely moving price signals reflecting demand and supply conditions have historically provided one pretty good means of coordination. They have facilitated increasingly complex social divisions of labour and increases in what is termed 'the roundaboutness of production' (signalling the number of independent production steps involved prior to arriving at the finished product). The increasing number of components incorporated in the final product (cars which incorporate sophisticated electronic devices like GPS systems, for example) increases the complexity of supply flows. This necessitates the creation of more or less 'honest' and reliable market structures with proper price signals to ensure the continuity of capital circulation. This inner connection between the expansion of capital at a compound rate and the use of market signals to coordinate flows calls forth state regulation against, for example, monopolisation, cornering or manipulating markets, at the same time as it requires the reduction of any social barriers (tariffs, quotas or unnecessary delays) to commodity movement. The removal of frontier checks in the 1980s on truck traffic in Europe had a huge impact on smoothness of flows of inputs into many production processes. Conversely, geopolitical tensions between states can disrupt the free flow of vital inputs and act as a check upon capital accumulation. The disruptions of Russian oil and natural gas flows through the Ukraine because of political disputes in 2008 created serious problems for producers and consumers as far west as Germany and Austria.

But the market is not the only means for coordination. Increasingly, producers deal with suppliers directly and, with optimal scheduling and supply models, transmit orders for components directly back down their supply chain and take delivery on a 'just-in-time' principle that minimises the cost of idle inventories. In many industries (autos, electronics, etc.) these direct coordinations have come to supplant the open market. Producers signal in advance how much extra means of production they will need and supplier firms calculate their output accordingly. And in certain instances of market failure, the state can step in with its own models of input–output structures to plan either the totality or a key component in a supply chain that capital has difficulty organising (such as power or water supply and a whole panoply of physical infrastructures for production). While it is a commonly held belief, particularly in the United States, that state interventions lead to inefficiency, the history of Japan's or Singapore's industrialisation leads a long list of examples in which the state planning, coordination, intervention and reorganisation of capital flows has been more effective than the anarchy of open market coordinations. If corporations themselves have successfully avoided the anarchy of open markets by efficient optimal scheduling arrangements with their suppliers, then why cannot society do likewise on an even broader terrain?

Leaving aside the ideological fight over state planning versus market, what this all means is that the continuity of capital flow in a world of increasingly complicated social divisions of labour rests upon the existence of adequate institutional arrangements that facilitate the continuity of that flow across space and time. Where those arrangements are defective or do not exist, capital will encounter serious barriers. While ways can be found for capital to operate successfully under, say, conditions of lawlessness, corruption and indeterminate property rights, this does not in general constitute an optimal environment in which capital can flourish. What to do about 'failed states' and how to ensure the creation of 'a good business climate' (including the suppression of corruption and lawlessness) have therefore become leading missions of international financial institutions such as the IMF and the World Bank, as well as a project of various arms of contemporary US and European imperialist practices in many parts of the world. The WTO agreements, for example, codify 'good behaviour' for the states that have signed up (and many states have no option except to sign if they wish to continue to trade with the US and Europe) in such a way as to favour the freedoms of corporations to do business without excessive state regulation or interference.

Unfortunately, such projects invariably attack forms of value production and valuation other than those given by the market and, if successful (which they often are not), dissolve forms of cultural meaning and social solidarities that play an important role in sustaining daily life, both materially and socially, outside of ordinary commodity production. Non-market and non-capitalist-based modes of living are, in short, considered a barrier to capital accumulation and they therefore must be dissolved to make way for the 3 per cent compound growth rate that constitutes the capitalist juggernaut. The complicated history of how the absolute limit against capital accumulation in China under communist rule was dissolved after the reforms of 1978 into a series of barriers, each of which was gradually transcended or circumvented, is, of course, one of the most significant political and economic stories of our times.

But there are also, it turns out, some tensions and potential contradictions within the supply chains that can lead to what are called 'crises of disproportionality'. At the end of volume 2 of *Capital*, Marx set up what he called 'reproduction schemas' to analyse the dynamic relations between two broad sectors of the economy, those producing 'wage goods' (to feed, sustain and reproduce the labourer, later broadened to include 'luxury goods' for the personal consumption of the capitalist class) and those producing means of production (for the capitalist to use in production). Marx then asked how capital could shift from one sector to another, given the tendency for capitalists to equalise the rate of profit across all sectors through competition. What Marx showed was that situations could easily arise in which capital reinvestment would flow in such a way as to create disproportionalities between the sectors and that these disproportionalities could spiral into crises. The problem arose because, in striving to maximise the rate of profit, individual capitalists tended towards a systematic misallocation of capital flow across the two sectors. Later investigations that built on Marx's arguments, using far more sophisticated mathematical models, suggested that Marx was correct in his general reasoning. The twentieth-century Japanese economist Michio Morishima, for example, showed that, depending upon the dynamics of technological change and capital intensity in the two sectors, you would either get 'explosive oscillations' or 'monotonic divergence' around a balanced growth path in the economy. This insight confirmed the conclusions from earlier modelling (based indirectly on Marx's pioneering work on the reproduction schemas) of economic growth by the economists Roy Harrod and Evsey Domar, back in the 1930s and 1940s, that economic growth was always on a 'knife edge' of balanced growth that could all too easily fall off that narrow path and plunge headlong into major crises.

What they also showed was that crises are, in effect, not only inevitable but also necessary, since this is the only way in which balance can be restored and the internal contradictions of capital accumulation be at least temporarily resolved. Crises are, as it were, the irrational rationalisers of an always unstable capitalism. During a crisis, such as the one we are now in, it is always important to keep this fact in mind. We have always to ask: what is it that is being rationalised here and what directions are the rationalisations taking, since these are what will define not only our manner of exit from the crisis but the future character of capitalism? At times of crisis there are always options. Which one is chosen depends critically on the balance of class forces and the mental conceptions as to what might be possible. There was nothing inevitable about Roosevelt's New Deal any more than the Reagan-Thatcher counter-revolution of the early 1980s was inevitable. But the possibilities are not infinite either. It is the task of analysis to uncover what might now be possible and to place it firmly in relation to what is likely given the current state of class relations throughout the world.

———

At the base of the long supply chain that brings the means of production to the capitalist, there lurks a deeper problem of potential natural limits. Capitalism, like any other mode of production, relies upon the beneficence of nature. The depletion and degradation of the land and of so-called natural resources makes no more sense in the long run than the destruction of the collective powers of labour since both lie at the root of the production of all wealth. But individual capitalists, working in their own short-term interests and impelled by the coercive laws of competition, are perpetually tempted to take the position of *après moi le déluge* with respect to both the labourer and the soil. Even without this, the track of perpetual accumulation puts enormous pressures on the supply of natural resources, while the inevitable increase in the quantity of waste products is bound to test the capacity of ecological systems to absorb them without turning toxic. Here, too, capitalism is likely to encounter limits and barriers which will become increasingly hard to circumvent.

Nowhere has the idea of limits to capital been more stridently and persistently asserted throughout capitalism's history than with respect to scarcities in nature. The famous Enlightenment economists Thomas Malthus and David Ricardo both held that diminishing returns in agriculture would eventually lead the profit rate to fall to zero, thus spelling the end of capitalism as we know it because all profit would be absorbed by rent on land and on the supply of natural resources. Malthus went still further, of course, insisting (in the first version of his population theory) that the conflict between population growth and natural limits was bound to produce (and already was producing) crises of famine, poverty, pestilence and war, no matter what policies were implemented.

While Marx was not averse to contemplating the end of capitalism, he fiercely disputed the views of Malthus and Ricardo. With respect to Ricardo, Marx objected that falling transport costs and the opening up of new lands of remarkable fertility, particularly in the Americas, gave the lie to the idea that falling profits (a tendency which Marx readily accepted) and crises had anything whatsoever to do with natural scarcities. When faced with a crisis, Marx ironically observed, Ricardo 'takes refuge in organic chemistry'. In the case of Malthus, Marx's central objection was that capitalism creates poverty by virtue of its class relations and its compelling need to maintain an impoverished labour surplus for future exploitation. But the attribution of low living standards to scarcities in nature (rather than to the oppressions of capital) has been periodically resurrected. Environmental explanations were rife during the crisis of the 1970s (Donella H. Meadows' influential book *Limits to Growth* was published in 1972 and the first 'earth day' was in 1970) and it is no surprise that in the times of economic turmoil since 2006 a wide range of environmental issues, varying from peak oil and rising commodity prices (at least until autumn 2008) to global warming, have been invoked as underlying explanations for, or at least components of, our current economic difficulties.

There are all sorts of ways, it turns out, in which supposed limits in nature can be confronted, sometimes overcome and more often than not circumvented. The difficulty is that the category 'nature' is so broad and so complicated that it can encompass virtually everything that materially exists (including, of course, the so-called 'second nature' produced through human activities which we will consider separately below). It is, therefore, extremely difficult to come up with any comprehensive accounting of the role played by scarcities in nature (as opposed to scarcities arising from market manipulations) in crisis formation. The concept of natural resources are, for example, technical, social and cultural appraisals and so any apparent natural scarcity can in principle be mitigated, if not totally circumvented, by technological, social and cultural changes. But, it turns out, cultural forms are frequently just as fixed and problematic as anything else.

Sea sharks are being senselessly hunted close to extinction to satisfy the Chinese cultural predilection for shark's fin soup, as are African elephants for their ivory tusks which, when ground to powder, are supposed to have aphrodisiacal powers (the advent of Viagra may save the African elephant yet!). Western cultural preferences for meat-based diets have enormous implications for energy use and for global warming, both directly (cattle produce vast clouds of methane gas) and indirectly (the energy inputs in cattle feed are exorbitant relative to the energy imparted by meat-eating to human populations). The 'anglo' cultural preference for a 'home of one's own' on a plot of land has generated patterns of suburbanisation that are energy profligate as well as wasteful of land. In none of these instances would it be formally correct to blame capitalism *per se* for the development and persistence of these environmentally perverse cultural preferences, though it has to be said that an equally perverse capitalism is perfectly suited to fulfil, trade upon and in some instances go to great lengths to promote such cultural preferences (such as suburbanisation and meat-eating), whenever and wherever a profit is to be had by so doing.

Furthermore, 'nature' is far too simple a term to capture the immense geographical diversity of life forms and the infinite complexity of intertwined ecosystems. In the broad scheme of things the disappearance of a wetlands here, a local species there and a particular habitat somewhere else may seem trivial as well as inevitable given the imperatives of human population growth, let alone the continuity of endless capital accumulation at a compound rate. But it is precisely the aggregation of such small-scale changes that can produce macro-ecological problems such as global deforestation, loss of habitat and biodiversity, desertification and oceanic pollution.

Construing the relation to nature as inherently dialectical indicates a range of possible transformations in human behaviours as well as a process of natural evolution, including the human production of nature itself, that renders this relation dynamic and perpetually open. While on the one hand such a formulation would appear to deny the possibility of any out-and-out or prolonged, let alone 'final', environmental crisis, it also carries within it the prospect for cascading unintended consequences with widespread disruptive effects for the continuity of daily life as we currently know it. Who would have thought that refrigeration, which has saved so many lives and made possible large-scale urbanisation through the preservation of food quality, would ultimately produce the ozone hole by way of the chlorofluoral carbons used for cooling; that DDT would get so dispersed through the food chain as to lead to the deaths of Antarctic penguins; or that asbestos and lead-based paints would have such dire health effects on human populations many decades after their first use? It has long been understood (ever since the ancient Greeks, at least) that the unintended environmental consequences of human activities can be extensive and that the mere ability since ancient times to use fire or to unleash sheep and goats upon the landscape, to say nothing of the vast range of more contemporary effects of chemical wizardry on the toxicity of ecosystems, can result in such extensive forms of environmental modification to the point where nothing we now call nature is bereft of human influence.

But the compound rate of growth of capital accumulation inevitably suggests that the environmental modifications become both deeper and more extensive in their consequences over time. When the Manchester cotton factories started belching out smoke around 1780 or so, the peat moors on the Pennine hills shortly thereafter collapsed from acid deposition. But this is a far cry from the Ohio valley power stations destroying the ecology of New England forests and lakes and the British power stations doing the same to Scandinavia from the 1950s onwards.

What we call the natural world is not some passive entity but, as the philosopher Alfred North Whitehead once put it, 'a system in perpetual search of novelty'. To begin with, tectonic movements beneath the earth's surface generate instabilities that give us earthquakes, volcanic eruptions, tsunamis and other events, while instabilities in atmospheric and oceanic circulations give us hurricanes, tornadoes, snow storms, droughts and heat waves that have all manner of human consequences, albeit unevenly distributed both geographically and socially. Furthermore, trading upon and profiting from human disasters induced by natural events is far too frequent a feature of capitalism to be taken lightly.

While human action has successfully eliminated the bubonic plague and smallpox, it now has to confront entirely new pathogens and diseases such as HIV/AIDS, SARS, the West Nile virus, Ebola and avian flu, to say nothing of the potential for a new mutated influenza pandemic of the sort that killed millions back in 1918. Climates have long been subjected to a whole range of forces that uncomfortably mix together human-induced and non-human elements in such a way as to make it difficult to determine which is which, even when the very best scientific minds are collectively put to work to figure

75

out the global climatic consequences of human action. While the effects are indisputable, the full range of consequences is almost impossible to determine. Past changes, before human beings set to work to change the face of the earth, have sometimes been quite rapid – at least as measured in geological time (hundreds of years) – and quite unpredictable, with wide-ranging effects (such as waves of species extinction). Other things remaining equal, the indisputably humanly-induced effects are subject to the compound growth rate rule, which surely must give cause for serious concern and at the very minimum command serious investigation and precautionary international regulatory action (of the sort accomplished in the 1989 Montreal Protocol that curbed the use of CFCs). But even then, anyone who thinks they can predict climatic futures with even modest certainty is fooling themselves.

The historical geography of capitalism has, however, been marked by an incredible fluidity and flexibility with respect to the relation to nature coupled with wide-ranging unexpected consequences (both good and bad, from the perspective of human welfare). Hence, it would be false to argue that there are absolute limits in our metabolic relation to nature that cannot in principle be transcended or bypassed. But this does not mean that the barriers are not sometimes serious and that overcoming them can be achieved without going through some kind of general environmental crisis (as opposed to the collapse of the shark population, which could be construed as 'merely' regrettable were it not for the unknown but probably wide-ranging effect it will have upon the whole oceanic ecosystem).

A lot of capitalist politics, particularly these days, is about ensuring that the free gifts of nature are both available to capital on an easy basis and also sustained for future use. The tensions within capitalist politics over these sorts of issues can sometimes be acute. On the one hand, for example, the desire to maintain an expanding flow of cheap oil has been central to the geopolitical stance of the United States over the last fifty to sixty years, precisely because capital surplus absorption by suburbanisation after 1945 was conditional upon the availability of cheap oil. Making sure that the world's oil supplies are open for exploitation has drawn the US into conflict in the Middle East and elsewhere and energy politics, just to take one example of a crucial relation to nature, has often emerged as a dominant issue within the state apparatus and in inter-state relations.

But on the other hand the politics of cheap oil have posed problems of excessive depletion, as well as global warming and a host of other air quality issues (ground level ozone, smog, particulate matter in the atmosphere, and the like) that pose increasing risks to human populations. High-energy-consuming urban sprawl has produced chronic land use degradation conducive to flooding, the siting of waterways and the production of urban 'heat islands'. These environmental impacts complement the depletion of the natural resources required to support an automobile industry which played such a pivotal role in capital surplus absorption from the 1930s onwards.

Some Marxists, led by the Californian economist Jim O'Connor, who founded the journal *Capitalism, Nature, Socialism*, refer to the barriers in nature as 'the second contradiction of capitalism' (the first being, of course, the capital–labour relation). In our own times it is certainly true that this 'second contradiction' is absorbing as much if not more political attention than the labour question and there is a wide-ranging field of concern, of political anxiety and endeavour, that focuses on the idea of a crisis in the relation to nature, as a sustainable source of raw materials, as mere land for further capitalist (urban and agricultural) development, as well as a sink for an increasing stream of toxic waste. But there is always a danger in overemphasising supposedly 'pure' natural limits at the expense of concentrating upon the capitalist dynamics that force environmental changes in the first place and on the social (particularly class) relations that drive those dynamics in certain environmentally perverse directions. The capitalist class, it goes without saying, is always delighted, on this point at least, to have its role displaced and masked by an environmental rhetoric that lets them off the hook as the progenitors of the problem. When oil prices spiked in the summer of 2008, it was

helpful to claim natural scarcity when the oil companies and speculators were to blame.

In O'Connor's work, this second contradiction of capitalism
came to displace the first after the defeats of the labour and socialist
movements of the 1970s onwards. For him, the environmental
movement constitutes (or should constitute) the cutting edge of
anti-capitalist agitation and during the 1980s and 1990s it did indeed
sometimes seem as if the environmental movement was the only
anti-capitalist movement that had any life in it. I leave you to make
up your own mind on how far that sort of politics should be pursued.
But what is certain is that the barrier in the relation to nature is not
to be taken lightly and that the stresses are becoming, along with
everything else, more global.

There may be an imminent crisis in our relation to nature that
will require widespread adaptations (cultural and social as well as
technical) if this barrier is to be successfully circumvented, at least
for a time, within the framework of endless capital accumulation.
The fact that capitalism has, in the past, successfully navigated
around natural barriers, and that it has often done so profitably
since environmental technologies have long been big business and
can certainly become much bigger (as the Obama administration
proposes), does not mean that the nature question can never constitute some ultimate limit. But in terms of the immediate crisis of our
time that began in 2006, the question of natural limits cannot, on
the surface at least, be accorded primacy of place, with the possible
exception of the role of so-called 'peak oil' and its impact on energy
prices. The issue of peak oil requires, therefore, some commentary.

As background it is worth noting that what began to appear as
the greatest of all potential natural limits to capitalist development
in eighteenth-century Britain was neatly transcended by the turn to
fossil fuels and the invention of the steam engine. Before that time
the land had to be used for both food and energy production (from
biomass) and it became increasingly clear that it could not be used
for both at a compound rate of growth given the transport capacities

of the time. After 1780 or so, energy could come from underground (in the form of coal reserves laid down in the Carboniferous period) and the land could be used for food production alone. A century or so later the immense energy reserves of the Cretaceous period could likewise be tapped in the form of oil and natural gas. I make this observation in order to point up the obvious stupidity of trying to respond to supposed contemporary oil shortages by resort to ethanol production, which takes energy production back on to the land (using for the most part more energy in its production than it actually makes) with immediate and serious impacts on food grain prices. The perversity of a policy that takes us right back into the energy versus food trap of eighteenth-century Britain is nothing short of shocking. How did this come about?

The idea of 'peak oil' goes back to 1956 when a geologist then working for Shell Oil, M. King Hubbert, predicted, on the basis of a formula linking rates of new discoveries and rates of exploitation, that oil production within the US would peak in the 1970s and then gradually contract. He lost his job at Shell but his predictions proved correct and since the 1970s the United States has daily become more and more dependent upon foreign oil as domestic sources have continued to decline. The US now imports close to $300-billion-worth of oil annually, which accounts for almost one third of a burgeoning foreign trade deficit that has to be covered by borrowing from the rest of the world at well over $2 billion per day. The recent turn to ethanol combined a drive to diminish the political and economic vulnerabilities of the US to this foreign dependency with a delicious subsidy to a powerful agribusiness lobby which dominates the very undemocratic US Senate (where small rural states command 60 per cent of the votes) and which has long been one of the most powerful lobbies in Washington (the high level of agricultural subsidies in the US have been one of the most contentious issues in WTO negotiations with the rest of the world). The subsequent utterly predictable rise in food grain prices was also good news for agribusiness even as New Yorkers suddenly found their bagels increasing in price by 50 per cent. The consequent exacerbation of world hunger is no joke. As one critic of the Hubbard thesis noted, 'Filling a twenty-five gallon tank of an SUV with pure ethanol requires 450 pounds of corn, enough calories to feed one person for a year. On present trends (2008), the number of chronically hungry people could double by 2025 to 1.2 billion.'

This was all backed by increasing evidence (and plenty of rhetoric) that the 'peak oil' formula that Hubbert had applied to the US could usefully be applied to predict global oil supplies. Since global rates of discovery peaked, according to the data, in the mid-1980s, then it could widely be anticipated that oil production would itself peak no later than around 2010. Several oil-producing countries other than the US have roughly conformed to Hubbert's peak formula, including Kuwait, Venezuela, the United Kingdom, Norway and Mexico. While the situation elsewhere, particularly in Saudi Arabia (where there are rumours that peak production has already been achieved), the Middle East generally, Russia (where President Putin recently declared, though almost certainly for political rather than factual reasons, that peak oil has been passed) and Africa, is harder to monitor, the rise in oil prices from less than $20 a barrel in 2002 to $150 a barrel (and a doubling of gas prices at the pump for US consumers) by the summer of 2008 provided all the popular evidence needed to show that peak oil had arrived and was here to stay. Fortunately or unfortunately, depending on your view, oil prices suddenly plunged to less than $50 a barrel by the end of 2008, putting a big popular question mark over the relevance of the theory and opening the path towards central bank relaxation of fears over an oil-price rise led inflation and a consequent reduction of interest rates to close to zero in the United States at the end of 2008. Since oil at $50 a barrel is often cited as the break point above which ethanol becomes profitable, the vast investment in nearly doubling the number of ethanol plants in the US since 2006 may now be in jeopardy.

How and why the scarcity supposedly given by nature and represented so neatly by the formula of peak oil can be so volatile in the

ion. To get into this requires
e category, which Marx char-
er': rent on land and natural
t that matter (I discount here
called 'absolute rent' because,
irst category that does work is
n the first instance because of
nds and mines relative to the
that needs to be brought into
ands of the market. Differen-
a locational component (land
y more valuable than land on
e easier to exploit than those
In the case of oil, the costs of
l least accessible wells have to
t added at the average rate for
is this that sets the basic price
profits since their production
heir yield higher than on the
is excess profit accrue? Given
over the land and the oil well,
s (individuals or the state) can
d or the resource for others to
yment (rent) for the use of the
ed by the company exploiting
n oil sold directly in the world
te-owned oil company) that
holds the property right to the resource that it itself exploits. In all of
these cases, however, the property owner has a reserve price which
they typically demand and extract before they release the resource to
others to exploit. They can claim all or most of the differential rent if
they are savvy enough and still have production proceed.

The very existence of this reserve price testifies to the monopoly
rent that attaches to all forms of property rights claims under the

institutional arrangements that characterise capitalism. Any holder of a property right can withhold access to that property, and refuse to release it until a reserve price is reached. In competitive situations this reserve price is typically rather low because if there is abundant land available, producers have choices as to where they go and if you do not release your land to them (by sale, lease or rental agreement) at a reasonable price, then others will. In some instances this reserve price goes close to zero, though in that case there seems to be no point in property owners releasing the land anyway.

But at this point we have also to acknowledge that the fertility or productivity of the resource is not entirely due to nature but to the investments in technologies and improvements that raise the productivity of the original resource to new levels. Land fertility is as much made as given by nature. The owner of the property right to the land has a vested interest in the user improving its productivity. In the successful period of 'high farming' in nineteenth-century Britain, before the long agricultural depression that began in 1873, owners favoured long leases since this encouraged tenants to undertake long-term improvements (such as drainage, fertilisation and crop rotation techniques) that improved fertility rather than degraded it. In this case differential rent would accrue to the user during the time of the lease as a return on capital investment in long-term improvements. But how do we account for the extremely fertile land that was drained or reclaimed from the sea in the sixteenth century? While differential rent is a single category it rather beautifully encapsulates the problem of how hard it is eventually to distinguish what is given by nature and what arises as a result of human action, even as it highlights the strategic question that has to be faced by any owner of a resource: to mine an existing resource (no matter whether its productivity is due to nature or to human action) with ruthless efficiency until it is exhausted, or to husband or improve the resource for future and potentially long-term sustainable use.

In the case of oil wells, however, we are here dealing with a non-renewable resource, the reserve price on which is given by conditions of relative scarcity. Differential rent on oil wells (no matter whether it arises from superior production technologies or natural conditions of, say, high pressure and large quantities underground) here shades into monopoly rent, as has so obviously been the case with OPEC's control over the release of oil into the world market at a rate which maintains or stabilises prices at a given level. OPEC's range of action is limited, of course, by the fact that not all states belong to the cartel. But, in spite of all the usual objections, both producers and users generally benefit from reasonable stability in market prices that can be achieved by OPEC's actions. So why, then, such volatility in oil prices?

This brings us to the crux of the problem, because the market for oil is driven as much by scarcities created by social, economic and political conditions as it is by so-called natural scarcities. Oil rents and oil futures are targets for speculative investment and belief in some impending scarcity (whether it be due to political instabilities, wars or peak oil) drives up prices dramatically, particularly under conditions where there is even a temporary shortfall in the supply to match some 'peak' in demand such as that which arose when in the mid-1990s both China and India entered into the oil market in ways that matched their strong spurts of economic growth. Oil rents and oil futures therefore get capitalised as a form of fictitious capital and claims also circulate in such a way that all operators in these markets hedge their bets, create all manner of derivatives and then seek to manipulate the market in ways that match their bets. As oil prices rise, of course, all sorts of marginal fields get exploited (or in some cases re-opened) simply because the definition of the margin fluctuates with singular volatility. Canada's Athabaska tar sands are expensive to exploit but become highly profitable when oil goes to $150 a barrel. But the problem is that it takes considerable time to bring new fields into production and so the response time to a surge in demand is slow unless there is existing capacity, such as that controlled by OPEC, which can more easily be brought into play. But here, too, the whole operation including that of refining is capital-intensive and very sensitive both to conditions in capital markets, to profit margins and to what is happening in the oil futures market, which is one of the great markets for hedging and betting and so heavily influenced by the availability of surplus capital. When the world is awash with surplus liquidity, then why not put some of it into betting in the oil futures market? Particularly if someone tells you that peak oil is just around the corner!

What is clear from all this is that the relation to nature is a two-way street down which the vagaries and contingencies of naturally occurring evolutionary changes are matched by the vagaries and contingencies of the social, economic and political situations that define both the meaning of and the relation to nature. Barriers to accumulation are perpetually dissolving and re-forming around the issue of so-called natural scarcities and on occasion, as Marx might put it, these barriers can be transformed into absolute contradictions and crises.

———

Nature has been modified by human action over the ages. The environment is a category that has to include the fields that have been cleared, the swamps and wetlands that have been drained, the rivers that have been re-engineered and the estuaries that have been dredged, the forests that have been cut over and re-planted, the roads, canals, irrigation systems, railroads, ports and harbours, airstrips and terminals that have been built, the dams, power-supply generators and electric grid systems that have been constructed, the water and sewer systems, cables and communications networks, vast cities, sprawling suburbs, factories, schools, houses, hospitals, shopping malls and tourist destinations galore. These environments, furthermore, are inhabited by entirely new species (think of dogs, cats, cattle breeds and featherless chickens) that have either been engineered through selective breeding practices (supplemented now by direct genetic engineering practices that modify such crops as corn and tomatoes) or that have mutated or found new environmental niches (think of the patterns of diseases, like avian flu, that mutate and first gain a footing in the newly constructed environments of factory featherless chicken production). There is little left on the surface of planet earth that can be imagined as a pure and pristine nature absent any human modification. On the other hand there is nothing unnatural about species, including ours, modifying their environments in ways that are conducive to their own reproduction. Ants do it, bees do it, and beavers do it most spectacularly. In the same way that there is nothing unnatural about an ant hill, so there is, surely, nothing particularly unnatural about New York City.

But all of this has taken human energy and ingenuity to construct. The built environment that constitutes a vast field of collective means of production and consumption absorbs huge amounts of capital in both its construction and its maintenance. Urbanisation is one way to absorb the capital surplus.

But projects of this sort cannot be mobilised without assembling massive financial power. And capital invested in such projects has to be prepared to wait for returns over the long haul. This means either state involvement or a financial system robust enough to assemble the capital and deploy it with the desired long-term effects and wait patiently for the returns. This has usually meant radical innovations in the state–finance nexus. Since the 1970s, financial innovations such as the securitisation of mortgage debt and the spreading of investment risks through the creation of derivative markets, all tacitly (and now, as we see, actually) backed by state power, have permitted a huge flow of excess liquidity into all facets of urbanisation and built environment construction worldwide.

In each instance innovation in the state–finance nexus has been a necessary condition for channelling surpluses into urbanisation and infrastructural projects (e.g. dams and highways). But again and again over the last thirty years, excessive investment in such projects has become a regular catalytic trigger for crisis formation. As has been pointed out earlier, several of the financial crises since 1970 have been triggered by overextension in property markets.

The compounding rate of growth that lies at the heart of a capitalist mode of production cannot be achieved without the necessary physical infrastructural conditions first being put in place. An export-led economic boom in some country requires adequate prior transport and port facilities just as a factory cannot function without adequate (and sometimes copious) supplies of water and energy inputs and a transport and communications infrastructure that permits production to proceed without too many bottlenecks in the supply of inputs (including labour) and in the marketing of the product. Workers also have to live, shop, educate their kids and meet their leisure needs somewhere reasonably close by.

This vast infrastructure that constitutes the built environment is a necessary material precondition for capitalist production, circulation and accumulation to proceed. This infrastructure, furthermore, requires constant and adequate maintenance to keep it in good working order. An increasing portion of economic output has therefore to be put into maintaining these necessary infrastructures in an adequate condition. Maintenance failures (such as the breakdown of an electric grid, the failure of water supply or disruptions in transport and communications systems) are far from uncommon even in the most advanced capitalist economies (the United States has seen its share of infrastructural disasters such as collapsing bridges and malfunctioning power grids over the last few years). Further capital accumulation is, moreover, predicated upon building new infrastructures. The survival of capitalism, in short, depends upon the organisation and financing of material infrastructural investments appropriate to a compounding rate of growth. Capital has to create a landscape adequate to its own requirements – a second nature built in its own image as it were – at one point in time, only to revolutionise that landscape at a later point in time in order to accommodate further accumulation at a compound rate.

But what incentives exist for capital to invest in these infrastructures? An adequate rate of monetary return is the obvious answer and this means that payment for the use of these infrastructures has somehow to be extracted from those who benefit from them. While that is easy enough to imagine with respect to the houses, shops and factories that can be rented, leased or sold to users and also imaginable (though not necessarily desirable) for certain items of collective provision (such as highways, schools, universities, hospitals) that could be funded on a fee-for-service basis, there are still many aspects of the built environment that are held in common and for which it is very difficult to extract a direct payment. It is here that the state again has to enter into the picture and play a central role. To do this it needs to extract taxes. The theory of productive state expenditures pioneered in Second Empire Paris by the Saint-Simonian financiers and later generalised by Keynes suggests that the tax base should increase as private capital responds positively to possibilities generated by new infrastructural provisions. The result is a form of state–capital circulation in which state investments not only pay for themselves but also earn extra revenues to be put into more infrastructures.

Considerations of this sort require that we liberate the concept of production from its customary confinements. The usual image of production that prevails is of workers toiling away in a factory, perhaps on an assembly line making cars. But the workers who produce and maintain the highways, the water supply systems, the sewers and the houses and those who do the landscaping and the interior decorating are just as important. A multitude of firms and labourers are actively engaged in the (almost invariably debt-financed) production of urbanisation, or what is perhaps better more generically described as the production of new spaces, places and environments. The political struggles that arise in this arena typically exhibit rather distinctive qualities. While construction workers may wage a fierce war with contractors over wage rates, conditions of labour and safety, they are notorious for supporting both private and state-led development projects of no matter what sort. To the degree that such projects spark oppositions on environmental, political and social grounds, and to the degree that they invariably entail dispossession of the land rights of often vulnerable populations, then working-class factions are just as likely to collide in opposition as to unite in anti-capitalist struggle.

The production of spaces and places has absorbed, over time, vast amounts of capital surplus. New landscapes and new geographies have been created within which capital circulates in ways that are frequently haunted by deep contradictions. If the vast amount of fixed capital embedded in the land (look down upon the land next time you fly just to get a sense of how vast this is) is to be realised, then it must be used and paid for by capitalist producers in the here and now. Abandoning all those assets, as happened to many older industrial cities in the huge wave of deindustrialisation of the 1980s, incurs losses (social as well as infrastructural) and can itself be a source of crises that affect not only those that hold the debt on many of these infrastructural investments but also the economy at large. It is here that Marx's thesis that capitalism inevitably encounters barriers within its own nature (in this case, within the spaces, places and environments it has produced) becomes most visible.

―――――

The relations between capital and labour as well as those between capital and nature are mediated by the choice of technologies and organisational forms. Marx is, I think, at his very best in theorising the forces driving these choices and why it is that capitalists fetishise technologies (machinery in particular) and new organisational forms. Got a problem? There has to be a technological or organisational fix!

Machines cannot produce profits by themselves. But those capitalists with superior technologies and organisational forms typically gain a higher rate of profit than their competitors and eventually drive them out of business. As they do so, the cost of goods consumed by the workers typically declines because of rising productivity. Labour costs can then be reduced without lowering the standard of living of labour, generating greater profit for all capitalists. If productivity gains are very strong, material living standards of the workers can increase even as wages decline. This happened in the US after the 1990s with the Wal-Mart system of retailing based on cheap imports from China. Note that for Wal-Mart it was more organisational form than machinery that did the trick.

The upshot is a perpetual incentive for organisational and techno-logical dynamism. 'Modern industry,' Marx notes in *Capital*, 'never views or treats of the existing form of a production process as the definitive one. Its technical basis is therefore revolutionary, whereas all earlier modes of production were essentially conservative.' This is a persistent motif in Marx's works. As he and Engels presciently noted in *The Communist Manifesto*, 'the bourgeoisie cannot exist without constantly revolutionising the instruments of production, and thereby the relations of production, and with them the whole relations of society ... Constant revolutionising of production, unin-terrupted disturbance of all social conditions, everlasting uncertainty and agitation, distinguish the bourgeois epoch from all other ones.'

But why this revolutionary impulse in the heart of capitalism and why is capitalism so different from other modes of production? Human beings are clearly fascinated by the perpetual pursuit of novelty, but the social and cultural conditions under which such a fascination can become a central driving force in human evolution are very special. Most hitherto-existing social orders were inherently conservative. They sought to preserve the status quo, to protect a ruling class and repress human impulses towards innovation and new ideas. This was a persistent feature of the history of Chinese civilisation, for example. It ultimately proved to be the Achilles heel of actually existing communism. Bureaucratic and power-structure ossification became the problem.

For reasons that are much debated and which will probably never be finally settled, between the Catholic Church's inquisition and repression of Galileo in the early seventeenth century and Watt's invention of the steam engine in the late eighteenth century, there occurred in Europe, and in Britain in particular, a radical reconfiguration of the social, political, cultural and legal conditions that turned innovation and new ideas into an open sesame for the creation of wealth and power. A ruling class continued to rule, but not necessarily through the same personae or their biological descendants.

The kind of society that emerged was grounded in private property rights, juridical individualism, some version of free markets and free trade. The state increasingly saw its role as the management of this economy as a way to augment its wealth and power. None of this worked perfectly according to the rubrics of John Locke and Adam Smith, and one only has to read Charles Dickens's *Bleak House*, with its interminable legal struggles in Chancery, to recognise that British society was and still is constituted as a perpetual power struggle between the old and the new social orders. But in Britain and its erstwhile colony the United States the coercive laws of competition that flowed from these new institutional arrangements were allowed broadly to do their work unhindered by class and status repressions.

The primary mechanism that liberates innovation from repression and regulatory control is, therefore, competition. This typically produces a perpetual stream of innovations in technologies and organisational forms simply because those capitalists with more efficient, effective and productive labour processes gain higher profits than the rest. The quest for greater efficiency actually encompasses all aspects of the circulation of capital, from the procuring of labour supplies and means of production (hence the supply-chain structure of just-in-time delivery from subcontractors to the modern corporation) through to efficient and low-cost marketing strategies (the Wal-Mart syndrome). Capitalist entities, from individual entrepreneurs to vast corporations, are therefore forced to pay close attention to organisational and technological forms and are always on the look-out for those innovations that yield them excess profit, at least for a time. The trouble is that the excess profit that accrues to them is ephemeral because competitors can catch up with and even leap over their technological and organisational advantage.

Fierce, and what capitalists sometimes call 'ruinous' competition tends, therefore, to produce leap-frogging innovations that more often than not lead capitalists to fetishise technological and organisational innovation as the answer to all their prayers (including the disciplining of labour in both the market and the labour process). This fetishism is fed upon to the degree that innovation itself becomes a business that seeks to form its own market by persuading each and every one of us that we cannot survive without having the latest gadget and gismo at our command. The fear of the destructive and the potentially ruinous impacts of new technologies sometimes provokes attempts to control or even suppress threatening innovations. In recent times, monopolising or buying up patents or systematically destroying certain innovative paths (like electric cars) through monopoly control has not been unheard of, but as we are currently seeing in the case of the Detroit auto industry, in the long run this sort of response does not work.

But it is not only competition between capitalists that matters. There are other decision-making entities that play a decisive role in fostering innovation, the most important of which is the state apparatus. A putative inter-state system was consolidated in Europe through the Treaty of Westphalia in 1648. Sovereign entities formed whose territorial integrity was supposed to be respected or protected by main force if necessary. From this point onwards many states became involved in the pursuit of superior military technologies, organisational forms and transport and communications systems. State-sponsored, though nominally autonomous 'learned societies' – for example, the Académie Française and the British Royal Society – started to sponsor research initiatives, such as the celebrated search for a chronometer that would work on the high seas and thereby facilitate navigation (the aristocratic orders that still held power refused, however, to recognise the achievement of a mere artisan, John Harrison, who actually solved the problem in 1772). What later on came to be called a 'military–industrial complex' emerged in shadowy form early on in the history of capitalist state development (the 'Ponts et Chaussées' organisation, founded in 1747, became legendary in France for its scientific and technological expertise on infrastructural and military construction problems). But it was only during and after the Second World War that this aspect of innovative behaviour became paramount as Cold War arms races, space races and all the rest of it involved the state directly in research and development activity along with capitalist firms in different sectors of the economy (everything from nuclear energy to satellite imaging and public health). War periods or periods of political tension (such as the Cold War, and more recently, the so-called 'War on Terror') have thus played a crucial role in directing paths of innovation. In much the same way that the state–finance nexus came to play a key role in capitalist development, so a state–corporate nexus also emerges around questions of research and development in sectors of the economy considered to be of strategic (and not solely military) importance to the state. Surveillance becomes big business.

To the degree that R&D underpins comparative advantage in global economic competition, so a wide range of departments within the governmental apparatus (dealing with health, food and agriculture, transport and communications and energy, as well as the more traditional military arms and surveillance), backed by a huge semi-public research university system, have come to play a vital role in technological and organisational innovation in association with industry in the leading capitalist powers. In Japan it was the state that bureaucratically welded together corporate activities around an organisational and technological research programme that brought Japan into competitive pre-eminence through industrialisation (a model that was subsequently followed in South Korea, Taiwan, Brazil, Singapore and now plays a crucial role in China).

As all these forces come together, so the pace of technological and organisational change typically accelerates to produce a rapid succession of new frontiers in product innovation and development as well as in methods of production. Such waves of innovation can become destructive and ruinous even for capital itself, in part because yesterday's technologies and organisational forms have to be discarded before they have been amortised (like the computer I am working on) and because perpetual reorganisations in labour processes are disruptive to continuity of flow and destabilising for social relations. The devaluation of prior investments (machinery, plant and equipment, built environments, communications links) before their value has been recovered, for example, becomes a serious problem. Likewise, rapid shifts in labour quality require-ments (e.g. the sudden need for new skills such as computer literacy) that outpace existing labour force capacities generate stresses in the labour market. Social and educational infrastructures find it hard to adapt quickly enough and the perpetual need for 'retraining' several times in a worker's lifetime puts stresses on public resources as well as private energies. The production of chronic job insecurity through deskilling and reskilling is backed by technologically induced unem-ployment (about 60 per cent of job losses in the US in recent years are attributable to technological changes while only 30 per cent are due to the widely blamed offshoring of jobs to Mexico, China and elsewhere).

Spiralling crises of disproportionality can also arise out of the uneven development of technological capacities across different sectors, producing, for example, imbalances in the output of wage goods versus means of production. Dramatic shifts in spatio-temporal relations consequent upon innovations in transport and communications can revolutionise the global landscape of produc-tion and consumption (as we have already argued in the case of dein-dustrialisation) and produce 'switching crises' (sudden switches in flows of capital investment from one 'hot spot' to another) within a volatile system of uneven geographical development. Sudden accel-erations and general speed-ups in capital circulation (such as the computer trading in financial markets that are often blamed for the recent difficulties on Wall Street) can be chaotic and disruptive as well as advantageous and highly profitable for those whose math-ematical models work best (at least for a time).

The history of technological and organisational change within capitalism has been nothing short of remarkable. But it is, evidently, a double-edged sword that can be as disruptive and destructive as it can be progressive and creative. Marx himself felt that he had identified a critical means to explain the falling profitability that both Malthus and Ricardo had hypothesised. It was best explained, he argued, by the overall impact of labour-saving innovations on profit rates. Displacing labour, the source of making all new wealth, from production was bound to be counterproductive for profitability in the long run. The trend towards falling profits (which Ricardo had identified) and the crises to which it inevitably would give rise were internal to capitalism and not explicable at all in terms of natural limits. But it is hard to make Marx's theory of the falling rate of profit work when innovation is as much capital or means of production saving (through, for example, more efficient energy use) as it is labour saving. Marx himself actually listed a variety of counteracting influences to a falling rate of profit, including rising rates of exploitation of labour, falling costs of means of production (capital-saving innovations), foreign trade that lowered resource costs, a massive increase in the industrial reserve army of labour that blunts the stimulus for the employment of new technologies, along with the constant devaluation of capital, the absorption of surplus capital in the production of physical infrastructures, as well as, finally, monopolisation and the opening up of new labour-intensive lines of production. This list is so long that it renders the neat explanation for a solid 'law' of falling profits as a mechanical response to labour-saving technological innovation more than a little moot.

The very last item on Marx's list of counteracting influences deserves further elaboration because the capital surplus absorption problem would long ago have sounded the death knell of capitalism, had it not been for the opening up of new product lines. Since Marx's day the elaboration of new product lines and product niches has been a life-saver for capitalist development at the same time as it has transformed daily life, even down to the modest income levels of so-called developing countries (witness the rapid proliferation of transistor radios and cell phones throughout the world in a few decades). The household technologies now commanded by the professional bourgeoisie and the upper and middle classes of the advanced capitalist countries (which now include, in addition to Europe and North America, much of east and south-east Asia) are simply astonishing. Product innovation and development, like everything else, has in itself become big business applicable not only to the improvement of existing products (like automobiles) but also wholly new sectors of industry (such as computers and electronics and their huge fields of application in government, pharmaceuticals, health care, corporate organisation, entertainment, and the like, as well as in household goods). Much of this depends, of course, on the tastes of consumers and their level of effective demand (matters to be considered shortly). But the astonishing penchant for creating wholly new product lines and the acceleration that has occurred in new product development since the 1950s or so has placed the development of consumerism and a rising effective demand at the centre of the sustainability of contemporary capitalism in ways that Marx, for one, would have found hard to recognise.

The implication, however, is that any weakening in the coercive laws of competition, through, for example, patent laws and monopolisation, the increasing centralisation of capital or too heavily bureaucratised state intervention, will have an impact upon the pace and form of technological revolutions. In the United States, the research universities, which are hard to regulate and bring under centralised control even as they become more corporatised and increasingly reliant on state and corporate funds, play a crucial role in maintaining a technological comparative edge versus the rest of the world. The university's peculiarly loose form of organisation guards against the tendency towards ossification (and tacit corruption) in the overlap between state and corporate bureaucracies. Significantly and belatedly, the Europeans, the Japanese and the Chinese now recognise the significance of this sort of state-university R&D sector to their own competitive futures and are desperately trying to catch up by investing hugely in higher education and by financing research and development think-tanks.

Class struggle dimensions also deserve consideration. Broad-based oppositions (e.g. the Luddite movement of machine-breaking in the early nineteenth century that Marx considered), including the sabotage of new technologies and organisational forms on the shop floor, have a long history. This opposition arises because capital frequently uses new technologies as weapons in class struggle and workers instinctively resist. The more workers are positioned as appendages of the machines they operate, the less freedom of manoeuvre they have, the less their particular skills count and the more vulnerable they become to technologically induced unemployment. Hence, the frequently strong opposition of workers to the introduction of new technologies. The compromise, of course, has been productivity agreements between unions and capital in which both sides get to share some of the benefits that come from increasing productivity. The productivity agreements that became common in many of the advanced sectors of the capitalist world in the 1950s and 1960s (thus underpinning a rising standard of living for the privileged sectors of the working classes) became harder and harder to enforce after the crisis of the mid 1970s. Since then, most of the benefits of rising productivity have gone to capitalists and their upper-class agents, while the incomes of workers have stagnated by comparison.

But there are two further implications of technological and organisational dynamism that are of paramount importance if we are to understand the evolutionary trajectory of capitalism. While both of them are long-standing, they have both also become more and more salient since the Second World War, to the point where they have emerged as dominant from the 1970s onwards.

Firstly, it has long been argued that there are so-called 'long waves' or 'Kondratieff cycles' lasting on average fifty years in capitalist developmental history based upon technological innovations that bundle together in a particular place and time to set the stage for steady development and diffusion outwards until a new bundle of innovations comes along which supersedes the first. It is possible to look backwards and define 'eras' of capitalist development that roughly correspond to the railroads, steamships, the coal and steel industry and the telegraph; the automobile, the oil, rubber and plastics industries and the radio; the jet engine, refrigerators, air-conditioners, the light metals (aluminium) industry and TV; and the computer chip and the new electronics industry that underpinned the 'new economy' of the 1990s. What is missing from this account is an understanding of the revolutionary and contradictory social consequences of the capital–state dynamic and its associated shifts in organisational form (such as the move from family firms to vertically integrated corporations to horizontally networked systems of production and distribution).

The thesis of regularly spaced and mechanically occurring temporal (and spatial diffusion) waves in technological and organisational innovation does not, in my view, work. But the insight that technological and organisational forms become, as it were, paradigmatic for a time until their possibilities are exhausted, only to be replaced by something else, is important. It becomes even more significant as the capital surplus absorption problem becomes more acute. Where would the growing quantity of capital surplus find opportunities for profitable investment were it not for these innovation waves? The more surplus there is around, the more likely it will rush frantically into the new technologies in a vast speculative wave that puts to shame the railroad booms and crashes of the nineteenth century. The state–finance nexus here integrates with the state–corporate research nexus since, without the venture capital up front, many innovations would have languished in the shadows rather than surged so rapidly to prominence.

Institutional arrangements and state and bureaucratic cultures here play a critical role. Innovation waves are likely, however, to become faster, more compressed and more speculative in response to the compounding rate of capital accumulation and the crushing need to find new venues for capital surplus absorption. Where, then, will our next innovation-led speculative bubble come from? My current bet is biomedical and genetic engineering (this is where the big philanthropic organisations funded by those like Bill Gates and George Soros that have partially replaced the state in research financing are concentrating their activities), along with so-called 'green' technologies (which, I suspect, are more limited than generally imagined).

Consider, secondly, the revolutionary implications of technological and organisational changes for society in general. It has long been true that the drive to create new wealth and power through new product and organisational innovation has permitted a ruling class to continue to rule but not necessarily through the same personae or their biological descendants. Think of Andrew Carnegie, Jay Gould, the Vanderbilts, Andrew Mellon and the other 'robber barons' of post-Civil War America and the vast wealth they built from almost nothing on the basis of the railroads; think of Henry Ford, John D. Rockefeller (of Standard Oil) and all the others whose rising class power rested on the automobile; then think of Bill Gates, Paul Allen, Jack Welch, Michael Bloomberg and others who took over the reins after 1980 on the basis of the new electronic and communication technologies, along with the financial tycoons like George Soros, Sandy Weill, Robert Rubin, Bruce Wasserstein, Charles Sanford and all the rest of the Wall Street gang.

Plainly, the 'uninterrupted disturbance of all social conditions' and 'everlasting uncertainty and agitation', as Marx and Engels put it, applies as much to the composition of the capitalist class as it does to anything else. The capitalist class undergoes revolution after revolution, and not always peaceably so. Those who once held power often search to undermine the 'arrivistes' and 'nouveau riche' by entangling them in networks of exclusion and of culture that are hard to break when not actually manipulating their downfall (as the old-fashioned Rothschilds did to the 'arriviste' Péreire brothers and their new credit institutions in 1868 in Paris). The radical reconstitution of class relations through financialisation has yet to run its course.

But there is yet another dimension to the transformations of social relations consequent on new technologies and organisational forms. Marx held it to be a virtue of the technologies developed under capitalist modernity that they rendered transparent and understandable industrial processes that had long been opaque and mysterious. The science and technologies of pasteurisation, of steel-making, of steam power and of industrial materials and construction were all open for everyone to understand rather than locked into the minds and customary practices of artisans. But we have now come full circle, it seems. So many contemporary technologies (everything from nuclear power to materials science to electronics) are so complicated that we are increasingly subjected to a 'rule of experts'. We have all sat in the doctor's or dentist's office and had some blurry picture called an X-ray expertly interpreted as good or bad news; most of us would not know how to begin to construct an adequate interpretation. Diagnosing what is wrong with a computer system is no easy task (and dealing with hackers, viruses and identity robbers is even harder). Most of us rely on a user-friendly system that requires an expert (who often appears to speak in tongues even to those who are reasonably knowledgeable) to fix when it goes wrong. Much rests on trust in expert knowledge. Those who have that knowledge acquire a certain monopoly power, which can all too easily be abused (technofascism I have heard it called).

Any breakdown in trust can become catastrophic. Recent events in financial services are illustrative of exactly this problem. In the mid-1980s computers were both rare and primitive on Wall Street. Markets were still relatively simple, transparent and tightly regulated. Traders based their activities on some mix of information (insider if you did not get caught and prosecuted, as then indeed happened) and intuition. Twenty years later wholly new over-the-counter and hence unregulated and often undocumented markets in options and derivatives dominated trading ($600 trillion in business in 2008 relative to the total output of goods and services in the world economy of around $55 trillion!). One of the purposes of this innovation wave was to avoid regulation and to create new arenas in which the capital surpluses could be profitably deployed in 'free' (that is, unregulated) markets without constraint. Innovations were ad hoc and private, corresponding more to the activities of the 'bricoleur' than of the systematiser. This was the way to avoid the regulator and free the market. The traders were by the mid-1990s often highly trained mathematicians and physicists (many arriving with doctorates in those fields straight from MIT) who delighted in the complex modelling of financial markets along lines pioneered back in 1972 when Fischer Black, Myron Scholes and Robert Merton (who later became infamous for their role in the Long-term Capital Management crash and bail-out in 1998) wrote out a mathematical formula for which they earned a Nobel Prize in Economics on how to value an option. The trading identified and exploited inefficiencies in markets and spread risks but, given its entirely new patterns, this permitted manipulations galore that were extremely difficult to regulate or even to spot because they were buried in the intricate 'black box' mathematics of computerised over-the-counter trading programs.

So much for Marx's hope that the new technologies and organisational forms would render matters more readily understandable and transparent! Profits earned by many individual traders soared and bonuses went stratospheric. But so too did losses. By 2002, the writing should have clearly been on the wall. A young Singapore-based trader named Nicholas Leeson brought down the venerable bank of Baring, and companies like Enron, WorldCom, Global Crossing and Adelphia would bite the dust, as would Long-term Capital Management and the government of Orange County, California, all of them as a result of trading in these new unregulated markets (derivatives and options) and hiding their trades in all manner of shady accounting devices and mathematically sophisticated valuation systems.

Technological and financial innovations of this sort have played a role in putting us all at risk under a rule of experts that has nothing to do with guarding the public interest but everything to do with using the monopoly power given by that expertise to earn huge bonuses for gung-ho traders who aspire to be billionaires in ten years' time and thereby secure instant membership in the capitalist ruling class.

The more general point is to recognise technological and organisational innovation as a double-edged sword. It destabilises as it also opens up new paths of development for capital surplus absorption. Invariably, then, innovation waves in technological and organisational forms are associated with crises of 'creative destruction' in which one bundle of dominant forms is displaced by another. While Marx's account of how processes of technological and organisational change inevitably produce a tendency for the profit rate to fall may be unduly simplistic, his essential insight that such changes have a key role in destabilising everything and thereby producing crises of one sort or another is indubitably correct.

———

The application of human labour to reworking raw materials (either given in nature or already partially modified by human action) to make a new commodity takes us into the heart of the labour process where, under the control of the capitalist, old value is preserved and new value (including the surplus) is created. This is where profit is produced. Work is fundamental to all forms of human life because elements in nature have to be converted into items of utility to human beings. But under the social relations that dominate within capitalism, work takes on a very particular form in which labour, production technologies and organisational forms are brought together under the control of the capitalist for a predetermined time of contract for purposes of profitable commodity production.

The human relations involved within the labour process are always complex affairs, no matter how rigid the disciplinary apparatus, how automated the technology and how repressive the conditions of labour appear to be. It was one of Marx's most signal achievements to recognise that it is in fact the labourer – the person who actually does the work – that holds the real power within the labour process, even if it appears that the capitalist has all the legal rights and holds most of the political and institutional cards (through command over the state in particular). In the labour process, however, the capitalist is ultimately dependent upon the labourer. The worker produces capital in the form of commodities and so reproduces the capitalist. If the labourer refuses to work, downs tools, works to rule, or throws sand into the machine, then the capitalist is helpless. While the capitalist may organise the labour process, it is the worker who is the creative agent. Refusal to cooperate, as Marxists such as Mario Tronti who adopt the so-called 'autonomista' perspective have emphasised, is a crucial point of potential blockage where the labourer has the power to impose limits.

When we think of class struggle, too often our imagination gravitates to the figure of the worker struggling against the exploitations of capital. But in the labour process (as is indeed the case elsewhere) the direction of struggle is really the other way round. It is capital that has to struggle mightily to render labour subservient at that very moment where labour is potentially all-powerful. This it does both directly through the tactics of organisation of social relations on the shop floor, in the fields, offices and institutions and throughout the transport and communications networks. If capital is to be produced, then these social relations must be shaped in collaborative and cooperative ways. This can sometimes be achieved by brute force, coercion and technical modes of regulation but more often than not it involves forms of social organisation that entail trust, loyalty and subtle forms of interdependency that acknowledge the potential powers of labour while shaping it to capital's purpose. It is here that capital so frequently concedes to the labour movement certain powers, to say nothing of material advantages, provided of course that capital continues to be produced and reproduced.

To be sure, there are plenty of accounts of labour processes where labourers work under the whip of violent overseers, subject to all manner of verbal abuse and psychological and physical violence.

And one of the most persistent threads in the history of technological innovation has been the desire to disempower the labourer as much as possible and to locate powers of movement and of decision within the machine, or at least 'upstairs' in some remote control room. But the labour process is always a perpetual battleground which is both particular to the site of production and performed behind closed doors upon which are inscribed, as Marx observed, the capitalist creed: 'No Admittance Except on Business!' What happens behind those closed doors we do not generally know even as those that work within know full well and engage in forms of struggle and of compromise that have enormous implications in aggregate for the dynamics of how capitalism works (and indeed, if it continues to work and produce profitably at all).

Bourgeois constitutionality may perform beautifully in market affairs but it has an extremely hard time in extending its reach into production. Nevertheless, the power of labour over the years has yielded concessions over matters such as employment conditions, workplace safety, regulation of social relations (anti-harassment and equal treatment legislation), skill definitions, and the like. Legalised forms of labour organising may empower shop floor organisers (shop stewards in Britain) who can directly intervene in labour processes and regulate social relations within the workplace, while relating to broader class movements (such as national trade unions and left political parties). But workplace organising is not always easy and, even when it is achieved, it often regulates the labour process as much to the advantage of capital as it does for the benefit of labour. And as has again and again been revealed in recent years by scandals (ironically driven by anti-immigrant fervour) of employment of undocumented labour in the United States, the violations of labour laws are widespread in part because the capacity of government to enforce has been systematically gutted by a state increasingly ruled by corporate interests. The legal status of regulation of labour processes varies intensely from one place to another, however, such that the uneven geographical presence of unionisation movements and regulatory regimes over labour processes is very marked throughout the capitalist world.

The range of capitalist tactics in the labour process needs to be appreciated. It is here, in particular, that capitalists use the power of social differences to their own utmost advantage. Issues of gender often become paramount on the shop floor, as do issues of ethnicity, religion, race and even sexual preference. In the sweatshops of the so-called developing world it is women who bear the brunt of capitalist exploitation and whose talents and capacities are utilised to the extreme under conditions often akin to patriarchal domination. This is so because, in a desperate bid to exert and sustain control over the labour process, the capitalist has to mobilise any social relation of difference, any distinction within the social division of labour, any special cultural preference or habit, both to prevent the inevitable commonality of position in the workplace being consolidated into a movement of social solidarity and to sustain a fragmented and divided workforce. The culture of the workplace, in short, becomes a crucial feature and it is there that broader cultural values – such as patriarchy, respect for authority, social relations of dominance and subservience – are all imported to play their part in the actual practices of production. Go into any workplace – like a hospital or a restaurant – and note the gender, race and ethnicity of those doing the different tasks and it becomes evident how power relations within the collective labour process are distributed among different social groups. The recalcitrance of such social relations to change has as much to do with the tactics of capital as it does with inherent conservatism of social relations and the desire to preserve minor privileges (including even access to low-paid jobs) on the part of different groups.

We are now fortunate to have available to us innumerable ethnographic studies, primarily by anthropologists and sociologists of labour processes, conducted in a wide range of situations and in radically different cultural contexts. Leaving aside the vested interest such researchers have in elaborating upon cultures of difference and of specificity, the aggregate picture that emerges is indeed one of seemingly infinite varieties of social relations and cultural mores, albeit within an overall framing of constraints.

The constraint is, however, simply stated, even as the ideological and practical attempts to obscure its form multiply. Whatever else happens in the labour process, the potentiality for a revolutionary blockage of the sort the autonomists emphasise is always threatening. It must at all costs be averted by capital, because both capital and the capitalist must be perpetually reproduced by workers through the activity of labouring. The details of how this is done are infinite in their variety and certainly worthy of close investigation. Social struggles on the shop floor and in the fields, factories, offices, shops and spaces of construction, as well as over the production of spaces, places and built environments, define a potential blockage point to capital accumulation that is perpetually present and which perpetually needs to be circumvented if capitalism is to survive.

4

Capital Goes to Market

The final potential barrier to perpetual accumulation exists at the point where the new commodity enters the market either as a thing or as a service of some kind to be exchanged for the original money plus a profit. The particularity of the commodity has to be converted into the universality of money, which is much more problematic than going from money (the universal representation of value) to commodities. Somebody must need, want or desire the particular commodity for a sale to be possible. If no one wants it then it is useless and has no value. But those who need, want or desire the commodity must also have the money to buy it. Without money they cannot do so. If no one wants it or can afford to buy it then there is no sale and no profit is realised and the initial capital is lost.

An immense amount of effort, including the formation of a vast advertising industry, has been put into influencing and manipulating the wants, needs and desires of human populations to ensure a potential market. But something more than just advertising is involved here. What is required is formation of conditions of daily life that necessitate the absorption of a certain bundle of commodities and services in order to sustain it. Consider, for example, the development of the wants, needs and desires associated with the rise of a suburban lifestyle in the United States after the Second World War. Not only are we talking about the need for cars, gasoline, highways, suburban tract houses and shopping malls, but also lawn mowers, refrigerators, air-conditioners, drapes, furniture (interior and exterior), interior entertainment equipment (the TV) and a whole mass of maintenance systems to keep this daily life going.

Daily living in the suburbs required the consumption of at least all of that. The development of suburbia turned these commodities from wants and desires into absolute needs. The perpetual bringing-forth of new needs is a crucial precondition for the continuity of endlessly expanding capital accumulation. This is where the technologies and politics of new need creation come to the fore as a cutting edge of sustainable accumulation. It is now well understood that 'consumer sentiment' and 'consumer confidence' in the more affluent societies are not only keys to endless capital accumulation but are more and more the fulcrum upon which the survival of capitalism depends. Seventy per cent of US economic activity depends on consumerism.

But where does the purchasing power to buy all these products come from? There must be, at the end of the day, an extra amount of money that somebody holds somewhere to facilitate the purchase. If not, there is a lack of effective demand, defined as wants, needs and desires backed by ability to pay. What is called a crisis of 'under-consumption' results when there is not enough effective demand to absorb the commodities produced.

Workers spending their wages is one source of effective demand. But the total wage bill is always less than the total capital in circulation (otherwise there would be no profit), so the purchase of the wage goods that sustain daily life (even with a suburban lifestyle) is never sufficient for the profitable sale of the total output. A politics of wage repression only heightens the possibility of a crisis of underconsumption. Many analysts came to regard the crisis of the 1930s as primarily a crisis of underconsumption. They therefore supported unionisation and other state strategies (like social security) to bolster effective demand among the working classes. In 2008 the federal government in the US released a $600 tax rebate to most taxpayers below a certain income level in order to do the same thing. It would have been far better to have reversed the politics of wage repression put in place after the mid-1970s and raised real wages. This would have bolstered consumer demand and confidence permanently. But many capitalists, along with right-wing ideologues, were unwilling to contemplate any such solution. The Republicans in Congress blocked the initial plan to bail out the Detroit auto companies on the grounds that it did not reduce the wages and benefits of unionised labour to the level of those found in the non-unionised Japanese and German auto companies located in the American south. They therefore saw the crisis as an opportunity to engage in yet another bout of wage repression, which was exactly the wrong prescription for the ailment of lack of effective demand.

But worker demand, though an important base, can obviously never solve the problem of realisation of profits. Rosa Luxemburg, the famous leftist activist and theorist, paid great attention to this problem back in the early 1900s. First she took up the possibility that the extra demand could come from increasing the gold supply (or in our day by simply having the central banks print more money). Obviously this can help in the short run (injecting sufficient liquidity into the system, as during the financial crisis of 2008, was crucial to stabilising the continued circulation and accumulation of capital). But the impact is limited and in the long run the effect is to create yet another kind of crisis, that of inflation. Luxemburg's other solution was to presuppose the existence of some latent and mobilisable extra demand outside of the capitalist system. This meant the continuation of primitive accumulation through imperialist impositions and practices on non-capitalist societies. Whole populations had to be mobilised as consumers rather than as workers. In the nineteenth century the British used their imperial dominion over India to expand the market for British goods (and in the process destroyed indigenous forms of production). The Chinese market was also forcibly opened in the nineteenth century (only to be closed again after the communists took power in 1949).

In the transition to capitalism, and in the phase of primitive accumulation, the stores of accumulated wealth within the feudal order could play this role (often prised loose by the activities of the money-lenders and the usurers) along with the robbery and plundering of wealth from the non-capitalist world by merchant's capital. But what

Capital Goes to Market

might be called the 'gold reserves' of the non-capitalist world (such as India and China) were steadily depleted over time and the associated capacity of the peasantry to support the consumerism of a landed aristocracy (through the extraction of monetised land rents) or of a state apparatus (through taxation) was also increasingly exhausted.

As industrial capitalism consolidated in Europe and North America, so the plundering of wealth from India, China and other already developed non-capitalist social formations became more and more prominent, particularly from the mid-nineteenth century onwards. This was the phase of an immense transfer of wealth from east and south Asia, but also to some degree from South America and Africa, towards the industrial capitalist class located in the core capitalist countries of Europe and North America. But eventually, as capitalism grew and spread geographically, the ability to stabilise the system by these sorts of means became less and less plausible.

Since 1950 or so, but even more markedly since the 1970s, the capacity of imperialist practices of this sort to perform the role of grand stabiliser has been seriously impaired. With capitalism (of some sort) now firmly implanted in all of east and south-east Asia and developing strongly in India and Indonesia, to say nothing of all of the rest of the world, the problem of global effective consumer demand is placed on an entirely different footing. The effective demand that stabilises China's current growth, for example, is now largely located in the United States, which explains why China feels so compelled to cover US deficits because a collapse of US consumerism would have (and is having) devastating effects on industrial employment and profit rates in China. The obvious answer is for China to develop its own internal market, but that would require raising wage rates and undercutting its own competitive advantage in the global economy. It would also mean using more of its surplus for internal development which would mean less would be available to lend to the US. This would further diminish the effective demand for Chinese goods from the United States. What this presages, as we saw earlier, is a historic reversal of 150 years or more of wealth transfer from east and south Asia to the United States and Europe, and a radical change in the capacity of the US to dominate global capitalism as it has done since 1945.

The most important answer to the effective demand conundrum – one that Luxemburg failed to notice but which follows logically from Marx's analysis – is that the solution lies in capitalist consumption. This is of two sorts: a portion of the surplus value is consumed as revenues (e.g. as basic goods plus luxury goods and services) but the other portion is reinvested either in wage goods for the extra labourers to be employed or in fresh means of production. Given the wage repression that has occurred worldwide (though unevenly), the capitalist class in general has had an expanding stream of revenues at its command and the demand for luxury goods has plainly grown to a corresponding degree (go to any marina in Florida or around the Mediterranean, look at the yachts and cruise boats moored there, then contrast this with what you would have seen in 1970 and you will get the point). But for all of the conspicuousness of its consumption habits, there is still a physical limit to the number of yachts, MacMansions or pairs of shoes that the billionaire class can consume. Capitalist personal consumption, it turns out, is a very weak source of effective demand. The more that the centralisation of capital concentrates wealth in the hands of a very small group in the population (such as the 300 or so families that the UN development report of 1996 showed controlled 40 per cent of the world's wealth) the less effective is their consumption in bolstering demand.

So the answer has to lie in capitalist reinvestment. Assume that capitalists use their surpluses only in the further expansion of production. The extra demand for expansion today then mops up the surpluses of means of production and of wage goods produced yesterday. Surplus production internalises its own increasing monetary demand! Put more formally, the effective demand for yesterday's surplus product depends upon workers' consumption plus capitalist personal consumption plus the new demand generated out of tomorrow's further expansion of production. What appears as an underconsumption problem becomes a problem of finding reinvestment opportunities for a portion of the surplus produced yesterday!

For this reinvestment to happen, three fundamental conditions must be realised. Firstly, capitalists must immediately throw the moneys they gained yesterday back into circulation as new capital. But there is no compelling rule that says that the conversion of commodities into money must immediately be followed by the conversion of money back into commodities. Capitalists may prefer to hold money rather than reinvest. Circumstances arise in which it would make perfect sense for them to do this and it is at this point that an overlap emerges between Marx's and Keynes' thinking on the possibility of crises of underconsumption. Under conditions of uncertainty, hanging on to the universal form of wealth, money, rather than commodities makes sense, except under conditions of rapid inflation when it may prove more advantageous to hold on to cans of tuna and barrels of cooking oil rather than money. The more general case is one in which a loss of faith and of confidence in the economy leads people to hoard money and not to spend it. This can occur when profit prospects dim. But this in turn leads into what Keynes called the 'liquidity trap' – the more people or institutions (including banks and corporations) hoard money rather than spend it, the more likely that effective demand will collapse and the less profitable reinvestment in production will become. The result is a downward spiral (of the sort that occurred in the 1930s and which we are currently witnessing) that is difficult to reverse. Keynes sought to bypass this barrier by resort to state-led strategies of fiscal and monetary management. State-organised deficit financing (of the sort that emerged very conspicuously in the late autumn of 2008 in the United States, Britain and elsewhere) is seen as the immediate panacea.

The second condition is that the time gap between today's reinvestment and yesterday's surplus output can somehow be bridged. This requires the use of money as a means of account, and that means the existence of a credit system that can step into the circulation process to solve the problem of insufficient effective demand. As other options (such as raiding the gold reserves of preceding social orders or robbing the rest of the world of value) run out, so credit becomes the only main means to cover the effective demand problem. The solution is thereby internalised within the dynamics of capital accumulation. The price, however, is that the bankers and financiers who operate the credit system, along with the savers who deposit their money in credit institutions, can again claim their part of the future surplus value in the form of interest and fees for services.

The third condition is that the credit moneys received will be spent on the purchase of the extra wage goods and means of production that have already been produced. The general political argument for supporting the concentration of wealth in the upper classes is that they can and do use their wealth to reinvest and so create jobs, new products, and hence new wealth that can at the end of the day potentially benefit everyone (through trickle-down effects and the like) and so create more demand. What this story line misses is that capitalists, as we earlier saw, have a choice as to what they reinvest in: they can reinvest in the expansion of production or they can use their wealth to buy up assets, such as stocks and shares, property, art objects or shares in some speculative enterprise such as a private equity company, a hedge fund or some other financial instrument from which they can realise capital gains. In this case their reinvestments play no role in bolstering effective demand.

If we conclude that it is the further expansion of production that creates the demand for yesterday's surplus product and that credit is needed to bridge the temporal gap, then it also follows that credit-fuelled capital accumulation at a compound rate is also a condition of capitalism's survival. Only then can the expansion of today mop up yesterday's surplus. The reason that 3 per cent growth requires 3 per cent reinvestment then becomes clear. Capitalism, in effect, must generate and internalise its own effective demand if it is to survive under conditions where external possibilities are exhausted. If it fails to do so, as is currently the case, because of barriers to the continued expansion of production, a crisis ensues.

There is one further point to be noted. If it takes competition to keep the permanent expansion of production going, then it follows that keeping capitalism competitive is also necessary to capitalism's survival. Any slackening of competition through, for example, excessive monopolisation will in itself likely produce a crisis in capitalist reproduction. This was, of course, exactly the point made by the economists Paul Baran and Paul Sweezy in their *Monopoly Capital* (written during the 1960s). The tendency towards monopolisation and the centralisation of capital necessarily produces, as they clearly predicted, a crisis of stagflation (rising unemployment coupled with accelerating inflation) of the sort that so haunted the 1970s. The neoliberal counter-revolution that then occurred not only had to smash the power of labour; it had also to unleash the coercive laws of competition as 'executor' of the laws of endless capitalist accumulation.

This process is not without its potential complications. To begin with, the presumption is that all the other barriers (such as the relation to nature) have been superseded and that there is plenty of room for more production to occur. This implies that imperialism has to shift from robbing values and stripping assets from the rest of the world to using the rest of the world as a site for opening up new forms of capitalist production. The export of capital rather than of commodities becomes critical. Herein lies the big difference between nineteenth-century India and China, whose wealth was plundered by capitalist domination of their markets, and the United States, where unrestricted capitalist development produced new wealth in such a way as to absorb and realise the surplus product being generated in the older centres of capitalism (for example, the export of capital and machinery from Britain to the US in the nineteenth century). China in recent times has absorbed a vast amount of foreign capital in the development of production and in so doing has generated an enormous effective demand not only for raw materials but also for machinery and other material inputs. It is a primary market because it is a huge centre for investment in production.

There are, however, two problems inherent in this solution to the underconsumption problem. The first derives from the simple fact that accumulation becomes doubly speculative: it rests on the belief that tomorrow's expansion will not encounter any barriers so that today's surplus can effectively be realised. This means that anticipations and expectations, as Keynes well understood, are fundamental to the continuity of capital circulation. Any fall-off in speculative expectations will generate a crisis. In Keynes' *General Theory*, the technical solutions of monetary and fiscal policy occupy only a minor part of the argument compared with the psychology of expectations and anticipations. Faith in the system is fundamental and loss of confidence, as happened in 2008, can be fatal.

The second problem arises within the money and credit system itself. The possibility of 'independent' financial and monetary crises is omnipresent. The underlying problem lies in the contradictions of the money form itself, most easily understood when the monetary system had a clear metallic base. A particular commodity, gold, then represents the value of all forms of social labour, the particular (concrete and tangible) represents the universal (abstract), and private persons can command unlimited social power. There is a permanent temptation for individuals to hold on to money precisely because it is a form of social power. But the more people do this the greater the threat to the continuity of circulation. Releasing money back into circulation to get more social power takes either an act of faith, or requires safe and trustworthy institutions where you can put your personal money at someone else's disposal to pursue profit-making adventures (which is, of course, what banks traditionally do). Trust in the system becomes crucial. Ponzi schemes of whatever sort undermine that trust.

Loss of confidence in the symbols of money (the power of the state to guarantee monetary stability) or in the quality of money (inflation) butts up against the possibility of monetary famine and the freezing up of the means of payment of the sort that occurred in autumn in 2008. At the heart of the credit system there exist a range of technical and legal aspects (many of which can fail or badly distort, simply by virtue of their rules of operation) coupled with subjective expectations and anticipations. And to the degree that capitalism continues to expand, so the role of the credit system as a kind of central nervous system for directing and controlling the global dynamics of capital accumulation becomes more prominent. The implication is that the control over the means of credit becomes critical for the functioning of capitalism – a positionality that Marx and Engels recognised in *The Communist Manifesto* by making the centralisation of the means of credit in the hands of the state one of their key demands (presuming, of course, working-class control over the state). When this is added to the key role of the state with respect to the quality of the coinage and, even more importantly, symbolic moneys, then the further fusion of state and financial powers in the state–finance nexus appears inevitable.

But here is the chief problem. In the same way that capital can operate on both sides of the demand and supply of labour power (via technologically induced unemployment), so it can operate through the credit system on both sides of the production–realisation relation. An increasingly liberal supply of credit to prospective homeowners, coupled with an equally liberal supply of credit to property develop-ers, will fuel a massive boom in housing and urban development (as happened in Florida and California in recent years). It could then be imagined that the problem of continuous production and realisation of surpluses has been done away with. This concentrates immense social and economic power within the credit system. But to be sustained this also requires that credit itself expand at a compound rate, as indeed happened over the last twenty years. When the credit bubble bursts, which it inevitably must, then the whole economy plunges into a downward spiral of the sort that began in 2007. And it is at this point that capitalism has to create external power in order to save itself from its own internal contradictions. It needs to re-create

115

the equivalent of the external feudal or non-capitalist gold reserve that it has historically fed upon. This it does by locating the power of infinite money creation within a neofeudal institution like the Federal Reserve.

The realisation problem and the threat of underconsumption never goes away. But the problem of falling profits and devaluations due to lack of effective demand can be staved off for a while through the machinations of the credit system. In the short term, credit works to smooth out many minor problems, but over the long term it tends to accumulate the contradictions and the tensions. It spreads the risks at the same time as it accumulates them. The real problem is not the lack of effective demand, but the lack of opportunities for gainful reinvestment of the surplus earned yesterday in production. That this is the only conclusion to be drawn derives, it should be noted, from that condition of capital circulation that is essential to the survival of capitalism: the continuity of flow must be sustained at all times. And this, as we began by arguing, becomes much harder to do as we move on to the terrain of a $55 trillion global economy and look to double that over the next thirty years.

There has been a tendency within the history of crisis theorising to look for one dominant explanation for the crisis-prone character of capitalism. The three big traditional camps of thought are the profit squeeze (profits fall because real wages rise), the falling rate of profit (labour-saving technological changes backfire and 'ruinous' competition pulls prices down), the underconsumptionist traditions (lack of effective demand and the tendency towards stagnation associated with excessive monopolisation). The separations between these schools of thought became particularly fierce in the 1970s. The very term 'underconsumptionist' in some circles amounted to a dirty word (it seemed to mean you were a mere Keynesian and not a 'true' Marxist), while fans of Rosa Luxemburg became outraged at the mean-spirited dismissal of her ideas on the part of those who placed the falling rate of profit at the centre of their theorising. In recent years, for obvious reasons, far more attention has been paid to the environmental and financial aspects of crisis formation.

There is, I think, a far better way to think about crisis formation. The analysis of capital circulation pinpoints several potential limits and barriers. Money capital scarcities, labour problems, disproportionalities between sectors, natural limits, unbalanced technological and organisational changes (including competition versus monopoly), indiscipline in the labour process and lack of effective demand head up the list. Any one of these circumstances can slow down or disrupt the continuity of capital flow and so produce a crisis that results in the devaluation or loss of capital. When one limit is overcome accumulation often hits up against another somewhere else. For instance, moves made to alleviate a crisis of labour supply and to curb the political power of organised labour in the 1970s diminished the effective demand for product, which created difficulties for realisation of the surplus in the market during the 1990s. Moves to alleviate this last problem by extensions of the credit system among the working classes ultimately led to working-class over-indebtedness relative to income that in turn led to a crisis of confidence in the quality of debt instruments (as began to happen in 2006). The crisis tendencies are not resolved but merely moved around.

I think it is more in keeping with Marx's frequent invocation of the fluid and flexible character of capitalist development to recognise this perpetual repositioning of one barrier at the expense of another and so to recognise the multiple ways in which crises can form in different historical and geographical situations. It is also vital to remember that crises assume a key role in the historical geography of capitalism as the 'irrational rationalisers' of an inherently contradictory system. Crises are, in short, as necessary to the evolution of capitalism as money, labour power and capital itself. It takes, however, careful tracking and materialist analysis to locate the exact source or sources of the blockage in any particular place or time.

A synoptic view of the current crisis would say: while the epicentre lies in the technologies and organisational forms of the credit system and the state–finance nexus, the underlying problem is excessive capitalist empowerment vis-à-vis labour and consequent wage repression, leading to problems of effective demand papered over by a credit-fuelled consumerism of excess in one part of the world and a too rapid expansion of production in new product lines in another. But we need further tools of analysis to understand the historical geography of capitalism's evolution in all of its complexity. We must integrate the role of uneven development, both sectoral and geographical, in our analysis of crisis production. It is to this task that we now turn.

5

Capital Evolves

The forces unleashed by the rise of capitalism have re-engineered the world many times over since 1750. Flying over central England in 1820, we would have seen a few compact industrialised towns (with small factory smokestacks belching forth noxious fumes) separated by large areas of agricultural activity where traditional forms of rural life were preserved in scattered villages and farmsteads, even as lords of the manor waxed poetic about the new agricultural practices that underpinned rising agricultural productivity (and rising money rents). Compact industrial centres with names like Manchester and Birmingham were linked with each other and to the main commercial port cities of Bristol and Liverpool, as well as to the teeming capital city of London, by threads of dirt turnpikes and skinny slivers of canals. Barges full of coal and raw materials were laboriously towed along the canals either by sweating horses or, as Marx records in *Capital*, by almost starving women. Locomotion was slow.

Flying over the Pearl River delta in 1980, one would have seen tiny villages and towns with names like Shenzhen and Dongguan nestled in a largely self-sufficient agrarian landscape of rice, vegetable, livestock production and fish farming, socialised into communes ruled with an iron fist by local party officials who were also carrying an 'iron rice bowl' to guard against the threat of starvation.

Flying over both these areas in 2008, the landscapes of sprawling urbanisation below would be totally unrecognisable, as would be the forms of production and transportation, the social relations, the technologies, the ways of daily life and the forms of consumption on the ground. If, as Marx once averred, our task is not so much to understand the world as to change it, then, it has to be said, capitalism has done a pretty good job of following his advice. Most of these dramatic changes have occurred without anyone bothering first to find out how the world worked or what the consequences might be. Again and again the unanticipated and the unexpected has happened, leaving behind a vast intellectual and practical industry engaged in trying to clean up the messy consequences of what was unknowingly wrought.

The saga of capitalism is full of paradoxes, even as most forms of social theory – economic theory in particular – abstract entirely from consideration of them. On the negative side we have not only the periodic and often localised economic crises that have punctuated capitalism's evolution, including inter-capitalist and inter-imperialist world wars, problems of environmental degradation, loss of biodiverse habitats, spiralling poverty among burgeoning populations, neocolonialism, serious crises in public health, alienations and social exclusions galore and the anxieties of insecurity, violence and unfulfilled desires. On the positive side some of us live in a world where standards of material living and well-being have never been higher, where travel and communications have been revolutionised and physical (though not social) spatial barriers to human interactions have been much reduced, where medical and biomedical understandings offer for many a longer life, where huge, sprawling and in many respects spectacular cities have been built, where knowledge proliferates, hope springs eternal and everything seems possible (from self-cloning to space travel).

That this is the contradictory world in which we live, and that it continues to evolve at a rapid pace in unpredictable and seemingly uncontrollable ways, is undeniable. Yet the principles that underpin this evolution remain opaque in part because we humans have made so much of this history more in accord with the competing whims of this or that collective and sometimes individual human desire, rather than according to some governing evolutionary principles of the sort that Darwin uncovered in the realm of natural evolution. If we are to change this world collectively into a more rational and humane configuration through conscious interventions, then we must first learn to understand far better than is now the case what we are doing to the world and with what consequences.

The historical geography of capitalism cannot be reduced, of course, to questions of capital accumulation. Yet it also has to be said that capital accumulation, along with population growth, have lain at the core of human evolutionary dynamics since 1750 or so. Exactly how they have done so is central to uncovering what the enigma of capital is all about. Are there evolutionary principles at work here to which we can appeal for some sort of illumination?

————

Consider, first, capitalist development over time, laying aside for the moment the question of its evolving spatial organisation, its geographical dynamics and its environmental impacts and constraints. Imagine, then, a situation in which capital revolves through different but inter-related 'activity spheres' (as I shall call them) in search of profit. One crucial 'activity sphere' concerns the production of new technological and organisational forms. Changes in this sphere have profound effects on social relations as well as on the relation to nature. But we also know that both social relations and the relation to nature are changing in ways that are in no way determined by technologies and organisational forms. Situations arise, furthermore, in which scarcities of labour supply or in nature put strong pressures to come up with new technologies and organisational forms. These days, for example, the US media are full of commentary on the need for a range of new technologies to free the country of its dependency on foreign oil and to combat global warming. The Obama administration promises programmes to that end and is already pushing the auto industry towards making electric or hybrid cars (unfortunately the Chinese and Japanese got there first).

Production systems and labour processes are likewise deeply

implicated in the way daily life is reproduced through consumption. Neither of these are independent of the dominant social relations, the relation to nature and the duly constituted technologies and organisational forms. But what we call 'nature', while clearly affected by capital accumulation (habitat and species destruction, global warming, new chemical compounds that pollute as well as soil structures and forests whose productivity has been enhanced by sophisticated management), is most certainly not determined by capital accumulation. Evolutionary processes on planet earth are independently occurring all the time. The emergence of a new pathogen – such as HIV/AIDS – has had, for example, an immense impact upon capitalist society (and calls forth technological, organisational and social responses that are embedded in capital circulation). The effects on the reproduction of daily life, on sexual relations and activities, and on reproductive practices have been profound, but have been mediated by medical technologies, institutional responses and social and cultural beliefs.

All of these 'activity spheres' are embedded in a set of institutional arrangements (such as private property rights and market contracts) and administrative structures (the state and other local and multinational arrangements). These institutions also evolve on their own account even as they find themselves forced to adapt to crisis conditions (as we now see happening) and to changing social relations. People act, furthermore, on their expectations, their beliefs and their understandings of the world. Social systems depend on trust in experts, adequate knowledge and information on the part of those making decisions, acceptance as to reasonable social arrangements (of hierarchies or of egalitarianism), as well as constructions of ethical and moral standards (vis-à-vis, for example, our relations to animals and our responsibilities to the world we call nature as well as to others not like us). Cultural norms and belief systems (that is, religious and political ideologies) are powerfully present but do not exist independently of social relations, production and consumption possibilities and dominant technologies. The contested inter-relations between the evolving technical and social requirements for capital accumulation and the knowledge structures and the cultural norms and beliefs consistent with endless accumulation have all played a critical role in capitalism's evolution. For purposes of simplification, I will collect together all of these last elements under the rubric of 'mental conceptions of the world'.

This way of thinking yields us seven distinctive 'activity spheres' within the evolutionary trajectory of capitalism: technologies and organisational forms; social relations; institutional and administrative arrangements; production and labour processes; relations to nature; the reproduction of daily life and of the species; and 'mental conceptions of the world'. No one of the spheres dominates even as none of them are independent of the others. But nor is any one of them determined even collectively by all of the others. Each sphere evolves on its own account but always in dynamic interaction with the others. Technological and organisational changes arise for all manner of reasons (sometimes accidental), while the relation to nature is unstable and perpetually changing only in part because of human-induced modifications. Our mental conceptions of the world, to take another example, are usually unstable, contested, subject to scientific discoveries as well as whims, fashions and passionately held cultural and religious beliefs and desires. Changes in mental conceptions have all manner of intended and unintended consequences for acceptable technological and organisational forms, social relations, labour processes, relations to nature, as well as for institutional arrangements. The demographic dynamics that arise out of the sphere of reproduction and daily life are simultaneously autonomous but deeply affected by their relations to the other spheres.

The complex flows of influence that move between the spheres are perpetually reshaping all of them. Furthermore, these interactions are not necessarily harmonious. Indeed, we can reconceptualise crisis formation in terms of the tensions and antagonisms that arise between the different activity spheres as, for example, new technologies play against the desire for new configurations in social relations or disrupt the organisation of existing labour processes. But instead of examining these spheres sequentially as we did earlier in the analysis of capital circulation, we now think of them as collectively co-present and co-evolving within the long history of capitalism.

In a given society at a particular point in space and time – Britain in 1850, or the Pearl River delta of China now, say – we can define its general character and condition largely in terms of how these seven spheres are organised and configured in relation to each other. Something can also be said about the likely future development of the social order in such places given the tensions and contradictions between the activity spheres, even as it is recognised that the likely evolutionary dynamic is not determinant but contingent.

———

Capital cannot circulate or accumulate without touching upon each and all of these activity spheres in some way. When capital encounters barriers or limits within a sphere or between spheres, then ways have to be found to circumvent or transcend the difficulty. If the difficulties are serious, then here too we find a source of crises. A study of the co-evolution of activity spheres therefore provides a framework within which to think through the overall evolution and crisis-prone character of capitalist society. So how can this rather abstract framework for analysis be put to work in concrete ways?

An anecdote may help here. Back in the autumn 2005, I was co-chair of a jury to select ideas for the design of a completely new city in South Korea. The city then called 'The Multifunctional Administrative City' (now Sejong) was originally planned to be a new capital city, but constitutional objections led to it being reduced to a satellite city, about halfway between Seoul and Busan, but with many of the administrative functions of government to be placed there. The jury's task was to adjudicate on ideas rather than to select any final design. Those in charge of the project were tasked to undertake the final design, incorporating whatever we (and they) thought was useful from the submissions to the competition. The jury was half Korean and half foreign and weighted heavily with engineers, planners and some prominent architects. It was clear that the South Korean government, tired of the formulaic urbanisation that had hitherto dominated in South Korea and much of Asia, was interested in doing something different, perhaps generating a new worldwide model for an innovative urbanisation.

As prelude to our decision making, we discussed the kind of criteria that would be most relevant in judging the many designs that had been submitted. The initial discussion focused around the differing views of the architects on the relative strengths of circles and cubes both as symbolic shapes and as physical forms that could accommodate different kinds of development strategies. Looking at the various map-like designs, it was easy to see differences of this sort clearly displayed. But I intervened to suggest that we broaden the discussion and think of a number of other criteria such as: the proposed relation to nature and the technological mixes to be deployed in the city; how the designs addressed the forms of production and employment to be generated and the associated social relations (how should we approach the problem that the city would be dominated by a scientific, technological and bureaucratic élite, for example); the qualities of daily life for differently positioned inhabitants; and the mental conceptions of the world, including political subjectivities, that might arise from the experience of living in this new kind of city (would people become more individualistic or incline towards forms of social solidarity?) I concluded by saying that I thought it would be wrong to imagine that physical designs could answer all of these issues but that we should do our best to think about building this new city in ways that were sensitive to these criteria.

There was considerable interest in my way of thinking. Debate over my ideas proceeded for a while until one of the architects, evidently impatient with the complexity of the discussion, intervened to suggest that, of all of these doubtlessly valid perspectives, there was one that stood out as paramount, and that was mental conceptions. From this standpoint the most important question was one of symbolic meanings. In short order we were back to the discussion of the symbolic, conceptual and material potentialities of circles and squares in urban design!

It may sound utopian, but were I in charge of constructing a wholly new city, I would want to imagine one that could evolve into the future rather than a permanent structure that is fixed, frozen and completed. And I would want to imagine how the dynamics of relations between these different spheres might not only work but be consciously mobilised not so much to achieve some specific goal but to open up possibilities. To be sure, the city would have to be built in the first instance according to the dominant social relations, employment structures and the available technologies and organisational forms. But it could also be viewed as a site for the exploration of new technologies and organisational forms consistent with the development of more egalitarian social relations, respectful of gender issues, for example, and a more sensitive relation to nature than that demanded in pursuit of the increasingly unholy grail of endless capital accumulation at a 3 per cent compound rate.

This framework of thought does not originate with me, however. It derives from elaboration upon a footnote in chapter 15 of *Capital*, volume 1, in which Marx comments, interestingly after a brief engagement with Darwin's theory of evolution, that 'technology reveals the active relation of man to nature, the direct process of production of his life, and thereby it also lays bare the process of production of the social relations of his life and of the mental conceptions that flow from these relations'. Here Marx invokes five (perhaps six if 'the direct process of production of his life' refers both to the production of commodities and their consumption in daily life) of the different spheres of activity that I have identified. Only the institutional arrangements are missing.

The positioning of this footnote in the preamble to a lengthy examination of how the dominant technological and organisational forms of capitalism came into being is significant. Marx is concerned to understand the origins of the factory system and the rise of a machine tool industry (producing machines by way of machines) as an autonomous business dedicated to the production of new technologies. This is the key industry that underpins 'the constant revolutionising of production, uninterrupted disturbance of all social conditions, everlasting uncertainty and agitation' identified in *The Communist Manifesto* as the hallmark of what capitalism has been and still is about.

In this long chapter on machinery, the different spheres co-evolve in ways that accommodate and consolidate the permanently revolutionary character of capitalism. Mental conceptions of production as an art were displaced by scientific understandings and the conscious design of new technologies. Class, gender and family relations shifted as workers were increasingly reduced to the status of flexible appendages to the machine rather than as individuals endowed with the unique skills of the artisan. At the same time, capitalists mobilised new technologies and organisational forms as weapons in class struggle against labour (eventually using the machine to discipline the labouring body). The entry of a large number of women into the labour force, then as now, had all sorts of social ramifications. Public education became necessary as flexibility and adaptability of labour to different tasks became a crucial requirement. This brought forth other institutional changes, notably the educational clauses in the Factory Act of 1848 passed by a state dominated by capitalists and landlords. The factory inspectors appointed by that state provided Marx with abundant ammunition with which to bolster his arguments. New organisational forms (the corporate factory) promoted new technologies under new institutional arrangements that had ramifications for social relations and the relation to nature. At no point does it seem as if any one of the spheres dominated the others.

Yet there are uneven developments between the spheres that create stresses within the evolutionary trajectory. At some crucial turning points these stresses redirect the trajectory in this direction rather than that. Could a new and 'higher' form of the family arise out of this dynamic? Would the public education eventually required to produce a literate, flexible and well-trained workforce lead to popular enlightenment that would allow working-class movements to take command? Could technologies be devised that would lighten the load of labour rather than tie it more ruthlessly to the juggernaut of endless capital accumulation? Different possibilities were inherent in the situation even as the choices actually made pushed capitalism down ever more repressive paths. The British penchant for policies of free market 'laissez faire' did not have to triumph in the nineteenth century. But once they did, the evolution of capitalism took a very specific and not particularly benevolent turn.

So let me summarise. The seven activity spheres co-evolve within the historical evolution of capitalism in distinctive ways. No one sphere prevails over the others, even as there exists within each the possibility for autonomous development (nature independently mutates and evolves, as do mental conceptions, social relations, forms of daily life, institutional arrangements, technologies, etc.). Each of the spheres is subject to perpetual renewal and transformation, both in interaction with the others as well as through an internal dynamic that perpetually creates novelty in human affairs. The relations between the spheres are not causal but dialectically inter-woven through the circulation and accumulation of capital. As such, the whole configuration constitutes a socio-ecological totality. This is not, I must emphasise, a mechanical totality, a social engine in which the parts strictly conform to the dictates of the whole. It is more like an ecological system made up of many different species and forms of activity – what the French philosopher/sociologist Henri Lefebvre refers to as an *'ensemble'* or his compatriot the philosopher Gilles Deleuze calls an *'assemblage'* of elements in dynamic relation with each other. In such an ecological totality, the inter-relations are fluid and open, even as they are inextricably interwoven with each other.

Uneven development between and among the spheres produces contingency as well as tensions and contradictions (in much the same way that unpredictable mutations produce contingency in Darwinian theory). Furthermore, it is entirely possible that explosive developments in one sphere, in a given time and place, can take on a vanguard role. The sudden development of new pathogens (e.g. HIV/AIDS, avian flu or SARS), or the rise of some strong social movement around labour rights, civil or women's rights, or a burst of technological innovation as in the recent rise of electronics and computer-chip-based technologies, or a heady burst of utopian politics, have all in various times and places come out in front of the co-evolutionary process, putting immense pressure on the other spheres, either to play catch-up or to form centres of recalcitrance or active resistance. Once technology became a business in its own right (as it increasingly did from the mid-nineteenth century onwards) then a social need sometimes had to be created to use up the new technology rather than the other way around. In the pharmaceutical sector we see in recent times the creation of whole new diagnostics of mental and physical states to match new drugs (Prozac is the classic example). The existence of a dominant belief within the capitalist class and the social order more generally that there is a technological fix for every problem and a pill for every ailment produces all sorts of consequences. The 'fetish of technology' therefore does have an unduly prominent role in driving bourgeois history, defining both its astonishing achievements and its self-inflicted catastrophes. Problems in relation to nature have to be solved by new technologies rather than by revolutions in social reproduction and daily life!

Historically it seems as if there are periods when some of the spheres become radically at odds with each other. In the United States, for example, where the pursuit of science and technology appears to hold supreme, it would seem strange that so many people do not believe in the theory of evolution. While the science of global climate change is well established, many are convinced it is a hoax. How can the relation to nature be better understood in the face of overwhelming religious or political beliefs that give no credence to science? Situations of this kind typically lead either to phases of stasis or to radical reconstruction. Crises usually betoken the occurrence of such phases. Here, too, the crisis tendencies of capitalism are not resolved but merely moved around.

But there is a bottom line to all this. No matter what innovation or shift occurs, the survival of capitalism in the long run depends on the capacity to achieve 3 per cent compound growth. Capitalist history is littered with technologies which were tried and did not work, utopian schemes for the promotion of new social relations (like the Icarian communes in the nineteenth-century US, the Israeli kibbutz in the 1950s, or today's 'green communes'), only to be either co-opted or abandoned in the face of a dominant capitalist logic. But no matter what happens, by hook or by crook, capital must somehow organise the seven spheres to conform to the 3 per cent rule.

———

In practice capitalism seems to have evolved in ways somewhat similar to Stephen Jay Gould's 'punctuated equilibrium' theory of natural evolution: periods of relatively slow but reasonably harmonic co-evolution between the spheres are punctuated by phases of disruption and radical reform. We are possibly now in the midst of such a disruptive phase. But there are also signs of a desperate attempt to restore the pre-existing order, and to proceed as if nothing of consequence has really changed, nor should it.

Consider how this idea of punctuated equilibrium looks when we cast our eye backwards over the last major phase of capitalist reconstruction that occurred during the crisis of 1973–82. In my 2005 book *A Brief History of Neoliberalism*, I attempted an account of capitalist restructuring that began during these years. Throughout the capitalist world, but particularly in the United States (the undisputed dominant power of that time), capitalist class power was weakening relative to labour and other social movements and capital accumulation was lagging. The heads of leading corporations, along with media barons and wealthy individuals, many of whom, like the Rockefeller brothers, were scions of the capitalist class, went on the counter-attack. They set in motion the radical reconstruction of the state–finance nexus (the national and then international deregulation of financial operations, the liberation of debt-financing, the opening of the world to heightened international competition and the repositioning of the state apparatus with respect to social provision). Capital was re-empowered vis-à-vis labour through the production of unemployment and deindustrialisation, immigration, offshoring and all manner of technological and organisational changes (e.g. subcontracting). When later coupled with an ideological and political attack on all forms of labour organisation in the Reagan/Thatcher years, the effect was to solve the crisis of declining profitability and declining wealth by way of wage repression and the reduction in social provision by the state. Mental conceptions of the world were reshaped as far as possible by appeal to neoliberal principles of individual liberty as necessarily embedded in free markets and free trade. This required the withdrawal of the state from social provision and the gradual dismantling of the regulatory environment that had been constructed in the early 1970s (such as environmental protection). New forms of niche consumerism and individualised lifestyles also suddenly appeared, built around a postmodern style of urbanisation (the Disneyfication of city centres coupled with gentrification), and the emergence of social movements centred around a mix of self-centred individualism, identity politics, multiculturalism and sexual preference.

Capital did not create these movements but it did figure out ways to exploit and manipulate them, both in terms of fracturing hitherto important class solidarities and by commodifying and channelling the affective and effective demands associated with these movements into niche markets. New electronic technologies with widespread applications in both production and consumption had a huge impact upon labour processes, as well as on the conduct of daily life for the mass of the population (laptops, cell phones and iPods are everywhere). That the new electronic technologies held the answer to the world's problems became the fetish mantra of the 1990s. And all of this presaged an equally huge shift in mental conceptions of the world such that an even more intensive possessive individualism arose, along with money-making, indebtedness, speculation in asset values, privatisation of government assets and the widespread acceptance of personal responsibility as a cultural norm across social classes. Preliminary studies of those caught up in the foreclosure wave now indicate, for example, that many of them blame themselves rather than systemic conditions for not being able, for whatever reason, to live up to the personal responsibility entailed in home ownership. The view of the appropriate role of the state and of state power shifted dramatically during the neoliberal years, only now to be challenged as the state was forced to step in, after the bankruptcy of Lehman Brothers in September 2008, with massive financial aid to rescue a banking system on the brink of failure.

Of course, the details were much more complicated than this, and the myriad forces at work flowed in all manner of cross-cutting directions. On the world stage, uneven geographical developments of neoliberalism were everywhere in evidence, along with differentials of resistance. All I wish to illustrate here is how much the world changed, depending upon where one was, across all of these spheres between 1980 and 2010. The co-evolutionary movement has been palpable to anyone who has lived through it.

The danger for social theory as well as for popular understandings is to see one of the spheres as determinant. When the architect on the South Korean urban jury said only mental conceptions matter, he was making a very common move doubtless impelled by an understandable desire for simplification. But such simplifications are both unwarranted and dangerously misleading. We are, in fact, surrounded with dangerously oversimplistic monocausal explanations. In his bestselling 2005 book *The World is Flat*, the journalist Thomas L. Friedman shamelessly espouses a version of technological determinism (which he mistakenly attributes to Marx). Jared Diamond's *Guns, Germs and Steel* (1997) argues that the relation to nature is what counts, thus transforming human evolution into a tale of environmental determinism. Africa is poor for environmental reasons, not, he says, because of racial inferiorities or (what he does not say) because of centuries of imperialist plundering, beginning with the slave trade. In the Marxist and anarchist traditions there is a good deal of class struggle determinism. Others place social relations of gender, sexuality or racialisation in the vanguard of social evolution. Still others preach that our current problems arise out of arrant individualism and universal human greed. Idealism, in which mental conceptions are placed in the vanguard of social change, has an immensely long tradition (most spectacularly represented by Hegel's theory of history). There are, however, many other versions in which the visions and ideas of powerful innovators and entre-preneurs or of religious leaders or utopian political thinkers (such as some versions of Maoism) are placed at the centre of everything. Changing beliefs and values are, it is said, what really matter. Change the discourses, it is sometimes said, and the world will change, too.

The workerist wing of the Marxist tradition, on the other hand, treats the labour process as the only position from which truly revo-lutionary change can come because the real power of labour to change the world lies exclusively in the activity of labouring. From this starting point, and only from this starting point, is it possible, claimed John Holloway in 2002, to *Change the World without Taking Power*. In yet another popular text, *Blessed Unrest* (2007), Paul Hawken makes it seem as if social change in our times can only emanate, and already is emanating, from the practical engagements of millions of people seeking to transform their daily lives in the particular places in which they live, casting aside all of those political ideologies and utopian mental conceptions (from communism to neoliberalism) that have proven so disastrous in the past. The left version of this now sees the politics of everyday life in particular locales as the fundamental seedbed for both political action and radical change. The creation of local 'solidarity economies' is the exclusive answer. On the other hand, there is a whole school of historians and political philosophers who, by choosing the title of 'institutionalists', signal their adherence to a theory of social change that privileges command over and reform of institutional and administrative arrangements as fundamental. Capture and smash state power is the revolutionary Leninist version of this. Another radical version derives from Michel Foucault's focus on questions of 'governmentality', which interestingly analyses the intersections between two spheres – institutional and administrative systems and daily life (construed as body politics).

Each position in this pantheon of possibilities has something important, albeit unidimensional, to say about the socio-ecological dynamism of capitalism and the potentiality to construct alternatives. Problems arise, however, when one or other of these perspectives is exclusively and dogmatically viewed as the only source, and hence the primary political pressure point for change. There has been an unfortunate history within social theory of favouring some spheres of activity over others. Sometimes this reflects a situation in which one or other of the spheres – such as class struggle or technological dynamism – seems to be in the forefront of the transformations then occurring. In such a situation it would be churlish not to acknowledge the forces that are in the vanguard of socio-ecological change in that place and time. The argument is not, therefore, that the seven spheres should always be given equal weight but that the dialectical tension within their uneven development should always be born in mind.

What appears minor in one era or in one place can become major in the next. Labour struggles are not now in the forefront of the political dynamic in the way they were in the 1960s and early 1970s. Much more attention is now focused on the relation to nature than formerly. Contemporary interest in how the politics of the everyday unfold is clearly to be welcomed simply because it has not received the attention it should have commanded in the past. Right now we probably do not need yet another exposition on the social impacts of new technologies and organisational forms, which have in the past too often been thoughtlessly prioritised.

Marx's whole account of the rise of capitalism out of feudalism can in fact be reconstructed and read in terms of a co-evolutionary movement across and between the seven different activity spheres here identified. Capitalism did not supplant feudalism by way of some neat revolutionary transformation resting on the forces mobilised within only one of these spheres. It had to grow within the interstices of the old society and supplant it bit by bit, sometimes through main force, violence, predation and seizures of assets, but at other times with guile and cunning. And it often lost battles against the old order even as it eventually won the war. As it achieved a modicum of power, however, a nascent capitalist class had to build its alternative social forms at first on the basis of the technologies, social relations, administrative systems, mental conceptions, production systems, relations to nature and patterns of daily life as these had long been constituted under the preceding feudal order. It took a co-evolution and uneven development in the different spheres before capitalism found not only its own unique technological base but also its belief systems and mental conceptions, its unstable but clearly class-ridden configurations of social relations, its curious spatio-temporal rhythms and its equally special forms of daily life, to say nothing of its production processes and its institutional and administrative framework, before it was possible to say that this was truly capitalism.

Even as it did so, it carried within it multiple marks of the differential conditions under which the transformation to capitalism had been wrought. While too much has probably been made of the differentials between Protestant, Catholic and Confucian traditions in marking out significant differences in how capitalism works in different parts of the world, it would be foolhardy to suggest that such influences are irrelevant or even negligible. Furthermore, once capitalism found its own feet, so it engaged in a perpetual revolutionary movement across all the spheres to accommodate the inevitable stresses of endless capital accumulation at a compound rate of growth. The daily habits and mental conceptions of the working classes that have emerged (along with a redefinition of what constitutes a 'working class' social relation in the first place) in the 1990s bear little relationship to working-class habits and moves of Britain in the 1950s and 1960s. The process of co-evolution that capitalism sets in motion has been perpetual.

Perhaps one of the biggest failures of past attempts to build socialism has been the reluctance to engage politically across all of these spheres and to let the dialectic between them open up possibilities, rather than close them down. Revolutionary communism, particularly that of the Soviet sort – especially after the period of revolutionary experimentation of the 1920s was terminated by Stalin – too often reduced the dialectic of relations between the spheres to a single-track programme in which productive forces (technologies) were placed in the vanguard of change. This approach inevitably failed. It led to stasis, stagnant administrative and institutional arrangements, turned daily life into monotony, and froze the possibility to explore new social relations or mental conceptions. It paid no mind to the relation to nature, with disastrous consequences. Lenin, of course, had no option but to strive to create communism on the basis of the configuration given by the preceding order (part feudal and part capitalist), and from this standpoint his embrace of the Fordist factory, its technologies and organisational forms as a necessary step in the transition to communism is understandable. He plausibly argued that if the transition to socialism and then communism was to work it had to be initially on the basis of the most advanced technologies and organisational forms that capitalism had produced. But there was no conscious attempt, particularly after Stalin took over, to move towards the construction of truly socialist, let alone communist technologies and organisational forms (though they did make major advances in robotisation and in the mathematical planning of optimal production and scheduling systems that could have lightened the burden of labouring and enhanced efficiency if they had been properly applied).

Mao's overwhelming dialectical sense of how contradictions worked, as well as his recognition, in principle at least, that a revolution had to be permanent or nothing at all, led him consciously to prioritise revolutionary transformation in different activity spheres in different historical phases. The 'Great Leap Forward' emphasised production and technological and organisational change. It failed in its immediate objectives and produced a massive famine, but almost certainly had a huge impact upon mental conceptions. The Cultural Revolution sought to radically reconfigure social relations and mental conceptions of the world directly. While it is contemporary received wisdom that Mao failed miserably in both of these endeavours, the suspicion lurks that in many respects the astonishing economic performance and revolutionary transformation that has characterised China since its shift towards institutional and administrative reforms from the late 1970s onwards has rested solidly on the real achievements of the Maoist period (in particular the break with many 'traditional' mental conceptions and social relations within the masses as the Party deepened its grasp over daily life). Mao completely reorganised the delivery of health care in the 1960s, for example, by sending an army of 'barefoot doctors' out into the hitherto neglected and impoverished rural regions to teach elementary preventive medicine, public health measures and pre-natal care. The dramatic reductions in infant mortality and increases in life expectancy that resulted just happened to produce the labour surpluses that fuelled China's growth surge after 1980. It also led to draconian limitations on reproductive activity through enforcement of a one child per family policy. That all of this opened the path towards a certain kind of capitalist development is an unintended consequence of huge significance.

How, then, might revolutionary strategies be construed in the light of this co-evolutionary theory of social change? It provides a framework for enquiry that can have practical implications for thinking through everything from grand revolutionary strategies to redesign of urbanisation and city life. At the same time it signals that we perpetually confront contingencies, contradictions and autonomous possibilities, as well as a host of unintended consequences. As with the transition from feudalism to capitalism, there are plenty of interstitial spaces to start alternative social movements that are anti-capitalist. But there are also plenty of possibilities for well-intended moves to be co-opted or go catastrophically wrong. Conversely, seemingly negative developments (such as Mao's Great Leap Forward or the Second World War that set the stage for rapid economic growth after 1945) may turn out surprisingly well. Should that deter us? Since evolution in general and in human societies in particular (with or without the capitalist imperative) cannot be stopped, then we have no option but to be participants in the drama. Our only choice is whether or not to be conscious of how our interventions are working and to be ready to change course rapidly as conditions unfold or as unintended consequences become more apparent. The evident adaptability and flexibility of capitalism here provides an important role model.

So where shall we start our revolutionary anti-capitalist movement? Mental conceptions? The relation to nature? Daily life and reproductive practices? Social relations? Technologies and organisational forms? Labour processes? The capture of institutions and their revolutionary transformation?

A survey of alternative thinking and of oppositional social movements would show different currents of thought (more often than not unfortunately posed as mutually exclusive) as to where it is most appropriate to begin. But the implication of the co-evolutionary theory here proposed is that we can start anywhere and everywhere as long as we do not stay where we start from! The revolution has to be a *movement* in every sense of that word. If it cannot move within, across and through the different spheres then it will ultimately go nowhere at all. Recognising this, it becomes imperative to envision alliances between a whole range of social forces configured around the different spheres. Those with a deep knowledge of how the relation to nature works need to ally with those deeply familiar with how institutional and administrative arrangements function, how science and technology can be mobilised, how daily life and social relations can most easily be re-organised, how mental conceptions can be changed, and how production and the labour process can be reconfigured.

But in what space does a revolutionary movement occur and how does it make space as it goes? That is the geographical question we now have to consider.

6

The Geography of It All

The crisis that began in highly localised housing markets in the United States in 2007 quickly spread around the world via a tightly networked financial and trading system that was supposed to spread risk rather than financial mayhem. As the effects of the credit crunch spread, it had differential impacts from one place to another. Everything depended on the degree to which local banks and other institutions like pension funds had invested in the toxic assets being peddled from the United States; the degree to which banks elsewhere had copied US practices and pursued high-risk investments; the dependency of local firms and state institutions (such as municipal governments) upon open lines of credit to roll over their debts; the impact of rapidly falling consumer demand in the US and elsewhere on export-led economies; the ups and downs in the demand for and prices of raw materials (oil in particular); and the different structures of employment and of social support (including flows of remittances) and social provision prevailing in this place rather than that. When, how and why did this crisis hit a particular country, region or neighbourhood, if at all? Why does unemployment within the European Union (averaging 8.9 per cent in April 2009) vary from 2 per cent in the Netherlands to 17.5 per cent in Spain? Why does it matter that US households in recent years have been saving almost nothing, the British around 2 per cent and the Germans 11 per cent of their income? Why did Lebanon, with all of its tumultuous recent history, feel almost no effects of the crisis as of summer 2009? (Answer in part: because of the huge economic stimulus already underway in rebuilding the country from the ruins of the Israeli bombardment of 2006.)

In China and much of the rest of Asia the problem was almost entirely registered through the collapse of export markets, whereas in Iceland it was almost entirely due to exposure of national banks to toxic assets. Tightly regulated Canadian banks have so far reported no difficulties, but industries dependent on trade with the US have been seriously hit. Britain was badly hit because it had followed the US model in almost all respects, whereas Germany had to cope mainly with falling exports, even as rumours flew that there were many toxic assets hidden within the German banking system. China, with huge foreign exchange reserves, had abundant financial resources to confront the difficulties, whereas Iceland had none.

The responses of both populations and of state authorities have varied remarkably from one country to another according to the depth and nature of the local problem, ideological predilections, dominant interpretations of primary causes, institutional arrangements (the much stronger social safety net in many European countries, for example, compared to the United States, where welfare provision is parsimonious in the extreme), customary habits (with respect to personal savings, for example) and the availability of local resources (budget surpluses, in particular) to deal with local impacts. Germany, with awful memories of the impacts of the Weimar inflation that brought Hitler to power, feared that excessive debt-financing would spark inflation and so stuck rigidly to neoliberal orthodoxies, whereas the US cheerfully subscribed (to the embarrassment of the born-again fiscal conservatives in the Republican Party) to the Reagan doctrine that 'deficits do not matter'. If the responses and the impacts are so diverse, then this poses the question of whence either the recovery or some innovative turn towards an alternative political economy might come? We know the answer to the east and south-east Asian crisis of 1997–8: booming but debt-fuelled US consumer markets allowed the economies of that region to export their way back to economic health. So where might it be this time? Emerging markets in Brazil, India and China that are still showing signs of growth? We simply cannot tell this time around, though there are a lot of signs that point to east Asia as the epicentre of recovery. Both the effects of the crisis and, we have to anticipate, the geographical paths whereby the so-called 'green shoots' of economic recovery might spread are almost impossible to predict.

To illustrate the strange pathways by which financial contagion can spread, consider the following example.

Like many other municipalities around the world, Berlin was having problems financing its public transport system during the 1990s. The increasingly neoliberal central government was reluctant to provide support. Financial advisers came up with a neat way to help out. Lease the transport equipment long term to investors in the United States and then lease it back. The investors in the United States, who received tax credits on depreciation of foreign investment, shared their tax break with the Berlin transit authority (who received around $90 million in the late 1990s). In effect US taxpayers were subsidising German municipal governments, many of which struck similar deals on everything from water supply and sewage systems to convention centres. When the US tax authorities figured out the scam they moved to close the loophole after 2004. But the contracts, complicated and written in English, stayed in force. The contract specified that the value of the leased assets had to be insured with a highly rated insurer. Berlin was eventually persuaded by the US investment bank JP Morgan to insure through a collateralised debt obligation (CDO) backed by many financial institutions deemed highly credit-worthy, including Lehman Brothers, AIG and the Icelandic banks. When all of these crashed in September 2008, and the CDO went toxic, Berlin had to either find another highly rated insurer (by then impossible) or deposit its own monies as collateral. It was liable for $200 million or more. Many other German municipalities found themselves in the same predicament (Leipzig was particularly hard hit because that city had leased almost everything it had). But it was very difficult, as one German municipal official noted, not to be lured into such a scheme when so many other municipalities were gloating at their good fortune back in the 1990s.

The fiasco of cross-border leasing in Germany then added fuel to an all-too plausible but erroneous European interpretation, articulated by both German and French leaders, that the crisis was a distinctively Anglo-American production rather than a systemic failure of capitalism. The broadly nationalist (and, in some instances, dangerously right-wing) responses to the crisis – as evidenced in the European elections of June 2009, when right-wing parties substantially increased their vote – throughout much of Europe then become easier to understand. But the idea that the export industries of Germany thrived all on their own, as if the debt-laden consumer boom on the other side of the Atlantic had nothing to do with it, is a great example of how narrow national perceptions distort the realities of what globalising capitalism is all about.

———

So what guides the geographical trajectory of unfolding crises, and how do local impacts and local political responses relate to global dynamics? Is there, in short, some theory of the uneven geographical development of capitalism to which we can appeal that will help us understand the intricate geographical dynamics of capital accumulation and so contextualise how this particular crisis unfolded?

Processes of capital accumulation do not exist, obviously, outside of their geographical settings and these settings are by nature immensely diverse. But capitalists and their agents also take an active and prominent role in changing these settings. New spaces and space relations are constantly being produced. Wholly new transport and communications networks and sprawling cities and highly productive agrarian landscapes are being made. Much of the land has been deforested, resources have been extracted from the bowels of the earth, habitats and atmospheric conditions (both locally and globally) have been modified. The oceans have been trawled incessantly for food and all manner of wastes (some toxic in relation to all forms of life) have been spread across the earth. The long-term environmental changes wrought by human actions throughout the whole of our history have been enormous. The changes wrought under capitalism have been even more so. What was given us by nature has long been superseded by what has been humanly constructed. Capitalism's geography is increasingly self-produced.

Capitalists are not, however, the only ones engaged in its production. Since around 1700, the world's population has grown at a compound rate that, interestingly, parallels the compounding rate of capital accumulation. Global population topped 1 billion around 1810. It rose from 1.6 billion in 1900 to 2.4 billion by 1950 and to over 6 billion by 2000. Estimates now put it at 6.8 billion. Projections put it at 9 billion or so by 2050.

The exact nature of the relation between capital accumulation and population growth is a matter of debate. But what is almost certain is that capitalism could not have survived and flourished in the way it has, had it not been for the perpetual expansion of the populations available as both producers and consumers. This has been so even when those populations have not been organised according to capitalist social relations, technologies, production forms and institutional arrangements. The contributions of slavery, of Inca gold, of raw material supplies extracted from indigenous populations, and of non-capitalist markets to the production and absorption of capital surpluses have been fundamental to sustaining capitalist growth across the centuries. The booming cotton industries of Manchester in 1860 rested upon raw cotton being produced on plantations in the United States using slave labour transported from Africa, while the finished products were sold, *inter alia*, to the vast and ever-growing populations in non-capitalist but British-imperialist-controlled India. But the converse proposition also applies: without the growth supplied through capital accumulation, populations could well have starved, unless some other way of provisioning them had been devised.

In more recent times, the newly and in many instances only partially proletarianised populations of rural China have laid the foundation for a phenomenal phase of capitalist growth. This growth has helped keep an increasingly volatile capitalism on a compounding growth path, even as stresses have been registered in those regions that could not compete with China's low-wage industry. To take another example, the massive movement of expanding populations into urban areas has put enormous pressures on land uses and played therefore a key role in the rising land values and land rents that have been captured by landed capitalists and developers.

The accommodation of more and more people on planet earth has entailed in itself massive geographical changes. Migratory and pioneering movements have taken sparsely populated continents, such as North America in 1700, and turned them into dynamic growth centres for the accumulation of people and eventually capital, too. Early on in the history of capitalism settler colonies and frontier pioneering activity played a key role in opening up new territories for capitalist development. Even today, there are millions of peasants, small farmers and producers, artisans and workshop producers and repairers along with those pursuing alternative lifestyles or more simply coping with lack of opportunities for incorporation within the capitalist system, whose connection to the accumulation of capital is either loose or tangential. Their involvements are largely orchestrated through their contacts with the market system and limited participation in commodity exchange. Taxation by the state, however, provides a long-standing means whereby populations of this sort are brought into the general orbit of capital accumulation through the necessity to sell something in order to pay the tax man.

This vast army of people provides both a potential labour reserve as well as a potential market. In recent years, for example, what was once referred to in the official language of international institutions as 'the informal sector' (and therefore somehow outside of the logic of capital accumulation) has been redefined as a world of 'microenterprises'. The fate of these enterprises is then linked to that of capital through the extension of microcredit and microfinance schemes to these microenterprises. These schemes extend small amounts of credit (at very high rates of interest) to collectives (usually a fairly small group of women) from within the 2 billion people who live on less than 2 dollars a day. The purported aim is to permit the population to raise themselves out of poverty and join the merry business of capital accumulation. Some succeed, but for the rest it means debt peonage.

These populations make their own geography in innumerable ways. Their demographic and economic situations vary a great deal, however. In east and south Asia, populations have continued to surge even as vast wealth has been drained from them – at least until recently – from the seventeenth century onwards by virtue of aggrandising colonial and imperialist practices. The more advanced centres of capital accumulation, such as much of western Europe and Japan, have slipped into negative population growth (with attendant problems of ageing populations which pose all manner of problems for sustained capital accumulation), while the rest of Asia, Latin America and Africa continue to increase. China, meanwhile, through draconian restriction on family size, seeks to contain the growth of its already huge 1.2 billion population while the United States has sustained its demographic growth through a more open but now increasingly challenged immigration policy (supplemented by a significant influx of illegal immigrants who provide much of the low-wage labour required for agribusiness, construction and domestic services in particular).

People occupy space and have to live on the land somewhere and somehow. How they live, sustain themselves and reproduce the species varies enormously from place to place, but in the process people create places within which they dwell, from the peasant hut, the small village, the favela, the urban tenement, to the suburban tract house or the multimillion-dollar homes in the Hamptons of Long Island, in China's gated communities or in Sao Paulo's or Mexico City's high rise penthouses. Place-making, and the creation of a dwelling place that becomes the secure environment called house and home, is as extensive as capital accumulation in its impacts upon the land, even as the production of such places becomes a major vehicle for surplus production and absorption. The production of 'the urban', where most of the world's burgeoning population now lives, has become over time more closely intertwined with capital accumulation, to the point where it is hard to disentangle one from the other. Even in the shanty towns of self-built housing, the corrugated iron, the packing boxes and the tarpaulins were first produced as commodities.

Surplus populations are no more anchored in place than is capital. They flow everywhere in search of pioneering opportunities or employment, in spite of barriers to migration sometimes put up by nation states. Captive labour forces of indentured domestic servants, migrant gangs of construction workers and agricultural labourers vie with local populations and individuals who move in search of better chances in life. Polish women clean the hotels around Heathrow airport in London, Latvians serve in Irish pubs, itinerant labourers from Mexico and Guatemala build condominium towers in New York or pick strawberries in the fields of California, Palestinians, Indians and Sudanese work in the Gulf States, and so on. Remittances from the Gulf States to India and south-east Asia or back into the Palestinian refugee camps parallel the flows of remittances from the United States to Mexico, Haiti, the Philippines, Ecuador and many other less-developed countries. Diasporas of all kinds (of both business and labour) form networks that intricately weave into the spatial dynamics of capital accumulation. And it is exactly through such networks that we now see the effects of the financial crash spreading into almost every nook and cranny of rural Africa or peasant India. Malnutrition and outright starvation stalk Haiti as the remittances that were flowing from the US dry up because women domestic workers in New York City and Florida are losing their jobs.

Human landscapes of geographical difference are thus created in which social relations and production systems, daily lifestyles, technologies and organisational forms and distinctive relations to nature come together with institutional arrangements to produce distinctive places of different qualities. Such places are in turn marked by distinctive politics and contested ways of life. Consider, for a moment, the various ways in which all these elements hang together in the place where you live. This intricate physical and social geography bears the imprint of the social and political processes, as well as the active struggles that produced it.

The uneven geographical development that results is as infinitely varied as it is volatile: a deindustrialised city in northern China; a shrinking city in what was once East Germany; the booming industrial cities in the Pearl River delta; an IT concentration in Bangalore; a Special Economic Zone in India where dispossessed peasants revolt; indigenous populations under pressure in Amazonia or New Guinea; the affluent neighbourhoods in Greenwich, Connecticut (until recently, at least, hedge fund capital of the world); the conflict-ridden oil fields in the Ogoni region of Nigeria; the autonomous zones carved out by a militant movement such as the Zapatistas in Chiapas, Mexico; the vast soy bean production zones in Brazil, Paraguay and Argentina; the rural regions of Darfur or the Congo where civil wars relentlessly rage; the staid middle-class suburbs of London, Los Angeles or Munich; the shanty towns of South Africa; the garment factories of Sri Lanka or the call centres of Barbados and Bangalore 'manned' entirely by women; the new megacities in the Gulf States with their star-architect-designed buildings – all of this (and of course much more) when taken together constitutes a world of geographical difference that has been made by human action.

At first blush, this world would appear to be so geographically diverse as to escape principled understanding, let alone rationalised control. How on earth does it all relate? That there are intertwinings and inter-relationships is obvious. The civil wars in Africa, in many ways sad legacies of European colonial practices, reflect the long history of corporate and state-led struggles to control Africa's valued resources, with China these days an increasingly important player. The factory in northern China or Ohio closes down in part because the factories in the Pearl River delta open up. The call centre in Barbados or Bangalore services customers in Ohio and London and the shirts or skirts worn in Paris have labels from Sri Lanka or Bangladesh, just as the shoes that were once made in Italy now come from Vietnam. The Gulf States build spectacular buildings on the back of an oil trade that depends in part on the profligate use of energy to service a predominantly suburban lifestyle in the United States.

How is all this geographical difference produced? How is its seemingly infinite and uncontrollable variety internally knit and woven together to form the dynamic geography in which we have our being?

———

In what space does the co-evolutionary process outlined earlier occur? Consider, first, a typical US suburb in a major metropolitan area such as Washington DC in the year 2005, before the financial crisis broke. The population is relatively homogeneous (mainly white but with a scattering of educated African Americans and equally educated recent immigrants from countries as diverse as India, Taiwan, South Korea and Russia) and reasonably affluent. The suburban tract housing is laid neatly out and the schools, supermarkets and shopping malls (incorporating entertainment functions), medical facilities and financial institutions, gas stations and auto showrooms, sports facilities and open spaces are all within easy driving distance. Local employment is heavily involved in services (particularly finance, insurance and real estate, software production and medical research) and whatever production there is, is either oriented to supporting a middle-class suburban lifestyle (car repair, garden centres, ceramics, carpentry, medical equipment) or involved in the reproduction or further production of the built environment (all facets of the construction industry and its suppliers such as plumbers, roofers and road menders). The tax base is stable and adequate and the local administration, apart from engaging in the usual suburban practices of cosying up to construction interests and developers, is reasonably efficient. Commuting times are longish but bearable, particularly with the help of all that electronic equipment that turns the interior of a car into an entertainment centre. Daily life is reasonably well ordered, apart from a few scandalous family break-ups or egregious crimes; social relations are individualistic but loosely integrated through social forms, particularly those associated with the churches, schools and local golf clubs. Home ownership (mortgage induced and tax subsidised) is widespread, which guarantees that the defence of individual housing value is a collective norm, upheld by homeownership associations, even in the midst of plenty of isolated individualism. The houses are all laden with different kinds of electronics and of course everyone has iPods and cell phones which are in perpetual use.

In this world, relations between the seven spheres of activity are roughly harmonised in ways that most people accept as secure and reassuring, even though a bit dull. Conflicts are minor (for the most part of the 'not in my back yard' sort) and even the two political parties vying for office run moderate candidates. The flows of capital into, through and out of this produced place are steady and the particular configuration of relations between the different spheres of activity successfully facilitates the profitable continuation of these flows.

Contrast this with a second area not too far away (in Pennsylvania, say) that was once a thriving steel and metal-working town that has recently suffered deindustrialisation and plant closures. The population was once homogeneous enough, built around seemingly secure and unionised male blue-collar jobs with family structures based on that source of income plus casual part-time low-paid female employment. But all of this has now disappeared. Many of the men are unemployed and on welfare, working-class housing is deteriorating (some houses stand empty and vandalised), many local stores have closed down, the tax base is weak and the schools and services correspondingly degraded, and welfare, pension and health care rights are fragile. The union halls that used to be the centres of socialising are either abandoned or almost empty and only the churches still offer sanctuary for socialising and solace. Petty crime is rampant. Problems of alcoholism and substance abuse are mounting. Gender relations are radically transformed and family break-ups escalate as women become the primary breadwinners and a traditional male working class finds itself reduced to the status of a disposable underclass. Various attempts to revive the area are underway but nothing much seems to stick. Some women armed with rudimentary computer skills create a barter and collective support network (an example of what is now called the 'solidarity economy'). A local entrepreneur tries to rally local merchants to support an art event that might attract visitors, and the cheap property prices find a market with disillusioned populations from a nearby metropolis where living has become too expensive, such as New York City. But these populations are immigrants, gays and bohemians whose values are radically different from the predominantly white working class who once lived here so securely. Ethnic and sexual tensions escalate. Itinerant immigrant labourers doss down in some empty houses and are greeted with hostility by local residents. Anti-immigrant violence flares. The collapse of the production base has here set in motion a chain reaction across all the other spheres, forcing stressful, grating and conflictual co-evolutionary adjustments in mental conceptions, social relations, patterns of daily living and social reproduction, as well as in technologies and systems of governance. The disharmony between the spheres is palpable and how they might get back into balance is uncertain.

Now consider what in India is legally defined as a 'slum'. Thousands of people are crammed together in a settlement where no formal title to land or housing exists. Governance is largely exercised through informal power structures that derive either from economic wealth, accumulated legally or illegally, or from status. Charismatic religious or political figures emerge as local bosses. Formal state power is rarely exercised directly and, when it is, it is either through violent police and military interventions, bureaucratic and legalistic impositions or through outright corruption in the name of protection. Some economic activity can be found – rubber tyres turned into sandals are marketed on the streets and some subcontracting networks for leather products or artisanal objects that end up in Manhattan stores can be found in the midst of dense and chaotic structures. Running water and sewage disposal are generally lacking and fetid odours are everywhere. Electricity is pirated on an occasional basis. Life expectancy is short and infant mortality shockingly high.

Meanwhile, social relations are just as often predatory as they are mutually supportive and violence is frequently resorted to as a way to preserve social power, if not life itself. New migrants from the countryside are treated as the lowest of the low and gender relations and family structures are as unstable as they are ephemeral, even as some groups form strong ties of mutual support. Rudimentary attempts by NGOs to upgrade conditions exist and a pilot project to bring microfinance projects into the slum as a solution to poverty is having a hard time gaining traction.

Some plan exists in a faraway planning office for upgrading the physical environment, but most local people see it as a plot to evict them from potentially high-value land. There is no health care (apart from local folkloric medicines and indigenous cures) and education is either non-existent or haphazard. Some flow of labour into the rest of the city occurs (men into construction or landscaping work and women sweep the floors for middle-class families for almost no remuneration, though at least they eat well from the scraps off the rich folks' tables). Transistor radios are everywhere and, in the absence of landlines, cell phones (often stolen) are now ubiquitous. Indeed, the main market activity is either in stolen goods or in the bartering of the cheapest of products. In this space, sharply bounded by a highway and a winding river, the seven activity spheres co-exist in a unique configuration. While radically different from the US suburb, we can still describe the internal relations within the totality of this space and dissect the processes of often tense and contradictory co-evolution that make this slum such a dynamic ecological space.

In these three places the co-evolutionary trajectories point in seemingly different directions. Here the economic, social and political winds blow in one way, there they are stagnant and somewhere else they blow in a completely different direction. But in each case we are able to grasp how lives are lived and how circumstances are changing. We have available to us, in fact, innumerable historico-geographical, sociological and anthropological monographs describing in intricate detail the interactions and changes occurring in this or that place (often tacitly invoking relations between different spheres of activity). The media provide descriptions of how things are going – well or badly as the case may be – in 'older US suburbs', Kazakhstan, Cairo, Wuppertal, Chenai, Mombassa or Canton, Ohio. The big problem arises when we try to put all of these different accounts from around the world together in a way that highlights both their interdependency and their undoubted particularity.

If we could somehow map the movement of capital occurring in different places across the globe, then the picture would look something like the satellite images taken from outer space of the weather systems swirling across the oceans, mountains and plains of planet earth. We would see an upwelling of activity here, becalmed zones there, anticyclonic swirls in another place and cyclonic depressions of various depths and sizes elsewhere. Here and there tornadoes would be ripping up the land and at certain times typhoons and hurricanes would be coursing across the oceans posing imminent dangers for those in their paths. Refreshing rains would turn pastures green while droughts elsewhere leave a scorched earth brown.

At first sight, all this motion within weather systems appears chaotic and unpredictable. But careful observation and analysis have revealed patterns within their swirling chaos. Long-term changes in climatic signals are also detectable. Climatologists and meteorologists can grasp the underlying fluid dynamic forces, heat budgets and the like that impel much of the movement even as they turn to chaos theory to frame their thinking on the details. They can even gain some traction, though never perfect, over forecasting short-term weather patterns and predicting longer term shifts such as global warming. They have certainly arrived at a point where retrospective understandings of what happened are pretty convincing.

The economic geographer is faced with analogous problems of finding some distinctive patterns and longer-term signals of change within the seeming chaos of social, economic and political activity observable on the ground. A synoptic map of economic activity in the 1980s, for example, would have depicted a series of highs building and swirling around the Pacific edge of much of east and south-east Asia (from Japan to Hong Kong) as well as down the west coast of the USA and throughout Bavaria and Tuscany. It would have depicted most of Latin America stagnant but prone to violent political and economic upheavals, and a series of deep depressions passing across the Ohio valley and Pennsylvania, the British industrial heartlands as well as across the Ruhr valley of Germany. The big difference to the study of weather and climate, however, is that, whereas the laws of fluid dynamics can be presumed to remain constant over time, the laws of capital accumulation are constantly evolving as human behaviours adapt reflexively to new circumstances.

The art and the science of geographical analysis and forecasting remain lamentably underdeveloped relative to, say, the effort put into understanding the world's weather and climate. The social sciences, too, often collectively turn their back on the problem of geography. By and large (and there are, of course, always wonderful exceptions) anthropologists prefer to view the messiness of the global as intractable in order to justify an exclusive focus on local ethnographies; sociologists focus on something called community or, until recently, confine their studies within state borders; and economists place all economic activity on the head of a pin. The complex geography of it all, from local to global, is either ignored or reduced to some banal version of physical geographical determinism of the sort peddled recently by Jared Diamond in *Guns, Germs and Steel* or by the economist Jeffrey Sachs in *The End of Poverty* (2005) or, even worse, revives dangerous (because sometimes self-fulfilling) theories of Darwinian struggles between states for geopolitical domination.

The result is a doubly serious lacuna. We do not well understand what happens where and why and how events here affect conditions elsewhere. Nor can we assess how dependent the reproduction of capitalism is upon the seemingly chaotic forms of uneven geographical development. As a result, we have even less idea what to do about it all in the midst of a crisis, even though we are collectively in a potential position to change the laws of social reproduction and capital accumulation (hopefully for the better) through conscious action.

Are there, then, some geographical principles to which we can tentatively appeal to understand all this seeming chaos on the ground and the role it plays in capitalism's reproduction? In what follows I lay out some broad-brush ideas.

———

Principle number one is that all geographical limits to capital accumulation have to be overcome. Capital, Marx wrote in the *Grundrisse*, must 'strive to tear down every spatial barrier to intercourse, i.e., to exchange, and conquer the whole earth for its market'. It must also perpetually strive to 'annihilate this space with time'. What does this mean and why is this so?

Early on, urban-based merchants and traders learned that their power to survive within a land-based feudal or imperial power lay in cultivating a superior ability to manoeuvre in space. Merchant and trading capital (along with a nascent banking capital) circumvented and eventually subverted the feudal order in large part by spatial strategies, albeit by protecting certain places – the early trading cities – as networked islands of liberty in a world of feudal restraints. To this day, the capitalist class and its agents (including a variety of ethnic business diasporas) maintain much of their power of domination by virtue of superior command over and mobility in space. These same powers are also fundamental, as every general knows, to the maintenance of military superiority. The so-called 'space race' of the 1960s and 1970s between the US and the Soviet Union was perhaps the most dramatic version of this omnipresent ambition in recent times. There thus emerges a joint imperative within the state–corporate nexus constituted within capitalism, to fund the technologies and organisational forms that assure the continued dominance of space and spatial movement by state and capital. Hence the British Royal Society's competition in the eighteenth century to construct a chronometer that could work on the high seas and so pinpoint locations accurately. In the early years, maps were guarded as state secrets and kept under lock and key. Now, of course, we have satellites, GPS systems and Google Earth to guide us, though this does not prevent the US from buying up all the satellite images of Afghanistan to protect its military interests. Drones flying over Afghanistan fire missiles on command from a base in Colorado. Computerised orders from Wall Street are executed in London and received instantaneously in Zurich and Singapore.

This penchant for the domination of space goes far deeper than mere economic rationality. The psychology of it all plainly matters. The fetish belief in the human capacity to transcend the chains that keep us tied down on planet earth long ago emerged as a central motif in bourgeois utopian desire. 'Ye Gods! annihilate but space and time/ And make two lovers happy' went the couplet from the eighteenth-century poet Alexander Pope. The grand rationalist philosopher René Descartes had his engineer survey the world from on high in the belief that nature could be dominated by man. Johann Goethe's Faust made a pact with the devil in order to gain omnipotence over planet earth. The novelist Honoré Balzac – always a great revelatory source as regards the fetish desires of the upstart classes – wildly imagined himself 'riding across the world, disposing all in it to my liking ... I possess the world effortlessly, and the world hasn't the slightest hold upon me ... I am here and I have the power to be elsewhere! I am dependent upon neither time, nor space, nor distance. The world is my servant.'

The conquest of space and time and the mastery of the world (of both 'mother earth' and the world market) appear in many capitalist fantasies as displaced but sublime masculine expressions of sexual desire and millennial charismatic belief. Is this the fetish belief that impels onwards the ever rising 'animal spirits' of the financiers? Is this why so many financiers and hedge fund wizards are men? Is this how people feel when they bet the whole of the New Zealand currency in one go? What astonishing power to ride the world and bend it to one's will!

Marx and Engels spelled out the secular consequences of this in their 1848 *Communist Manifesto* in ways that every worker who has experienced deindustrialisation over the last forty years will readily understand:

> All old-established national industries have been destroyed or are daily being destroyed. They are dislodged by new industries, whose introduction becomes a life and death question for all civilised nations, by industries that no longer work up indigenous raw material, but raw material drawn from the remotest zones; industries whose products are consumed not only at home, but in every quarter of the globe. In place of the old wants, satisfied by the productions of the country, we find new wants, requiring for their satisfaction the products of distant lands and climes. In place of the old local and national seclusion and self-sufficiency, we have intercourse in every direction, universal interdependence of nations ...

What we now call 'globalisation' has been in the sights of the capitalist class all along.

Whether the desire to conquer space and nature is a manifestation of some universal human longing or a product of specifically capitalist class passions we will never know. What can be said with certainty is that the conquest of space and time, along with the ceaseless quest to dominate nature, have long taken centre stage in the collective psyche of capitalist societies. In spite of all manner of critiques, objections, revulsions and political movements of opposition, and in spite of the massive unintended consequences in the relation to nature that are increasingly felt, the belief still prevails that the conquest of space and time, as well as of nature (including even human nature), is somehow within our reach. The result has been an inexorable trend for the world of capital to produce what I call 'time–space compression' – a world in which capital moves faster and faster and where distances of interaction are compressed.

There is a more prosaic way to look at this. The coercive laws of competition (often resisted) impel both corporations and states to seek out advantages conferred by superior command over space and time, as well as technological advances. Superiority in either yields clear economic, political and military benefits. The fetish belief then takes hold that there is either a technological or a spatio-temporal fix for every problem capital encounters. Difficulties absorbing surplus capital? Either: invent a new technology and product line. Or: expand geographically and find a market elsewhere, in another space, by colonial or neocolonial domination if necessary (this is what British capital did with India after 1850 or so). What if there is no external market readily available? Then export capital to create a new centre of production overseas where accelerating production (as in contemporary China) rather than 'individual consumption' (as in the debt-sodden United States) creates the demand to mop up the surplus capital.

When these two fetish beliefs in technological and spatio-temporal fixes collide, they feed off each other in frenzies of technological innovation designed to circumvent all temporal and spatial limits to the circulation of capital. How many of the technological innovations throughout the history of capitalism have been about reducing the frictions of distance or speeding up capital circulation? The list is endless. Where would we be without canals, railroads, steamships, automobiles, highways, air transport, telegraphs, radios, telephones, electronic communications, and the like? Computerised trading in financial centres linked by near instantaneous flows of information now flip $600 trillion in derivatives around the world in milliseconds. Even pigs have twice as many litters in a year as was their previous wont (no wonder they get the flu).

————

The second set of principles emerges from the simple fact that the circulation of capital does not take place on the head of a pin. Production entails geographical concentration of money, means of production and labour power (largely contained in localised labour markets). These are brought together in a particular place where a new commodity is produced. They are then shipped off to markets to be sold and consumed somewhere else. Proximity to means of production (including natural resources), labour power and consumer markets lowers costs and raises profits in favoured locations.

But where might capital accumulation begin? The answer: wherever and whenever somebody who has some money decides to use it to make more money by exploiting wage labour. But what conditions permit individuals to start and, even more importantly, to sustain their money-making over time? Obviously, a monetised economy must already exist (along with market exchange) and money must already be a significant form of social power. Furthermore, wage labour must either already be in existence or at least procurable through either expelling people from the land or attracting them into the labour market by some means. For this to happen requires that social and political barriers to individual capital accumulation must be overcome. When the Chinese leader Deng Xiaoping pronounced that making money and getting rich was good, he let the capitalist genii out of the bottle across the length and breadth of China – with astonishing results. But a mere pronouncement and the loosening of administrative constraints does not guarantee success. Success can be gauged only after the coercive laws of competition have determined that this initiative has been successful in this particular place rather than that.

This point is crucial. The laws of capital accumulation operate after the fact and not before. It is sometimes said that Marx held that everything is economically determined and economically rational- ised in advance. There is, it is claimed he said, no room for individual initiative and agency. Nothing could be further from the truth. It is precisely the genius of capitalism that it relies upon the instincts, enterprise and sometimes crazy ideas (the 'animal spirits' invoked by both Marx and Keynes) of individual entrepreneurs operating in particular places and times. It is only where a modicum of individual liberty is tolerated or fostered that an inherently speculative capital- ism can develop and propel itself forward. Capitalism is founded, both in terms of its ruling ideologies and in its necessary practices, upon individual freedoms and liberties to engage in speculative money-making activities. Marx understood and appreciated that full well.

The seeming chaos of geographical differentiation, we can conclude, is a necessary condition for capital accumulation to begin. It was, after all, in small villages and townships with names like Manchester and Birmingham where social and political controls were lacking, not in the large urban centres like Norwich and Bristol where corporatist political controls and guild labour prevailed, that the industrial revolution began in Britain. And it was in small trading posts with names like Chicago in the United States where it continued.

The so-called laws of capital accumulation operate after the fact rather than before. It was, for example, a very particular set of circum- stances that led a man called William Morris to begin to build cars (rather than mend bicycles) in the unlikely location of east Oxford in England. The same was true for Henry Ford in Detroit. But in both instances the initial circumstances – access to raw materials, wage labour, markets – were good enough to succeed. Initial success led to the construction of more and more supportive local infrastructures (both social and physical) that made the chosen locations even better for car production. Successful enterprises often collect infrastructural developments around them (including other enterprises) that make them even more profitable. Only now, after nearly a century, are we seeing the rationalisations of competition and of crises pushing car production in these hitherto successful locations either to the brink of elimination or into a phase of radical restructuring.

It is through the coercive laws of competition and through crises that 'after the fact' rationalisations and geographical restructurings to capital accumulation occur. This is why both competition and crises are so fundamental to the evolutionary trajectory of capitalism. But this also explains why it is that capitalism flourishes best in a geographical world of such immense diversity of physical attributes and social and cultural conditions. Since it can never be known in advance whether or not a profit-seeking venture can succeed here rather than there, then probing the possibilities everywhere and finding out what works where becomes fundamental to the reproduction of capitalism. The failures, of which we rarely hear in an otherwise triumphalist economic historical geography, are far more numerous than the success stories. Who would have known that IT activities would become so successful in Bangalore, India? Why did Henry Ford's attempt to build a new rubber plantation community in Amazonia in the inter-war years fail so miserably? Geographical diversity is a necessary condition for, rather than a barrier to, the reproduction of capital. If the geographical diversity does not already exist, then it has to be created.

The necessity for continuity in the geographical flows of money, goods and people requires that all this diversity be woven together through efficient transport and communications systems. The resultant geography of production and consumption is deeply sensitive to the time and cost of traversing space. These times and costs have been much reduced through technological and organisational innovations and the falling costs of energy. The frictions of distance now play less and less of a restraining role in capitalism's geographical mobility. This does not mean, however, that geographical differences no longer matter. Precisely the opposite: highly mobile capital pays close attention to even slight local differences in costs because these yield higher profits.

———

The fact that capitalists are drawn to and survive best in maximum profit locations often leads to the concentration of many activities in particular places. The cotton-spinning factory benefits from having the machine tool workshop, the chemical dye producer and the shirt maker nearby. 'External economies' (economic benefits one capitalist receives from being close to another) produce geographical agglomerations of capitalist activities. The noted nineteenth-century economist Alfred Marshall called where many firms cluster together 'industrial production districts'. This is a familiar feature in the geographical world that capitalism constructs. Collective legal, financial, infrastructural, transport and communications services, along with access to a common labour pool and supportive civil administration, can also provide lower costs for all capitalists in a given locale up until the point where congestion costs escalate to offset the benefits. In the early stages of capitalism the rise of the industrial city epitomised such agglomeration economies in action. In more recent times much has been made of the rise of 'Marshallian' industrial production districts like Silicon Valley or the 'Third Italy' centred around Bologna, where many small firms have come together to share economies of production and marketing. In the financial world today, having legal, accounting, tax advice, information, media and other activities alongside the core financial functions produces the typical profile of the great financial centres such as the City of London and Wall Street.

Very early on, capitalist enterprises also drew on a vast network of spatially disparate market connections. Commodities like wool, cotton, exotic dyes, timber and leather often came from far away and, while most wage goods that supported the daily lives of labourers in the past came from close by, salt, spices, sugar, tea, coffee, cacao, wine, resins, dried cod, as well as wheat, rice, rye and barley were often traded over very long distances thanks to the activities of the merchants. In some instances trading networks were formalised, as happened early on with the Hanseatic League. Trading houses and merchants from many cities formed a mutually supportive network stretching from the Baltic to the Iberian Peninsula from the thirteenth century on. Alongside this there grew up international networks of finance houses, the bankers of Augsburg and Nuremberg in the sixteenth century, or later on, in the nineteenth century, the great finance houses like the Rothschilds with their different family branches in Vienna, Paris, London, Madrid and Berlin. Today, Goldman Sachs and HSBC ('The World's Local Bank') have offices all over the globe. In other instances, trading networks were developed, as in early China, within a structure of periodic markets carefully monitored by tax collectors and other agents of imperial power. Commodities have always travelled immense distances (though slowly), as, for example, along the legendary 'silk road' from China to the West. Ethnic diasporas of businesses continue to do much the same. (Go to any Chinatown in any city of the world to see what I mean.)

Tentacles of trading networks intertwined and stretched onwards and outwards to infiltrate everywhere. Wool from remote regions of Tibet finds its way into Indian market places just as medicinal herbs and animal body parts from Mongolia and Western China get assembled in Hong Kong before being dispersed across the markets of south-east Asia. Street corner currency traders in North Africa or in Kerala become conduits for flows of remittances from the Gulf States. The establishment of these networks, the knowledge of routes, passages and paths, their compulsive mapping, and knowledge of the kinds of commodities that could be traded for what where became one of the immense contributions of merchant and trader capital. Without this, capitalism as we now know it could not have emerged. And to this day that is what merchants and traders do with increasing sophistication. They work out and uncover paths to markets for capital surplus absorption that would otherwise remain hidden.

Competition forces individual capitalists and corporations to seek out better places to produce, just as they are forced to seek out superior technologies. As new locations with lower costs become available, so capitalists under the gun of competition have to respond by moving, if they can. Producers move from Ohio to the Pearl River delta, from California to the Tijuana maquiladora factories, or from Lancashire to Turkey, for example.

But competition for superior locations is a peculiar kind of competition. While firms can adopt identical technologies, they cannot occupy identical locations. Spatial competition between firms, as Adam Smith long ago noted, is a monopolistic form of competition. Twelve competing railways from London to Glasgow would be ridiculous. Twelve supermarkets on the same street makes no economic sense. One line from London to Glasgow and supermarkets spread throughout a metropolis does. On the other hand, putting all the diamond or antique dealers together in the same quarter (or on the same street, as in New York City) does make sense because of mutually supportive agglomeration economies: in the search for an old gold watch it is good to have many stores together for the searcher to rummage around in.

The monopolistic element in spatial competition has far-reaching consequences in a market-based economy. When transport costs are high, for example, many producers in local markets are protected from outside competition. They become, in effect, local monopolists. When transport costs come down this localised monopoly power weakens. Beer, which used to be brewed and sold only in local markets, became a big item in international trade after transport costs fell dramatically from the mid-1960s on. Even bottled water now travels from Fiji and Evian, France, to New York! That would have seemed a ridiculous idea fifty years ago (and in many respects still is ridiculous, when you think about it. New York tap water is just as good).

But there are other ways to protect the power of spatial monopoly by claiming there is no place like this one for the production of this particular product. The wine from this region or indeed just from this plot of land – '*terroir*', as the French call it – is supposedly special because of the unique circumstances under which the grapes are grown. Claims are made about water from Evian or from Fiji, even though no chemical analyst or taste test can actually define anything special. The monopoly given by uniqueness of location is as powerful as any other kind of branding in the market place and producers go out of their way to protect it. (Try producing Roquefort cheese in Wisconsin and see what happens; the European Union says you can't use the word champagne for anything other than the sparkling wine produced in a particular district of France.) Beer trade may be international, but local microbrews are special everywhere. Competition for the monopoly power given by prime locations has always been, and continues to be, an important aspect of capitalism's dynamic.

The geographical landscape is likewise shaped by a perpetual tension between the economies of centralisation, on the one hand, and the potentially higher profits to be had from decentralisation and dispersal on the other. How that tension works out depends on the barriers posed to spatial movement, the intensity of agglomeration economies and divisions of labour. Financial firms may have their head offices in Wall Street, their back offices in New Jersey or Connecticut and some routine functions in Bangalore. As transport and communications costs decline, once optimal locations become inferior. Once vibrant and profitable factories, steel mills, bakeries and breweries close down. The fixed capital embedded in them is devalued, and localised crises roil the lives of everyone inhabiting such now-bereft locations. Sheffield lost around 60,000 steel jobs in about four years back in the 1980s. The huge Bethlehem steel plant in Pennsylvania now stands an empty and silent shell in the town it once dominated, apart from that bit of it being converted into a raucous gambling casino. Meanwhile factories, mills, bakeries and breweries open up elsewhere. The whole geographical pattern of production, employment and consumption is in perpetual motion.

Geographically localised crises have been endemic within the history of capitalism. The vein of ore runs out, the mine closes down and a ghost town is left behind. A local factory goes belly up for some reason and almost everyone is unemployed. Can such localised crises spiral out of control to create global crises of the geographical and economic order? Yes, they can. This is exactly what happened when a series of highly localised housing foreclosure crises occurring in 2006, particularly in Florida and the American south-west, went global in 2007–9. For those who continue to live in devalued places, the social costs are often incalculable and the misery extreme.

———

Consider, then, an extended example of how this all works. The production of space in general and of urbanisation in particular has become big business under capitalism. It is one of the key ways in which the capital surplus is absorbed. A significant proportion of the total global labour force is employed in building and maintaining the built environment. Large amounts of associated capitals, usually mobilised in the form of long-term loans, are set in motion in the process of urban development. These debt-fuelled investments often become the epicentre for crisis formation. The connections between urbanisation, capital accumulation and crisis formation deserve careful scrutiny.

From their very beginnings cities depended on the availability of surplus food and labour. These surpluses were mobilised and extracted from somewhere and from somebody (usually an exploited rural population or from serfs and slaves). The control over the use and distribution of the surplus typically lay in a few hands (such as a religious oligarchy or a charismatic military leader). Urbanisation and class formation have, therefore, always gone together. This general relation persists under capitalism, but there is a rather different dynamic at work. Capitalism is a class form of society given over to the perpetual production of surpluses. This means that it is always producing the necessary conditions for urbanisation to occur.

To the degree that the absorption of capital surpluses and growing populations is a problem, so urbanisation provides one crucial way to absorb both. Hence an inner connection arises between surplus production, population growth and urbanisation.

The specific history of this under capitalism is interesting. Consider, first, what happened in Paris during what is known as the Second Empire, which lasted from 1852 to 1870. The Europe-wide economic crisis of 1848 was one of the first clear crises of unemployed surplus capital and surplus labour existing side by side with seemingly no way to put them back together again. It struck particularly hard in Paris and the result was an abortive revolution on the part of unemployed workers and those bourgeois utopians who saw a social republic as the antidote to the capitalist greed and inequality that had prevailed in the 1830s and 1840s. The republican bourgeoisie violently crushed the revolution but failed to resolve the crisis. The result was the ascent to power of Louis-Napoleon Bonaparte, who engineered a coup in 1851 and proclaimed himself Emperor Napoleon III in 1852. To survive politically, the authoritarian emperor resorted to widespread political repression of alternative political movements, but he also knew that he had to find ways to absorb the capital surplus profitably. He announced a vast programme of infrastructural investment both at home and abroad. Abroad this meant the construction of railroads throughout Europe and down into the Orient, as well as support for grand works such as the Suez Canal. At home it meant consolidating the railway network, building ports and harbours, draining marshes, and the like. But above all it entailed the reconfiguration of the urban infrastructure of Paris. Bonaparte brought Baron Haussmann to Paris to take charge of the public works in 1853.

Haussmann clearly understood that his mission was to help solve the surplus capital and surplus labour problem by way of urbanisation. The rebuilding of Paris absorbed huge quantities of labour and of capital by the standards of the time and, coupled with authoritarian suppression of the aspirations of the Parisian workers, was a primary vehicle of social stabilisation. Haussmann drew upon the utopian plans pulled together by Fourierists and Saint-Simonians for the reshaping of Paris that had been debated in the 1840s, but with one big difference. He transformed the scale at which the urban process was imagined. He thought of the city on a grander scale, annexed the suburbs, redesigned whole neighbourhoods (such as the produce market of Les Halles so brilliantly described in Zola's 1873 novel *The Belly of Paris*) rather than just bits and pieces of the urban fabric. He changed the city wholesale rather than retail. He could do this in part because of new building technologies (iron and glass construction, gas lighting and the like) and new forms of organisation (the omnibus companies and the department stores). But he also needed new financial institutions and debt instruments (the Crédit Mobilier and Immobilier). He helped resolve the capital surplus disposal problem in effect by setting up a Keynesian-style system of debt-financed infrastructural urban improvements.

All of this entailed the co-evolution of a new urban way of life and a new kind of urban persona. Paris became 'the city of light', the great centre of consumption, tourism and pleasure. The cafés, the department stores (also brilliantly described in another Zola novel, *The Ladies' Paradise* (1883)), the fashion industry, the grand expositions, the opera and the spectacle of court life all played their part in creating new profit opportunities through consumerism. But then the overextended and increasingly speculative financial system and credit structures on which all this was based crashed in the financial crisis of 1868. Haussmann was forced from power, in desperation Napoleon III went to war against Bismarck's Germany and lost, and in the vacuum that followed arose the Paris Commune, one of the greatest revolutionary episodes in capitalist urban history.

Fast forward now to 1942 in the United States. Here the capital surplus disposal problem that had seemed so intractable in the 1930s (and the unemployment that went with it) was temporarily resolved by the huge mobilisation for the war effort. But what was going to happen after the war? Politically the situation was dangerous. The federal government was in effect running a nationalised economy (and doing so very efficiently). The US was in alliance with the communist Soviet Union in the war against fascism. Strong social movements with socialist inclinations had emerged during the 1930s and leftist sympathisers were integrated into the war effort (the Marxist philosopher Herbert Marcuse worked in the organisation that later became the CIA). Popular questioning of the legitimacy and effectiveness of corporate capitalism was rife. A hefty dose of political repression of the left was therefore initiated by the ruling classes of the time to preserve their power. McCarthyism, the witch-hunt against the 'reds under the bed', signs of which were already in evidence in 1942 in the Un-American Activities Committee hearings in the US Congress, provided the means to deal with all forms of anti-capitalist opposition after 1950 or so. But what of the capital surplus disposal problem?

The answer was symbolised by Robert Moses, who after the Second World War did to the New York metropolitan region what Haussmann had done to Paris. Moses changed the scale of thinking about urbanisation by thinking about the metropolitan region rather than the city itself. Through a system of debt-financed highways and infrastructural transformations, through suburbanisation and the total re-engineering (using new construction technologies pioneered during the war) not just of the city but of the whole metropolitan region, he defined a way to absorb the capital and labour surpluses profitably. This process of suburbanisation, when taken nationwide through the geographical expansion of capitalist development into the American south and west, played a crucial role in the stabilisation of not only the US economy but also US-centered global capitalism after the war. Where would the capital surplus have gone had it not been for the making of the New York metropolitan region, Chicago, Los Angeles and other places of their ilk after 1945?

But for all this to happen required a revolution in financial and administrative structures, a turn to debt-financing backed by an increasing ability of working people to pay for the suburban way of life. The compact between capital and labour after the Second

World War, in which a privileged segment of labour shared in the benefits of productivity gains, helped deal with the effective demand problem. The revolutions in financial institutions that began in the 1930s (particularly those designed to facilitate mortgage finance for housing), when supplemented by tax subsidies for homeowner-ship, a generous GI Bill that supported homeownership and college education for returning military personnel, all laid the groundwork for the suburbanisation of the US.

The suburbanisation of the United States was not merely a matter of new infrastructures. As happened in Second Empire Paris, it entailed a radical transformation in lifestyles, a new way of life based on the highway and the automobile. It relied upon the production and marketing of new products, from suburban tract housing and shopping malls to refrigerators, air-conditioners, TVs and tele-phones. It meant two cars in the driveway and a boom in the rubber, oil and steel industries. Even the demand for lawn mowers surged! After all, those suburban lawns had to be kept neat. Suburbanisa-tion (alongside militarisation) thus played a critical role in helping to absorb the surpluses of both capital and labour in the post-war years in the United States. The spread of similar tastes and technolo-gies – the automobile culture, in particular – helped spread these processes globally.

But it did so at a cost. It was profligate in its use of both land and energy. It rested upon a huge shift in the relation to nature. In the United States it led to an ultimate dependency on foreign oil sources and perpetual involvements in Middle East oil politics. Over-rapid suburbanisation also led to the hollowing-out of city centres, leaving them bereft of a sustainable economic basis. The suburban solution to the Great Depression produced the so-called 'urban crisis' of the 1960s, defined by revolts of impacted minorities (chiefly African-American) in the inner cities who had been denied access both to the suburbs and to the new prosperity.

But all was not well in the suburbs either. The new lifestyle had all manner of social and political consequences. The individualism, the defence of property values, the bland if not soulless qualities of everyday life, became topics of critique. Traditionalists increasingly rallied around the urbanist Jane Jacobs, who had very distinctive ideas as to what constituted a more fulfilling form of everyday life in the city. They sought to counter sprawling suburbanisation and the brutal modernism of Moses' large-scale projects with a different kind of urban aesthetic that focused on local neighbourhood development, historical preservation and, ultimately, reclamation and gentrification of older areas. Feminists proclaimed the suburb and its lifestyle as the locus of all their primary discontents. As happened to Haussmann, a crisis began to unfold such that Moses-style urbanisation (as well as Moses himself) fell from grace towards the end of the 1960s. And in the same way that the Haussmanisation of Paris had a role in explaining the dynamics of the Paris Commune, so the soulless qualities of suburban living played a role in the dramatic protest movements of 1968 in the USA.

Discontented white middle-class suburban students went into a phase of revolt. In Santa Barbara in California they buried a Chevy in the sand and burned down a Bank of America building to symbolise their disgust. They sought alliances with other marginalised groups, rallied against US imperialism (the Vietnam War) and a suburban consumerism that was environmentally unsustainable (the first Earth Day was in 1970). They initiated a powerful though inchoate movement to build another kind of world, including a different kind of urban experience and a different relation to nature.

To top it all, a financial crisis, centred in the US but global in scope, began to unfold in the state–finance nexus that had powered suburbanisation and underpinned international development throughout the post-war period. This crisis gathered momentum at the end of the 1960s. The solution was becoming the problem. The Bretton Woods Agreement of 1944 came under stress. The US dollar was under mounting international pressure because of excessive borrowing. Then the whole capitalist system fell into a deep recession, led by the bursting of the global property market bubble in 1973. The dark days of the 1970s were upon us with all the consequences earlier outlined.

Fitting, though, that it was the New York City fiscal crisis of 1975 that centred the storm. With one of the largest public budgets at that time in the capitalist world, New York City, surrounded by sprawling affluent suburbs, went broke. The local solution, orchestrated by an uneasy alliance between state powers and financial institutions, pioneered the neoliberal ideological and practical political turn that was to be deployed worldwide in the struggle to perpetuate and consolidate capitalist class power. The recipe devised was simple enough: crush the power of labour, initiate wage repression, let the market do its work, all the while putting the power of the state at the service of capital in general and of investment finance in particular. This was the solution of the 1970s that lies at the root of the crisis of 2008–9.

———

After the 1970s, urbanisation underwent yet another transformation of scale. It went global. The urbanisation of China over the last twenty years has been hugely important. Its pace picked up after a brief recession in 1997 or so, such that since 2000 China has absorbed nearly half of the world's cement supplies. More than a hundred cities have passed the 1 million population mark in the last twenty years and small villages, like Shenzhen, have become huge metropolises with 6 to 10 million people. Industrialisation, at first concentrated in the special economic zones, rapidly diffused outwards to any municipality willing to absorb the surplus capital from abroad and plough back the earnings into rapid expansion. Vast infrastructural projects, such as dams and highways – again, all debt-financed – are transforming the landscape. Equally vast shopping malls, science parks, airports, container ports, pleasure palaces of all kinds, and all manner of newly minted cultural institutions, along with gated communities and golf courses, dot the Chinese landscape in the midst of overcrowded urban dormitories for the massive labour reserves being mobilised from impoverished rural regions.

The consequences of this urbanisation process for the global economy and for the absorption of surplus capital have been enormous: Chile booms because of the demand for copper, Australia thrives and even Brazil and Argentina recover in part because of the strength of demand from China for raw materials. Bilateral trade between China and Latin America increased tenfold between 2000 and 2009. Is the urbanisation of China the primary stabiliser of global capitalism? The answer has to be a partial yes. But it is also the case that real estate development has been crucial to class formation in China. This is where immense personal fortunes have been made in very short order. A company founded in the mid-1990s to mass produce housing units on greenfield sites in the Pearl River delta went public (with the help of J. P. Morgan) on the Hong Kong stock exchange in 2007 and realised a net worth of $27 billion. The daughter of the person who launched the company holds 60 per cent of the shares and is therefore worth some $16 billion, which puts her up there with Warren Buffett and Bill Gates on the list of the world's wealthiest individuals.

But China is only the epicentre for an urbanisation process that has now become global, aided by the integration of the world's financial markets. Debt-financed urbanisation projects exist all over, from Dubai to Sao Paulo and from Madrid and Mumbai to Hong Kong and London. The Chinese central bank is active in the secondary mortgage market in the USA (it is heavily invested in Fannie Mae and Freddie Mac, which explains why, when the US had to nationalise these institutions, it protected the bondholders because of Chinese holdings). Goldman Sachs has been heavily involved in the surging property market in Mumbai and Hong Kong capital has invested in Baltimore. Every urban area in the world has had its building boom in full swing in the midst of a flood of impoverished migrants that is simultaneously creating a planet of slums.

Building booms have been evident in Mexico City, Santiago in Chile, in Mumbai, Johannesburg, Seoul, Taipei, Moscow, and all over

Europe (Spain and Ireland being most dramatic), as well as in the cities of the core capitalist countries such as London, Los Angeles, San Diego and New York (where more large-scale urban projects took shape under billionaire Mayor Michael Bloomberg's administration than ever before). Astonishing, spectacular and in some respects absurd urbanisation projects have emerged in the Middle East in places like Dubai and Abu Dhabi as a way of mopping up the capital surpluses arising from oil wealth in the most conspicuous ways possible (like an indoor ski slope in a hot desert environment). Many of these booms, including those in the Gulf States, are now, however, in deep trouble. Dubai World, the government-backed development corporation which had borrowed vast amounts of surplus capital from British and other European banks to build so spectacularly, suddenly declared it could not meet its obligations in late 2009, sending all manner of tremors through global markets.

This transformation in scale makes it hard to grasp that what may be going on globally is in principle similar to the processes that Haussmann managed so expertly for a while in Second Empire Paris. This new wave of urbanisation depended, as did all those before it, on financial innovation to organise the credit required to sustain it. The securitisation and packaging of local mortgages for sale to investors worldwide, and the setting up of new financial institutions to facilitate a secondary mortgage market, have played a crucial role. The benefits were legion: it spread risk and permitted surplus savings pools easier access to surplus housing demand. It brought aggregate interest rates down, while generating immense fortunes for the financial intermediaries who worked these wonders. But spreading risk does not eliminate risk. Furthermore, the fact that risk can be spread so widely encourages even riskier local behaviours because the risk can be transferred elsewhere. What happened to the Péreire brothers in 1867–8 in Paris and what happened to New York City in the mid-1970s (to say nothing of multiple other instances throughout capitalism's historical geography) has now happened yet again in the subprime mortgage and housing asset value crisis.

As in all the preceding phases, the remaking of urban geographies entailed transformations of lifestyle. In the United States, these transformations were in large part dictated by the need to assuage the suburban discontents of the 1960s. Quality of urban life has become a commodity for those with money, as has the city itself in a world where consumerism, tourism, niche marketing, cultural and knowledge-based industries, as well as perpetual resort to the economy of the spectacle, have become major aspects of urban political economy. With an economy that now relies more and more on consumerism and consumer sentiment as its driving force (it accounts for 70 per cent of the economy in the contemporary US, compared to 20 per cent in the nineteenth century), the organisation of consumption through urbanisation has become absolutely central to capitalism's dynamic.

The postmodern penchant for the formation of market niches – in urban lifestyle choices, consumer habits and cultural norms – suffuses the contemporary urban experience with an aura of freedom of choice, provided you have the money. Shopping malls, multiplexes and box stores proliferate (the production of each has become big business), as do fast food and artisanal market places, boutique cultures, coffee shops, and the like. And it is not only in the advanced capitalist countries where this style of urbanisation can be found – you will find it in Buenos Aires, Sao Paulo and Mumbai as well as in almost every Asian city you can think of. Even the incoherent, bland and monotonous suburban tract development that continues to dominate in many parts of the world now gets its antidote through a 'new urbanism' movement that touts the sale of community (supposedly intimate and secure as well as often gated) and a supposedly 'sustainable' boutique lifestyle as a developer product to fulfil urban dreams.

The impacts on political subjectivity have been huge. This is a world in which the neoliberal ethic of intense possessive individualism and financial opportunism has become the template for human personality socialisation. This is a world that has become increasingly characterised by a hedonistic culture of consumerist excess. It has destroyed the myth (though not the ideology) that the nuclear family is the solid sociological foundation for capitalism and embraced, however tardily and incompletely, multiculturalism, women's rights and equality of sexual preference. The impact is increasing individualistic isolation, anxiety, short-termism and neurosis in the midst of one of the greatest material urban achievements ever constructed in human history.

The darker side of surplus absorption through urban transformation entails, however, repeated bouts of urban restructuring through 'creative destruction'. This highlights the significance of crises as moments of urban restructuring. It has a class dimension since it is usually the poor, the underprivileged and those marginalised from political power that suffer primarily from this process.

Violence is often required to make the new urban geography out of the wreckage of the old. Haussmann tore through the old Parisian slums, using powers of expropriation for supposedly public benefit, doing so in the name of civic improvement, environmental restoration and urban renovation. He deliberately engineered the removal of much of the working class and other unruly elements, along with insalubrious industries, from Paris's city centre, where they constituted a threat to public order, public health and, of course, political power. He created an urban form where it was believed (incorrectly, as it turned out, in the revolutionary Paris Commune of 1871) sufficient levels of surveillance and military control were possible so as to ensure that the restive classes could easily be controlled by military power.

In reality, as Frederik Engels pointed out in his 1872 tract *The Housing Question*:

> the bourgeoisie has only one method of solving the housing question after its fashion – that is to say, of solving it in such a way that the solution perpetually renews the question anew. This method is called 'Haussmann' [by which] I mean the practice that has now become

general of making breaches in the working-class quarters of our big towns, and particularly in areas which are centrally situated, quite apart from whether this is done from considerations of public health or for beautifying the town, or owing to the demand for big centrally situated business premises, or, owing to traffic requirements, such as the laying down of railways, streets (which sometimes seem to have the aim of making barricade fighting more difficult) ... No matter how different the reasons may be, the result is always the same; the scandalous alleys disappear to the accompaniment of lavish self-praise by the bourgeoisie on account of this tremendous success, but they appear again immediately somewhere else ... The breeding places of disease, the infamous holes and cellars in which the capitalist mode of production confines our workers night after night, are not abolished; they are merely *shifted elsewhere*! The same economic necessity that produced them in the first place, produces them in the next place.

The processes Engels described recur again and again in capitalist urban history. Robert Moses 'took a meat axe to the Bronx' (in his own infamous words) and long and loud were the lamentations of neighbourhood groups and movements, which eventually coalesced around the rhetoric of the inveterate urban reformer Jane Jacobs, at the unimaginable destruction of valued urban fabric but also at the loss of whole communities of residents and their long-established networks of social integration. Once the brutal power of state expropriations and older neighbourhood destruction for purposes of highway construction and urban renewal had been successfully resisted and contained by the political and street agitations of '68 (with Paris once more an epicentre but with violent confrontations everywhere from Chicago to Mexico City and Bangkok), a far more insidious and cancerous process of transformation began through fiscal disciplining of democratic urban governments, the freeing up of land markets from controls, property speculation and the sorting of land to those uses that generated the highest possible financial rate of return.

Engels understood all too well what this process was about.

> The growth of the big modern cities gives the land in certain areas, particularly in those areas which are centrally situated, an artificially and colossally increasing value; the buildings erected on these areas depress this value instead of increasing it, because they no longer belong to the changed circumstances. They are pulled down and replaced by others. This takes place above all with workers' houses which are situated centrally and whose rents, even with the greatest overcrowding, can never, or only very slowly, increase above a certain maximum. They are pulled down and in their stead shops, warehouses and public buildings are erected.

It is depressing to think that all of this was written in 1872. Engels' description applies directly to contemporary urban processes in much of Asia (Delhi, Seoul, Mumbai), as well as to the contemporary gentrification of, say, Harlem and Brooklyn in New York. The making of new urban geographies inevitably entails displacement and dispossession. This is the ugly mirror image of capital absorption through urban redevelopment.

Consider the case of Mumbai, where 6 million people are considered officially slum dwellers, settled on land for most part without legal title (the places where they live are left blank on all maps of the city). With the attempt to turn Mumbai into a global financial centre to rival Shanghai, the property development boom gathers pace and the land the slum dwellers occupy appears increasingly valuable. The value of the land in Dharavi, one of the most prominent slums in Mumbai, is put at $2 billion and the pressure to clear it – ostensibly for environmental and social reasons – is mounting daily. Financial powers backed by the state push for forcible slum clearance, in some cases violently taking possession of a terrain occupied for a whole generation by the slum dwellers. Capital accumulation on the land through real estate activity booms as land is acquired at almost no cost. Do the people who have been forced out receive compensation?

The lucky ones receive a bit. But while the Indian constitution specifies that the state has an obligation to protect the lives and well-being of the whole population irrespective of caste and class, and to guarantee rights to livelihood housing and shelter, the Indian Supreme Court has rewritten this constitutional requirement. Illegal occupants who cannot definitively prove their long-term residence on the land they occupy have no right to compensation. To concede that right, says the Supreme Court, would be tantamount to rewarding pickpockets for their actions. So the slum dwellers are forced either to resist and fight or to take their few belongings and camp out on the highway margins or wherever they can find a tiny space.

Similar examples of dispossession (though less brutal and more legalistic) can be found in the United States through the abuse of rights of eminent domain to displace long-term residents in reasonable housing in favour of higher order land uses (such as condominiums and box stores). Challenged in the US Supreme Court, the liberal justices carried the day against the conservatives and declared it was perfectly constitutional for local jurisdictions to behave in this way in order to increase their property tax base. Progress is progress, after all!

In Seoul in the 1990s, the construction companies and developers hired goon squads of sumo wrestler types to invade whole neighbourhoods and smash down with sledgehammers not only the housing but also all the possessions of those who had built their own housing in the 1950s, on the hillsides of the city on what had become by the 1990s high-value land. Most of those hillsides are now covered with high-rise towers that show no trace of the brutal processes of land clearance that permitted their construction. In China millions are currently being dispossessed of the spaces they have long occupied. Since they lack private property rights, the state can simply remove them from the land by fiat offering a minor cash payment to help them on their way (before turning the land over to developers at a high rate of profit). In some instances people move willingly, but widespread resistances are also reported – the usual response to which is brutal repression by the Communist Party. Populations on the rural margins are also unceremoniously displaced as cities grow outwards. This is the case in India, too. Special economic development zones are now favoured by central and state governments, leading to violence against agricultural producers, the grossest of which was the massacre at Nandigram in West Bengal, orchestrated by the ruling Marxist political party, to make way for large-scale Indonesian capital that is as much interested in urban property development as it is in industrial development.

But these processes do not pass unresisted. Urban social movements are everywhere in evidence. Sometimes these movements are narrowly based – an anti-gentrification movement here and a movement in defence of affordable housing there. But in other instances such movements can begin to coalesce into a broader demand; around, for example, what the Brazilians call 'the right to dwell', or what others refer to as 'the right to the city' – the right to make a new urban geography more in accord with principles of social justice and respect for the environment.

The right to participate in the making of capitalism's geography is, therefore, a contested right. While the power relations at this conjuncture unquestionably favour the combination of capital and state over everyone else, there are significant forces of opposition. And both capital and state are currently on the defensive, their claims to act for the benefit of everyone severely damaged, as are their claims to be the benefactors of all humanity through endless market-based capital accumulation.

———

But behind all the contingencies and the uncertainties involved in the perpetual making and remaking of capitalism's geography there lurks a singular principle power that has yet to be accorded its proper place in our understanding of not only the historical geography of capitalism but also the general evolution of capitalist class power. The making of new geographies entails changes in and on the land. The owners of that land have everything to gain from these changes. They can benefit enormously from increases in land values and rising rents on both land and the 'natural' resources contained therein. Those rising rents and property values depend on both investments in place and investments that change space relations in ways that add land value by improving accessibility. Far from being a 'residual class' of landed aristocrats and feudal lords, this landed developer interest takes an active role in making and remaking capitalism's geography as a means to enhance its income and its power.

Investment in rents on land, property, mines and raw materials thereby becomes an attractive proposition for all capitalists. Speculation in these values becomes rife. The production of capitalism's geography is propelled onwards by the need to realise speculative gains on these assets. Once the process of suburbanisation got underway in the United States, for example, the rent on peripheral land began to increase and speculators soon descended on it like locusts. To realise speculative gains they had to ensure that public investments in highways, sewers, water supplies and other relevant infrastructures materialised to make the land they held more valuable. Developers and landholders either bribed or legally funded the political campaigns of elected officials to ensure such public investments were made. The wheels of rapid suburbanisation were greased magnificently by such activities and of course the process of suburbanisation became self-propelling, anchored by this drive to enhance land values. Overextension was always possible, of course. Look at the course of Japanese land prices since they peaked around 1990. A greased slope can result in downward slippage just as easily as it can facilitate upward momentum.

The money that can be made (and sometimes lost) out of creating new geographies and new space relations is too often ignored as a fundamental aspect of the reproduction of capitalism. The social critic Thorstein Veblen, writing in the early years of the twentieth century, surmised that the wealth of the 'leisure class' (as he called them) in the United States derived as much from speculations associated with land and urban development as it did from the more frequently touted sphere of industrial production. The same may have long been true even in Britain, since the rising land values and rents around London from the seventeenth century onwards appear to have contributed far more to augmenting the wealth of the upper classes than did the rise of the factory system. And as we earlier saw in China, much of the wealth that has fuelled class formation there has arisen out of speculative gains from urban development projects (just look at Shanghai's new skyline).

The power of land and resource owners has been much underestimated, as has the role of land and resource asset values and rents in relation to the overall circulation and accumulation of capital. This arena of activity accounts for as much as 40 per cent of economic activity in many of the advanced capitalist countries. Small wonder that urban infrastructures are a key component in the stimulus packages governments are currently devising to shore up their crumbling economies. Furthermore, it is vital to see this as an active rather than as a passive power, because it is precisely through the making of new geographies that landowners (in alliance with developers, construction interests and, of course, the omnipresent financiers) advance their own class position while contributing key solutions to the capital surplus absorption problem.

But this solution is a double-edged sword. To the degree that capitalists invest in land rents and trade capitalised land rents (even on old properties that were amortised decades ago), so they impose the equivalent of a tax on all other forms of capitalist activity, as well as upon all those who reside on the land. What should have functioned as 'free gifts of nature' (including free gifts of that 'second nature' created by millennia of human activity in the remaking of the land) now feature as a costly drag upon productive forms of capitalist activity. Some producers get forced out of high rent locations because they cannot afford to produce there. The pressure on local wages to keep pace with rising land and property prices in particular locations becomes irresistible. Public employees in London receive an extra allowance to cover the soaring costs of urban living. The rentiers and developers backed by the financiers play their part not only in reshaping capitalism's geography but also in producing crises and contributing to long-run stagnation. Lord Keynes wishfully imagined what he called 'the euthanasia of the rentier'. Unfortunately the rentier these days is both very much alive even though not particularly well, given the empty condominiums that litter the cityscapes of New York, Miami, Las Vegas and Dubai.

If rent and land value are the theoretical categories whereby political economy integrates geography, space and the relation to nature into the understanding of capitalism, then these become not residual or secondary categories within the theory of how capitalism works. As we earlier saw in the case of interest and credit, rent has to be brought forward into the forefront of the analysis, rather than being treated as a derivative category of distribution as happens in Marxist as well as in conventional economic theories. Only in this way can we bring together an understanding of the ongoing production of space and geography and the circulation and accumulation of capital and put them in relation to processes of crisis formation where they so clearly belong.

7

Creative Destruction on the Land

The so-called 'natural environment' is subject to transformation by human activity. Fields are cleared, marshes drained, cities, roads and bridges built, while plants and animals are domesticated and bred, habitats transformed, forests cut over, lands irrigated, rivers dammed, landscapes grazed (voraciously, by sheep and goats), climates altered. Whole mountains are cut in half as minerals are extracted, quarries scar landscapes, waste flows into streams, rivers and oceans, topsoil erodes and hundreds of square miles of forests and scrubland are eradicated accidentally as a result of human action, while the Amazonian rainforest burns as the cattle ranchers and the soybean producers hungrily but illegally gobble up the land just as the Chinese government announces a vast programme of reforestation. But the British love to walk in their misty countryside and admire their heritage of country houses, the Welsh love their valleys, the Scots their glens, the Irish their emerald green bogs, the Germans their forests, the French their distinctive 'pays' with their local wines and cheeses. The Apache believe that wisdom sits in places, and indigenous groups everywhere, from Amazonia to British Columbia and the mountains of Taiwan, celebrate their long-standing and unbreakable bond with the land wherein they dwell.

The long history of creative destruction on the land has produced what is sometimes called 'second nature' – nature reshaped by human action. There is now very little, if anything, left of the 'first nature' that existed before humans came to populate the earth. Even in the remotest regions of the earth and in the most inhospitable environments, traces of human influence (from shifts in climatic regimes, traces of pesticides and in the qualities of the atmosphere and the water) bear the imprint of human influence. Over the last three centuries marked by the rise of capitalism, the rate and spread of creative destruction on the land has increased enormously.

In the early years this activity was generally conceptualised in terms of a triumphalist human domination over nature (partly offset by aesthetic sentiments that romanticised the relation to nature). We are more circumspect now in our rhetoric, though not necessarily in our practices. Capitalist history is riddled with the unintended environmental consequences (sometimes long-term) of what has been wrought and some of these consequences (such as species and habitat extinctions) are irreversible. It is better to think not of domination, therefore, but of the development of human practices with respect to the physical world and within the web of ecological life that changes the face of the earth in often dramatic and irreversible ways.

While many agents are at work in producing and reproducing the geography of the second nature around us, the two primary systemic agents in our time are the state and capital. The geographic landscape of capital accumulation is perpetually evolving, largely under the impulsion of the speculative needs of further accumulation (including land speculation) and only secondarily in relation to the needs of people. But while there is nothing purely natural about the second nature with which we are surrounded, the co-evolutionary processes that are transforming geography are not entirely under the control of capital and the state, let alone of the people, however activist the latter may be. The colloquial phrase 'the revenge of nature' signals the existence of a stubborn, recalcitrant and unpredictable physical and ecological world that, like the weather, constitutes the environment in which we have our being.

How to understand the dialectical unfolding of the social relation to a nature that is itself perpetually evolving is the issue. The so-called 'green revolution' in agriculture is a fabulous example of how changes in all seven spheres of activity can co-evolve. Beginning in Mexico in the 1940s, new strains of wheat were bred in a new agricultural research institute under the direction of a young scientist, Norman Borlaug (who died in 2009). These new genetically modified strains of wheat led to the quadrupling of wheat yields by the end of the century and turned Mexico from a net importer to a net exporter of wheat in the decade after 1945. When taken to south Asia in the 1960s (promoted by US foundations like Ford and Rockefeller in alliance with Indian and Pakistani governments), new strains of wheat and rice doubled yields between 1965 and 1970, with huge impacts on food security and global food grain costs, which were cut in half. While the green revolution raised productivity and is credited with preventing mass starvation, it did so with all manner of negative environmental and social consequences. The vulnerabilities of monoculture meant heavy investments in oil-based fertilisers and pesticides (profitably produced by US-based corporations like Monsanto), while the capital layout involved (usually concerning water management and irrigation) entailed consolidation of a class of wealthy producers (often with the dubious help of credit institutions) and the reduction of everyone else to the status of a landless peasant. Genetically modified organisms (GMOs) have all along been ethically questioned and subject to moral objections from environmentalists ('Frankenstein foods', they are called in Europe). Geopolitical conflicts over trade in GMOs have since emerged.

The geography of capital accumulation and of creative destruction on the land cannot be brought into any kind of focus, nor is it possible without careful analysis of dynamics of this sort to get a better handle on how co-evolution works in different places. And without that we cannot assess the degree to which the relation to nature constitutes a limit to further capital accumulation that cannot be transcended or circumvented, no matter what technological, social and cultural fixes are in play.

Thanks to the environmental sciences, we have been made aware, of course, of a whole range of unintended consequences of human actions. Acid depositors from factory chimneys and power plants have been destroying local ecosystems like the Pennine peat bogs around Manchester after 1780 for years, but with the advent of tall smokestack technologies deposition fields went from local to regional as the sulphurous materials were projected high into the atmosphere. In the late 1960s, pollutants from Britain were destroying lakes and forests in Scandinavia and those from the Ohio valley were similarly affecting New England. Some difficult political consequences and negotiations then followed. Chlorofluorocarbons (CFCs) are a wondrous help in the refrigeration that became so crucial in securing untainted food supplies for burgeoning urban populations from the 1920s on, but when let loose in the atmosphere they deplete the upper stratospheric ozone layer and increase ultraviolet radiation penetration, thus posing a threat to all forms of life, particularly in the circumpolar regions. That too led to difficult international negotiations that ultimately resulted in the Montreal Protocol of 1987 to curb and then phase out the use of CFCs. Science suggests that human action is contributing to global warming (though at what pace has still to be agreed), reducing opponents (usually funded by the energy lobby) to the astonishing claim that global warming is a hoax perpetrated by the scientists upon the world's population. The wonder pesticide DDT that seemed such a marvellous solution to the scourges of mosquito-born infections when it was introduced as such in 1939 turned out to have disastrous impacts worldwide on the reproductive capacities of many species and therefore had to be banned in the 1960s (particularly after the publication of Rachel Carson's book *Silent Spring* in 1962).

Capitalists and their agents engage in the production of second nature, the active production of its geography, in the same way as they produce everything else: as a speculative venture, more often than not with the connivance and complicity, if not active collaboration, of the state apparatus. When the US Congress provided the railroad companies of the nineteenth century with land grants across the United States it helped launch a giant land speculation scheme which led, as might be expected, to cycles of boom and bust, generating innumerable local crises as it went.

The idea of nature as a social product has to be paralleled by the recognition that natural resources are cultural, economic and technological appraisals. This fact cuts two ways. On the one hand it permits one resource to be replaced by another through, say, the invention of new technologies that use different materials. If coal is scarce or too heavily polluting, then move over to natural gas or nuclear power. On the other hand, new technologies and lifestyle considerations may dictate the turn to very rare and highly localised supplies of material inputs. This is the case with many of the new electronic so-called 'green' technologies like wind turbines, which depend upon the availability of what are called 'rare earth metals' with names like indium, hafnium, terbium and neodymium. Demand for these rare earth metals with powerful magnetic qualities has been skyrocketing, and the fact that China currently commands nearly 95 per cent of the global supply is a cause for consternation. There are signs that China, producing these rare earth metals without regard for devastating environmental impacts, may restrict exports, thus forcing the producers of these new green technologies to relocate to China. Situations of this kind are not uncommon. Near-monopoly over supply because of geographical constraints has had a major impact upon the dynamics of capital accumulation throughout history, prompting major powers to try and ensure strategic supplies of raw materials by military means if necessary.

We can monitor the immense changes on the land and in the landscape. We can also track some of the more egregious and hubristic episodes of failed projects for environmental transformation. One of my favourite tales, told brilliantly in Greg Grandin's 2009 book *Fordlandia*, is that of Henry Ford's speculative attempt in the 1920s to tame the Amazon for rubber production. He bought up a huge tract of land in Amazonia, called his new town Fordlandia, and sought to impose upon the tropical rainforest an American Midwestern lifestyle for the rubber plantation and factory workers.

The idea was to secure the flow of rubber for the tyres of his cars (he had established control over almost everything else). 'Fordlandia had a central square, sidewalks, indoor plumbing, manicured lawns, a movie theater, shoe stores, ice cream and perfume shops, swimming pools, tennis courts, a golf course, and, of course, Model Ts rolling down its paved streets,' writes Grandin. Nothing came of it all, even after twenty years of trying and the outlay of astronomical amounts of money. The tropical rainforest won out. Abandoned in 1945, the place is now a ruin in the jungle. Not a drop of rubber latex ever materialised.

For Ford to engage in such a bizarre speculation in Amazonia presumed, of course, that the world was open for trade and investment and that there were no spatial barriers (such as state borders) to inhibit pursuit of his hubristic ambition. It was doubtless very reassuring for him to know that the whole military weight of a nascent US imperial globalising power would be deployed to rescue him should anything go wrong. After all, the marines were on the ground in Central America throughout the 1920s, practising entirely new techniques of aerial bombardment in order to suppress an indigenous peasant uprising, led by the charismatic Augusto Sandino in Nicaragua, which threatened the interests of the all-powerful United Fruit Company whose ambition was clearly to make real the appellation 'banana republic' to the form of government to be found there.

———

The creation and re-creation of ever newer space relations for human interactions is one of capitalism's most signal achievements. The dramatic reorganisation of the geographical landscape of production, exchange and consumption with changing space relations is not only a dramatic illustration of capitalism's penchant for the annihilation of space through time but it also entails fierce bouts of creative destruction – for example, the jet engine complements and even supplants the internal combustion engine as a primary means to define spatial accessibilities. The internet and the construction of cyberspace are the closest that capitalism has come so far to realising its ambition for frictionless movement. Unfortunately material goods and people cannot move through cyberspace, though all sorts of information and claims about them can. You can contract to buy instantaneously on eBay but it will still take a couple of days for UPS to deliver the product to your door.

This last example signals a field of contradictions within the drive to create a world without spatial barriers. The current crisis can partially be construed as a manifestation of a radical disjuncture in time–space configurations. The heads of the investment banks could not follow what their traders, most famously Nicholas Leeson of Barings Bank, were doing. The traders, armed with sophisticated mathematical computer models, worked in a newly constructed and quite different time–space frame. The result was loss of oversight and control from above with all the results we earlier noted.

The social order is riddled with problems of this kind. Raising a child in a city neighbourhood occurs in a radically different time–space from that defined by contemporary financial operations. People reasonably seek a secure personal space – a home – in which to live out their daily lives and to pursue their reproductive activity on, say, a twenty-year time horizon. But to do so they have to become titled property owners acquiring a mortgage in a debt market organised according to a different time–space logic. Some of them now live in tent cities because that logic went haywire.

This points to a long-existing but deep and abiding contradiction between the different time–space configurations that get constructed within and around the accumulation of capital. It is only through, for example, the active production of fixed spaces on the ground that capital in any form – from the immaterial flows of money to the tangible material flows of goods, people, services, etc. – can freely move across space. But capital invested in the land cannot be moved without being destroyed. The tension between stasis and motion here takes a peculiar twist. It induces a double motion. On the one hand, if the geographical landscape no longer serves the needs of mobile capital, then it must be destroyed and built anew in a completely different configuration. Either that, or flows of capital must conform to the remuneration requirements of capital invested in the land. An airport to which no flights come is neither profitable nor viable.

Fixed capital embedded in the land may facilitate ease of movement for mobile capital but loses its value when mobile capital fails to follow the geographical paths such fixed capital investments dictate. Capital embedded in the land usually has, moreover, a long life (it takes many years to build and amortise the debt incurred in an airport or an office complex). So as capitalism relentlessly pursues speed and the reduction of spatial barriers, it must also temper its flows to the capital that is both fixed in space and slow to circulate. From out of this tension crises can easily spring.

The spectacular nineteenth-century financial crashes due to overinvestment in the railroads were harbingers of things to come. The railroads were built at immense cost but enough traffic did not always materialise. The value embedded in the railroads was lost and investors, as the saying has it, 'took a bath'. The empty condominiums in Florida and New York, the shuttered shopping malls in California and the empty Caribbean luxury hotel all tell the same story. Capital, as Marx astutely once put it, here encounters barriers in its own nature. The disjunction between the quest for hypermobility and an increasingly sclerotic built environment (think of the huge amount of fixed capital embedded in Tokyo or New York City) becomes ever more dramatic.

———

The creation of territorial forms of social organisation, place-making, has been fundamental to human activity throughout history. How, then, has the circulation and accumulation of capital adapted to and transformed the territorial forms it inherited from preceding eras, made distinctive places and rejigged the map of global political power in ways that can accommodate the quest for endless compound growth? The rise of the modern state, for example, parallels the rise of capitalism and it was the main capitalist powers that partitioned much of the earth's surface into colonial possessions and imperial administrative forms, particularly in the period 1870 to 1925. These continue now to form the territorial basis for organised political power in the world. Capital accumulation has also played a crucial role, as we have seen, not only in reshaping places with ancient names like London, Rome and Edo (Tokyo), but also building vast new cities with names like Chicago, Los Angeles, Buenos Aires and Shenzhen, while colonial practices have shaped Johannesburg, Kinshasa, Mumbai, Jakarta, Singapore and Hong Kong in ways that feed into the ever-expanding demands located in the main centres of capital accumulation for means of production, markets, for new productive activity and for ruthless accumulation by dispossession.

But even today, it is not only capital that is involved in the construction of places like Detroit, Chenai or Fordlandia. The role of the sovereign individual is as extensive as it is ongoing. Go to any do-it-yourself' store in suburban New Jersey or in Oxfordshire and you will see myriads of people acquiring commodities that will be used to shape the space they call home and garden into something that is distinctly their own. The shanty town dwellers do much the same, though in their case it is often discarded commodities that form their raw materials and the space they occupy has no legal status and no infrastructures (unless the local state or a World Bank programme on sites and services has made some rudimentary attempt to provide them). Place-making, particularly around that place we call 'home', is an art that belongs largely to the people and not to capital, even as certain aspects of the places we call cities are fiercely fought over as capitalist developers struggle to provide the physical infrastructures so necessary for accumulation to occur on the ground. The deeper meanings that people assign to their relationship to the land, to place, home and the practices of dwelling are perpetually at odds with the crass commercialisms of land and property markets.

So, are our cities designed for people or for profits? The fact that this question is so often asked takes us immediately on to the terrain of the vast array of class and social struggles over place formation. These are the landscapes within which daily life has to be lived, where affective relations and social solidarities are established and where political subjectivities and symbolic meanings are constructed. Capitalist class and developer interests are all too well aware of this dimension and seek to mobilise it through community or city boosterism and the deliberate fostering of a sense of local or regional identity, sometimes successfully preying upon popular sensitivities derived from strong relations to the land and to place. The blandishments of the ad man are called upon to persuade the population that this new suburban development promises a more healthful relation to nature, a more satisfying form of sociality and of daily life, new technologies of living, and a brilliant location for future development. Failing persuasion, of course, capitalist developers are notorious for resorting to everything from political subversion, and legal manoeuvres to brute force to clear the land for their schemes.

Conversely, social solidarities are built within populations around entirely different values – those of history, culture, memory, religion and language – and these are often recalcitrant and resistant to the pure mechanics of capital accumulation and market valuations, in spite of all the efforts of the promoters and image makers. It is interesting to note that a whole new field of consultancy, called 'urban imagineering', has been invented to try and bridge this gulf.

For purposes of collective action, people and organisations come together to form territorial associations that seek to manage the spaces and places under their aegis and thereby give their place in the world a distinctive character. They do so according to their own distinctive cultural histories and beliefs, as well as according to their own material needs, wants and desires. Institutional arrangements are devised that declare the (relative) autonomy of these human associations and their exclusive control over at least some activities within the territory at their command. They form states or state-like entities. These entities can be neighbourhoods, cities or city regions, so-called 'nation states' (like France and Poland), federated states (like the United States and the United Kingdom) or state unions defined either loosely (like NAFTA) or more tightly (like the European Union). The administrative map of the world depicts a hierarchy of territorial units that exist at a variety of geographical scales (from urban neighbourhood to global power bloc) and these units, socially constructed, provide a framework for geopolitical and geoeconomic action and conflict. The borders that get constructed often then form barriers to movement. States just as often hinder as they facilitate the geographical motion of capital flow.

The degree of social cohesion and social bonding between individuals and groups within these territorial associations varies a great deal. Affective bonds – local, regional or national loyalties – can be strong (as in the case of intense nationalism) or weak as the case may be. The intensity of these bonds may reflect commonalities of religion, ethnicity, language or just simply history and tradition, giving to the state or regional government a distinctive character with well-defined common interests. The entity-like character of these territorial associations frequently leads them to compete with each other. Such competition often strengthens the affective loyalties and commonalities of purpose among those living within the territory at the same time as it tightens exclusions and emphasises differences.

What does all of this have to do with the reproduction of capital? The forms of human association based in territory that I am here describing preceded the rise of capitalism. They have characterised human societies, as I remarked at the outset, from the very beginning. Territory and place have always been used by institutions to organise populations and power relations. The Catholic Church, to take one example, early on organised space through parishes, dioceses and bishoprics within a hierarchical form of power with its apex in the Vatican. The Roman Empire for a while attempted the same sort of thing, as did the Q'ing dynasty in China and the Ottoman Empire. Territorial organisations of this sort defined the initial conditions to which capitalism either had to conform or transform in order to survive and flourish. Is there, then, a distinctive form of territorialisation associated with a distinctive history of institutional and administrative structures that arose with capitalism?

———

Capitalists, absent any prior form of territorial organisation, often produce, as we have seen, agglomerations of activity in particular places. Those aspects of capitalist activity that are complementary rather than competitive get organised in a collaborative way. The effect is to create a tendency towards an informal 'structured coherence' within geographical regions. Capitalists engaged in many different activities in a particular region come together to express and pursue collective common interests. Business associations and chambers of commerce arise, but in other instances powerful corporations (as with the auto industry of Detroit) or even a single local powerful boss (including drug cartel and mafia leaders) play key organising roles in bringing together local interests around a common purpose. Regional specialisations and territorial divisions of labour are actively produced. Detroit means (or meant) cars, Silicon Valley means computer electronics, Seattle and Bangalore mean software development, Bavaria means automotive engineering, the 'Third Italy' means small-scale engineering products and designer fashions, Taipei means computer chips and household technologies, and so on.

Within each of these regions, co-evolutionary dynamics operate in distinctive ways. Broadly common interests arise with respect to quality of labour supply, access to means of production, supportive research and development activities (often based in local universities like Carnegie Mellon, which specialises in metallurgy and technology in what was once the premier steel-making centre of Pittsburgh, as well as in the usual requirements of adequate transport and communications, efficient and low-cost infrastructural arrangements (water and sewage, for example), and in a civic administration that attends to social needs (such as education of the workforce, health and environmental qualities). All of these elements tend to hang together within a geographical region in a mutually supportive way. If they do not cohere, then economic development within the region tends to languish. Regions that develop superior qualities become grand attractors for further capitalist activity. In this way, what the Swedish economist Gunnar Myrdal dubbed 'circular and cumulative causation' operates to make rich and successful regions ever more prosperous, while poorer regions stagnate or decline.

Regional configurations in divisions of labour and of production systems are, in short, made by the conjoining of economic and political forces rather than dictated by so-called natural advantages. Their making inevitably involves a regional co-evolution of technological and organisational forms, social relations, relations to nature, production systems, ways of life and mental conceptions of the world (local cultural attitudes are often key). Specific patterns of relations between the activity spheres can then get sealed in and pinned down through the emergence of distinctive institutional and administrative territorial arrangements. The state emerges as the geographical container and to some degree as the guardian of these arrangements. But the state that emerges operates like a fixed net of administration cast over the ferment of capitalist activity constantly evolving into distinctive regional configurations on the ground. The evolving New York metropolitan region economy spreads across many state borders, posing a whole host of administrative and technical headaches for state authorities as it does so. The territorial organisation of London has gone through all manner of shifts, part politically and part economically inspired, over the last fifty years, in a complex history that is never neatly resolved.

———

State formation has been integral to capitalist development. But the details of this process escape easy analysis. To begin with, the design of territorialised institutional and administrative arrangements is not predetermined by its relations to all of the other spheres of activity. It exhibits a relative autonomy, both with respect to them and to the circulation and accumulation of capital. But states are produced out of social relations and through technologies of governance. To the degree, for example, that states are reifications of mental conceptions, so theories of state formation must pay careful attention to what it is that people were and are thinking the state should be in relation to them. As mental conceptions shift, so the state is subject to all manner of pressures to transform its functioning. The neoliberal movement that began in the 1970s, for example, constituted a radical ideological assault upon what the state should be about. To the degree it was successful (and often it was not) it led to wide-ranging state-sponsored changes in daily life (the promotion of individualism and an ethic of personal responsibility against the background of diminishing state provision), as well as in the dynamics of capital accumulation. Margaret Thatcher dissolved the Greater London Council in 1986 because it resisted her neoliberalising project, thus leaving the London region bereft of an adequate coordinating authority to match the boom in financial services and property values that engulfed the whole of south-east England. The Blair government finally had to restore some semblance of metropolitan government to rectify that situation.

The 'success' of a particular state (national or local) is often measured by the degree to which it captures flows of capital, builds the conditions favourable to further capital accumulation within its borders and achieves a high quality of daily life for its inhabitants. States are inevitably involved in competition with each other concerning how all the other spheres within the co-evolutionary process are brought together into some sort of working whole. The more capital accumulation can be captured within its borders, the richer the state becomes. State management of the co-evolutionary process emerges as a goal of governance.

The mental conceptions that guide these managerial practices often depend on attachment to some normative principles. For example, the international system that arose after 1945 rested upon fixed exchange rates against the dollar and the right of states to keep tight control over cross-border capital and money flows. My students are astonished when I tell them that when I first travelled abroad from Britain in the late 1950s I could not take more than £40 with me in any one year and that whatever I took was recorded in my passport to make sure I didn't evade the rule. Regulatory barriers of this sort kept most capitalist activity, except for large multinational companies, export-oriented firms and financial institutions, tightly confined within nation state borders during this period. When the fixed exchange rate system broke down at the end of the 1960s, capital controls gradually disappeared. The last time any major state seriously attempted to use them occurred when the socialist François Mitterrand came to power in France in 1981. He nationalised the French banks and sought to stem capital flight by imposing strict controls on the outflows of capital. There was, however, a near revolution when the French found they could not freely use their credit cards abroad. Controls were quickly abandoned. Malaysia, however, did go against conventional wisdom and successfully defended itself against the crash of 1997–8 by resorting to capital controls.

The diversity of state responses to the current crisis is indicative of how different interpretations and theoretical frameworks can underpin not only an uneven geographical development in responses but potentially an uneven geographical development of impacts. State managers and politicians are anything but omniscient even at the best of times, and at the worst of times can be refractory in the extreme. Again, the contingency and arbitrariness that attaches to geographical differentiation is emphasised rather than assuaged by such dynamics.

Nevertheless, capitalism requires sovereign territorial entities to render coherent (by force if necessary) the institutional and administrative arrangements (such as property rights and market laws) that underpin its functioning. But capitalism also requires the existence of sovereign individuals, free to engage in the speculative and innovative entrepreneurial activities that render capitalism so dynamic and keep the accumulation of capital in motion. This points to a central conundrum in political organisation: the relationship between the sovereign state with sovereign powers and the sovereign individuals – not only capitalists but a citizenry with all manner of different inclinations – endowed with a sovereign right to pursue profit (or some other objective such as the 'life, liberty and happiness' proposed in the US Declaration of Independence) without regard to spatial barriers.

This relationship between state and individual has always been unstable, contingent and deeply problematic. It is into this territorial space that questions of political organisation, of how public life should be constructed, of governance and democracy and of political authority are worked through in distinctive ways. Each state evolves its own unique and distinctive character, its own institutional, legal and administrative framework. Yet here too competition between states for mobile capital and for the accumulation of wealth and power tend to favour some configurations rather than others. The combination of authoritarian state powers with limited democratic rights but considerable free market individualism in economically successful countries like Singapore, Taiwan and South Korea in recent times, and now China surging to the forefront under one-party rule, suggests that there is no necessary relationship, particularly in early stages of development, between strong capital accumulation and individual democratic rights.

Political systems and the allegiances and loyalties that people have for their countries or the places they inhabit are obviously not just a byproduct of processes of capital accumulation. The will of the people always has a distinctive role, as do the mental conceptions that attach to political histories and traditions. The radical anti-authoritarianism and consequent anti-statist tradition that characterises the United States set it apart, for example, from countries like Germany and

France, where there is far greater acceptance of state interventions both in the economy and in the regulation of social life. Indian democracy is radically different from Chinese Communist Party rule and both have little in common politically with Zimbabwe or Finland. Within the United States, for example, most of the population, deeply attached, as opinion polls show, to radical egalitarianism and equally radical anti-statism, clearly want health care for all but fiercely resist the prospect that the government should provide it. The insurance companies and the Republicans consequently never argue against universal health care. They spend all their time decrying the overweening state power that might deliver it. So far they have used the latter sentiments successfully to thwart the egalitarian ideal of decent health care for all. Though why anyone would want to thwart universal health care is a mystery: until, that is, it is understood that it is the threat to the perpetuation of bloated but highly profitable private insurance companies, the darlings of Wall Street, that is at the root of the problem. So it is clear what the 'Party of Wall Street' wants.

The state system that has evolved throughout the historical geography of capitalism takes hierarchical form. Regional and local governments with limited powers to tax and to provide the public goods are embedded in sovereign states which have yielded some of their sovereignty to suprastate bodies. Organisations such as the International Monetary Fund, the World Trade Organization, the World Bank, the Bank of International Settlements and coordinations between major state powers (the G8, now expanded to the G20) have, for example, played an increasingly significant role in guiding capital flows and protecting capital accumulation. The formation of suprastate power blocs such as the European Union, North American Free Trade Association (NAFTA), Central American Free Trade Association (CAFTA), Latin American Southern Cone group (MERCOSUR), or even looser configurations of regional coordination such as the Association of South East Asian Nations (ASEAN), consolidates this tendency to define territorial units above and beyond the nation state largely for economic purposes. This is so because the regulatory environment in which capital (in money or commodity form) moves around the world requires institutionalised management if it is not to dissolve into chaos.

The powers residing at these different administrative scales diverge considerably, as do the instruments and forms of governance. The relations between capital accumulation and the different scales and layers of governance are notoriously unstable. But there are some discernible patterns. Some regional and local governments are held captive to capitalist interests, either through direct corruption or more subtly through the financing of pro-business candidates in elections and close collaboration between capitalist interests and the key departments in local administrations dealing with, for example, real estate and economic development.

One of the key transformations that occurred in the character of the state after the mid-1970s was the devolution of powers to local administrations. Controlled decentralisation turned out to be one of the very best means to exercise and consolidate centralised control. This was particularly marked in the reforms introduced into China after 1979. Authority not only was delegated to regional and metropolitan governments and in other instances corralled in special economic zones, but even extended to towns and villages that were invited to set up enterprises. The result was astonishing economic growth in aggregate and the centralisation of more and more power in Beijing. But across much of the capitalist world similar devolutions occurred. In the US, for example, a much greater emphasis was placed on an individual state's rights and metropolitan initiatives vis-à-vis the federal government after 1975 or so. The French state also introduced decentralisation reforms from the 1980s onwards and Britain conceded powers to a Scottish parliament, as did Spain to Catalonia, and so on.

Wars between states in the historical geography of capitalism have been earth-shaking episodes of creative destruction. Not only are physical infrastructures destroyed but labour forces are decimated, environments trashed, institutions reframed, social relations disrupted and all manner of new technologies and organisational forms designed (all the way from nuclear bombs, radar, burn surgery treatments to logistical systems and command and execute models of decision-making). Rebuilding in the aftermath of wars absorbs surplus capital and labour (as is currently happening in Lebanon and happened big time with the reconstruction of the Japanese and European economies after 1945). It is not, of course, that wars are deliberately designed by capital for this purpose, but capital certainly feeds off them to great effect.

State formation and interterritorial competition sets the stage for conflicts of all sorts, with war the ultimate resort. Capital, as it were, creates some of the necessary conditions for the modern forms of warfare but the sufficient conditions lie elsewhere, within the state apparatus and with the interests that seek to use state power for their own narrow benefit (including, of course, the 'military industrial complex' that survives largely through promoting fear of conflict, if not the conflict itself).

The coercive laws of interterritorial competition operate, however, with different effects at different geographical scales: between power blocs (such as Europe, North America, east Asia), between states, between regional entities (such as states in the United States or regional governments like Catalonia or Scotland in Europe), as well as between metropolitan regions, cities and even local townships and neighbourhoods. Making regions and states more 'competitive' in the global economy becomes foundational to the formation of public policies, just as making a neighbourhood more liveable in and attractive to the right sort of people often becomes the central aim of local civic associations (leading to a lot of 'not in my back yard' local politics). Local states compete with each other. Local solidarities that cut across class lines then become important in the attempt to lure mobile capital to town. The local chamber of commerce and local trade unions are more likely to collaborate rather than to struggle against each other when it comes to getting local development projects going that will bring in both investment capital and employment opportunities.

The selling and branding of place, and the burnishing of the image of a place (including states), becomes integral to how capitalist competition works. The production of geographical difference, building upon those given by history, culture and so-called natural advantages, is internalised within the reproduction of capitalism. Bring a signature architect to town and create something like Frank Gehry's Guggenheim Museum in Bilbao. This helps put that city on the map of attractors for mobile capital. If geographical differences between territories and states did not exist, then they would be created by both differential investment strategies and the quest for spatial monopoly power given by uniqueness of location and of environmental and cultural qualities. The idea that capitalism promotes geographical homogeneity is totally wrong. It thrives on heterogeneity and difference, although always within limits, of course (it cannot tolerate Cuba, Chile under Allende, the prospect of communism in Italy in the 1970s).

But the institutional and administrative arrangements within a territory are, theoretically at least, subject to the sovereign will of the people, which means they are subject to the outcomes of political struggle. This introduces a different dimension to the ways in which geographical organisation relates to the reproduction of capitalism. Oppositions to excessive commercialisation and crass capitalist development, as well as social movements against market-led capitalism, can all too easily arise within such a structure. These oppositions can come from both the left (such as communist-led insurgencies) or the right (religious fundamentalism or fascism). Whoever controls the means of violence – traditionally the state, but now disaggregated through terrorist and mafia-type organisations or placed at a higher level, as with an organisation like NATO – generally has the advantage in these struggles, increasingly so given the present sophistication of surveillance techniques and military technologies.

———

Imperialisms, colonial conquests, inter-capitalist wars and racial discriminations have played a dramatic role in the historical geography of capitalism. No account of the origins of capitalism can avoid confronting the significance of such phenomena. But does this mean that such phenomena are necessary to capitalism's survival? Could it evolve along anti-racist, non-militaristic, non-imperialist and non-colonial lines? What happens when, as Giovanni Arrighi suggests in *The Long Twentieth Century* (1994), we substitute the notion of hegemony for traditional theories of imperialist and colonial domination and insist that the former is a very different organisation of global power relations from the latter?

The rise of capitalism was associated with the rise of a distinctively capitalist form of state power – the 'fiscal military state' is how economic historians of the eighteenth century now like to characterise it. A variety of state–finance and state–corporate nexuses appeared within the expanding global space of capitalist development. Competition between them, sometimes fierce and war-torn, became generalised across the state system that then arose. State powers and territorialised forms of organisation have also evolved over time. This evolution, though autonomous, is embedded in the co-evolutionary processes earlier outlined.

A distinction thus arises between a logic of power, driven by territorial imperatives and political interests, captive to all of the complexities involved in place-making and the evolution of expressions of popular will (such as nationalism) in the public sphere, and a capitalistic logic of power that arises from the accumulation of money power in private and corporate hands searching for endless growth through profit-making.

By territorial logic I mean the political, diplomatic, economic and military strategies deployed by the state apparatus in its own interest. The first aim of these strategies is to control and manage the activities of the population within the territory and to accumulate power and wealth within the state borders. That power and wealth can be used either internally for the benefit of the people (or more narrowly to create a good business climate for capital and a local capitalist class) or externally to exert influence or exercise power over other states. Tribute can be extracted, for example, from colonial possessions or from weak states falling within the sphere of influence of some dominant state. Failing that, access to the resources, markets, labour power and productive capacity that exists in other countries can be secured so that surplus capital has some place to go when conditions at home are unfavourable for further accumulation. This opening up can involve violent conquests and colonial occupations (of the sort that the British engaged in over India from the eighteenth century onwards). But it can also be established more peacefully through negotiated access, trade agreements and commercial and market integrations of the sort that the British established with the United States, its former colony, after independence and the war of 1812.

The capitalist logic, on the other hand, focuses on the way in which money power flows across and through space and over borders in the search for endless accumulation. This logic is more processual and molecular than territorial. The two logics are not reducible to each other but they are closely intertwined. There is also, as I have earlier argued, a point of fusion where they come together to form the state–finance nexus (now represented by the world's central banks). But the motivations of those involved – business people versus politicians – are rather different and sometimes deeply contradictory even as they are inextricably intertwined. The capitalist holding money wishes to place it wherever profits are to be had and that is that. The capitalist therefore needs open spaces in which to move – and state borders can get in the way of that. Politicians and state bureaucrats typically seek to enhance the wealth and power of their state both internally and in external relations. To do so under contemporary conditions requires that they facilitate capital accumulation within their borders or find ways to extract wealth from elsewhere. Money is, after all, a primary form of social power and the state thirsts after it and is disciplined by it as much as anyone else. Historically, the most obvious variant of an explicit strategy along these lines was called 'mercantilism'. The state's mission, seventeenth- and eighteenth-century political economists suggested, was to accumulate money power (gold and silver) at the expense of other states. In his recent works, the American political commentator Kevin Phillips has taken to describing contemporary politics as being marked by what he calls 'a new mercantilism'.

One response to the financial crisis that engulfed east and south-east Asia in 1997–8, for example, was to 'go mercantilist'. Lack of cash (a crisis of liquidity) had made local economies vulnerable to external financial power. As viable businesses went under for lack of liquidity, foreign capital could take them over at fire-sale prices. When conditions recovered these businesses could be sold back at a huge profit that accrued to the foreign financiers. As Taiwan, South Korea, Singapore and Malaysia produced their way out of that crisis (selling to booming US consumer markets), they deliberately amassed the necessary foreign exchange reserves to defend themselves against predatory behaviour of this sort. China's foreign exchange reserves became even larger, giving it far greater flexibility in the face of crisis conditions than would otherwise have been the case. Surplus capital was therefore deliberately amassed in east and south-east Asia. But the surplus capital could not remain idle. It had to be placed somewhere. Much of it was invested in US treasury bonds to cover the growing indebtedness of the United States. The result has been a reversal of the historical drain of wealth from east to west. But does this imply that China and the other main powers in the region are assuming an imperialist role vis-à-vis the United States? Certainly, as was remarked in chapter 1, a shift in hegemony appears to be underway. But it would be wrong to call it imperialism or even neocolonialism, although there are disturbing hints of a neocolonial relation emerging between China and some African countries.

Command over space, we earlier stated, is always a crucial form of social power. It can be exercised by one group or social class over another or exercised imperialistically, as the power of one people over another. This power is both expansive (the power to do and to create) and coercive (the power to deny, prevent and, if necessary, to destroy). But the effect is to redistribute wealth and redirect capital flows to the benefit of the imperialist or hegemonic power at the expense of everyone else.

It then follows that the political and military power that accrues within the state can also be used to facilitate, check or even suppress the use of the money power that accumulates in private hands through capital accumulation. The history of socialist and communist states after 1917 is illustrative of the importance (as well as the inherent limits) of this counter-power located within the state apparatus to organise the global space according to a non-capitalistic logic. But, as earlier argued, the mere conquest of state power does not a true socialist or communist revolution make. Only when all the other spheres of activity within the co-evolutionary system move into some kind of alignment will we be able to speak of a full-scale revolutionary transformation away from capitalist domination. This does not mean, as some now argue, that the power of the state is irrelevant and that the prime locus for transformative politics has to shift exclusively to civil society and daily life.

While much of contemporary anti-capitalist thinking is either sceptical of or downright hostile to any turn to the state as an adequate form of counter-power to that of capital, some sort of territorial organisation (such as that devised by the Zapatista revolutionary movement in Chiapas, Mexico) is unavoidable in designing a new social order. The question is not, therefore, whether the state is a valid form of social organisation in human affairs, but what kind of territorial organisation of power might be appropriate in the transition to some other form of production. In the same way that pre-capitalist state forms were transformed into distinctively bourgeois and capitalist states from the seventeenth century onwards, so any transition away from capital accumulation as the dominant way of organizing the reproduction of social life has to anticipate a radical transformation and reconstruction of territorial power. New institutional and administrative apparatuses, operative within some territory, will need to be designed. While this may sound a tall order, we need only reflect upon how these apparatuses have changed over the last thirty years in the course of the neoliberal turn to see that wide-ranging transformations are not only possible but inevitable in the ongoing co-evolution of capitalism.

State forms have never been static. From the mid-nineteenth-century onwards the world was, for example, territorialised at the behest of and according to a logic imposed for the most part by the main imperial powers. Most of the world's territorial boundaries were laid down between 1870 and 1925 and most of these were drawn by British and French imperial power alone. Decolonisation after 1945 confirmed most of the boundaries (apart from some spectacular splits such as the partitioning of India) and produced many more nominally independent and nominally autonomous political states. I say 'nominally' because in most instances the subterranean tie of imperialistically imposed colonial institutions remained intact. Neocolonialism in Africa, for example, continues to this day, with immense implications for uneven geographical development of the whole continent.

The geographical configurations of state power achieved after 1945 remained fairly stable, once decolonisation was completed. But in recent times the map of the world has changed. The United Nations originally comprised 51 states but it now boasts 192 members. A whole series of reterritorialisations began after 1989 with the break-up of the Soviet Union and the subsequent dissolution of Yugoslavia. Changes have occurred at other levels of governance, too. Territorialisations may seem hard to change, but their history indicates they are never fixed in stone.

The big question this introduces is the shifting power relations within the evolving inter-state system and the resultant political conflicts between states or power blocs. This is not only a matter of examining inter-state competition and considering the outcomes in terms of winners and losers. It also concerns the capacity of some states to exert power over others and the mental framework within which political and military leaders that command the state apparatus interpret their position in the inter-state system. The sense of security and threat, fear of absorption, the need to manage internal struggles within a territory by invoking real or imagined external threats, all play a role. Mental conceptions become important.

———

It is in this world that the darker side of raw geopolitical thinking can all too easily flourish with potentially lethal effects. Once states are viewed, for example, as distinctive organisms that require sustenance (rather than as open forms of political organisation within a framework of international collaboration) then, as the German geographer Karl Haushofer, whose geopolitical institute laid the plans for Nazi expansionism, argued, they have a legitimate right to seek the necessary territorial dominance to secure their future. States, this argument went, are organisms that exist in a Darwinian world in which only the fittest will survive. There is no option except to engage in the struggle for existence on the world stage. The current revival of such modes of thought is and should be worrying. Is the Chinese government, rumoured to be enamoured of A. T. Mahan's landmark treatise *The Influence of Sea Power upon History* (published back in 1890), building a navy as part of a geopolitical strategy to protect its nascent but rapidly evolving geoeconomic relations with the Middle East, Africa and Latin America, whence it must procure the raw materials necessary for its further industrialisation? And what is that huge new port facility they have built in Pakistan about and all those ventures in inner Asia? Is there a geopolitical plan here for global domination? Are they also enamoured of the old geopolitical theories of the geographer Sir Halford Mackinder (published in 1904 as 'The

Geographical Pivot of History'), which say that whoever controls the 'heartland' of inner Asia controls 'the world island' constituted by Eurasia and therefore the world? If so, how should the United States respond to this threat?

Indeed, to what degree has US interventionism in Iraq and Afghanistan (and Obama's somewhat surprising commitment to continuing the struggle in Afghanistan) been driven by geopolitical considerations? Since 1945, the US has sought to dominate the Middle East, for that is where the global oil spigot lies. Whoever controls the global oil spigot controls the world. Its aim has been to prevent the formation of any independently powerful political force in the region and to protect the existence of a single world oil market denominated in dollars. This underpins the global hegemony of the dollar and accords to the United States the power of seignorage, the ability to print global money when in distress. The US has fought two Gulf wars and extended its reach into Afghanistan and Pakistan. It perpetually threatens the one state, Iran, that has refused to accept US hegemony and that has sought to maintain its position as an independent political power, in spite of a lengthy US-backed war with Saddam's Iraq in the 1980s. The extension of US control outwards from the core oil-producing states in Afghanistan and even into the heartland of central Asia bears all the marks of geopolitical pre-emption against Russian and Chinese aspirations.

Once geopolitical thinking of this sort, no matter how erroneous and unnecessary, grabs a hold on the foreign policy establishments of the leading states then it can and will likely be acted upon. The geopolitical visions and ambitions of Japan, Germany, Britain, France and the United States collided after 1914, with huge consequences for the making of a new global geography through war and struggles for political, economic and military supremacy. Strange, that it is through geopolitics that geography – so often, as we have seen, the neglected orphan of social theory – comes back into a social scientific understanding of the world. That it should do so in this sinister guise of geographical determinism, in a supposedly Darwinian and

Malthusian political world of competing states or power blocs, could have and has had tragic consequences. At times of crisis, such as now, the temptation to think in these terms is huge. It certainly was so after the crash of 1929 – and look what that led to.

The augmentation of state power certainly entails corralling as much wealth and money power as possible within a given territory out of the widening and deepening spatial flows that characterise capital accumulation on the world stage. This inevitably encourages a defensive politics in relation to the swirling depressions, recessions and economic hurricanes that characterise much of capitalism's history. The desire to protect against all forms of potential economic misfortune is understandable. But it can also lead to desperate and sometimes aggressive attempts to manage the uneven geographical development of capitalism by stymieing by whatever means (including military) the aspirations of other states while advancing those of one's own. Letting Lehman go bankrupt spread the effects of the US-centred crisis all around the world. Was that a deliberate move? At this point it is impossible to know.

The aggregate effect is to deepen and widen uneven geographical developments and to render the world's geography more unstable. Much then depends upon the policies set in motion. High tariff barriers, the protection of infant industries, substituting home-produced products for imported goods, along with state support for research and development, characterise the protectionist alternative within the overall patterns of world trade. Barriers erupt all over the place and interfere with the open spatial strategies that capitalists usually prefer. Protectionism typically provokes retaliation and heightened inter-state competition. Trade wars between states are by no means uncommon and their outcomes always contingent and uncertain.

Historically, of course, the empires built by the European powers and their distinctive colonial systems solved all of these problems by creating a grounded global geographical structure of administration, institution formation, and trade and development across fixed territories under the domination of the world's metropolitan centres (Madrid, London, Paris, Brussels, Amsterdam, Berlin, Moscow and Rome). Uneven geographical development, broadly managed from the metropoles, defined capital flows so as to accumulate the mass of the world's capital in the hands of those living in the advanced capitalist countries of the time. Decolonisation began to change all of this. Occurring early on in the case of the Americas and Oceania, decolonisation was ultimately embraced (following a lot of pressure from the United States) everywhere from 1945, though often after years of bitter struggles for national liberation, whose twists and turns had all manner of implications for the new states that emerged. Plainly, decolonisation did not end hegemony or dominance, nor did it prevent the organisation of uneven geographical development in ways that benefited the already existing centres of capital accumulation.

From the very beginning (and after a few false starts), the United States substituted pursuit of global hegemony for the practices of classical European (and later on, Japanese) forms of imperialism and colonialism based on territorial occupations. The US did not entirely abandon the objectives of territorial control but sought to exercise that control through forms of local governance that nominally preserved independence but which informally or in some instances formally (as in the cases of South Korea and Taiwan) accepted US hegemony in world affairs. This sometimes took covert violence on the part of the United States and certainly produced a networked set of neocolonial relations with weaker and usually smaller states that operated under US domination.

But one of the consequences of the huge burst of financial activity and of the global shifts in productive activity that have occurred over the last thirty years has been to render the language of imperialism and colonialism less relevant than that of the struggle for hegemony. The new imperialism is about the struggle for hegemony – financial hegemony, in particular, though the military dimension continues to be of great importance – rather than struggles for direct control over territory.

Uneven geographical development is not a mere sidebar to how capitalism works, but fundamental to its reproduction. Mastery over its dynamics is elusive. It generates many localised openings within which vulnerabilities become apparent and oppositional forces can rally. This makes it a fecund source for capitalist renewal. Had China not opened up after 1979 for reasons that remain difficult to pin down, then global capitalism would have been far more constrained in its overall development and far more likely to have run aground upon one or other of the barrier reefs to which the accumulation of capital is always prone. China, with its increasing influence not only in east Asia but also beyond, now has a major role to play in determining the kind of capitalism that may emerge from the current crisis. Hegemony is shifting geographically – as North America and Europe stagnate, China continues to grow – but this poses geopolitical dangers. How uneven geographical development unfolds both geoeconomically (through trading relations largely guided by corporate interests but sanctioned by state powers) and geopolitically (by state diplomacy and war, the latter famously referred to by the great nineteenth-century German military strategist Carl von Clausewitz as 'diplomacy by other means') will have immense implications for the future of humanity.

Behind all of this lies the complexity of geographical determinations. On the one hand, capitalists cannot abide geographical barriers of any sort – neither spatial nor environmental – and are engaged in a perpetual struggle to circumvent or transcend them. On the other hand, capitalists actively construct new geographies and geographical barriers in the form of physical built environments embodying vast quantities of fixed and immovable capital that must be fully used if their value is not to be lost. They also create regional divisions of labour which assemble around them all manner of supportive functions that then constrain geographical mobility of both capital and labour. Territorialised administrative arrangements and state apparatuses fix borders and boundaries in ways that often limit movement. To all of this must be added the multiple ways in which people create their own distinctive living spaces, reflective of their distinctive views on the proper relation to nature and appropriate forms of sociality, and of their mental conceptions as to what constitutes a satisfying, materially rewarding and meaningful form of daily life.

The reason that it is so difficult to integrate the making of geography into any general theory of capital accumulation, it should by now be clear, is that this process is not only deeply contradictory but also full of contingencies, accidents and confusions. The maintenance of heterogeneity rather than the achievement of homogeneity is important. But it is still possible to get some handle on where these difficulties are located and to what effect. The economic weather to which planet earth is subjected is, as it were, changeable and unpredictable in its details. Long-term economic changes are even harder to discern beneath all the surface churning, but they are definitely there. It is also abundantly clear that the reproduction of capitalism entails the making of new geographies and that the making of new geographies through creative destruction of the old is one very good way to deal with the perpetually present capital surplus disposal problem. But this search for a geographical 'fix' to the problem of surplus absorption also constitutes an ever-present danger. While there are innumerable parallels now being drawn between the crisis of the 1930s and the current one, the one potential parallel that is almost totally ignored is the collapse of international collaboration, the descent into geopolitical rivalries and the vast tragedy of one of the greatest of all episodes of creative destruction in human history: the Second World War.

8

What is to be Done? And Who is Going to Do It?

At times of crisis, the irrationality of capitalism becomes plain for all to see. Surplus capital and surplus labour exist side by side with seemingly no way to put them back together in the midst of immense human suffering and unmet needs. In midsummer of 2009, one third of the capital equipment in the United States stood idle, while some 17 per cent of the workforce were either unemployed, enforced part-timers or 'discouraged' workers. What could be more irrational than that?

For capital accumulation to return to 3 per cent compound growth will require a new basis for profit-making and surplus absorption. The irrational way to do this in the past has been through the destruction of the achievements of preceding eras by way of war, the devaluation of assets, the degradation of productive capacity, abandonment and other forms of 'creative destruction'. The effects are felt not only throughout the world of commodity production and exchange. Human lives are disrupted and even physically destroyed, whole careers and lifetime achievements are put in jeopardy, deeply held beliefs are challenged, psyches wounded and respect for human dignity is cast aside. Creative destruction is visited upon the good, the beautiful, the bad and the ugly alike. Crises, we may conclude, are the irrational rationalisers of an irrational system.

Can capitalism survive the present trauma? Yes, of course. But at what cost? This question masks another. Can the capitalist class reproduce its power in the face of the raft of economic, social, political and geopolitical and environmental difficulties? Again, the answer is a resounding 'Yes it can'. This will, however, require the mass of the people to give generously of the fruits of their labour to those in power, to surrender many of their rights and their hard-won asset values (in everything from housing to pension rights) and to suffer environmental degradations galore, to say nothing of serial reductions in their living standards which will mean starvation for many of those already struggling to survive at rock bottom. More than a little political repression, police violence and militarised state control will be required to stifle the ensuing unrest. But there will also have to be wrenching and painful shifts in the geographical and sectoral locus of capitalist class power. The capitalist class cannot, if history is any guide, maintain its power without changing its character and moving accumulation on to a different trajectory and into new spaces (such as east Asia).

Since much of this is unpredictable and since the spaces of the global economy are so variable, then uncertainties as to outcomes are heightened at times of crisis. All manner of localised possibilities arise for either nascent capitalists in some new space to seize opportunities to challenge older class and territorial hegemonies (as when Silicon Valley replaced Detroit from the mid-1970s onwards in the United States) or for radical movements to challenge the reproduction of an already destabilised and therefore weakened class power. To say that the capitalist class and capitalism can survive is not to say that they are predestined to do so, nor that their future character is given. Crises are moments of paradox and possibility out of which all manner of alternatives, including socialist and anti-capitalist ones, can spring.

So what will happen this time around? If we are to get back to 3 per cent growth, this will mean finding new and profitable global investment opportunities for $1.6 trillion in 2010, rising to closer to $3 trillion by 2030. This contrasts with the $0.15 trillion new investment needed in 1950 and the $0.42 trillion needed in 1973 (the dollar figures are inflation adjusted). Real problems of finding adequate outlets for surplus capital began to emerge after 1980, even with the opening up of China and the collapse of the Soviet bloc. The difficulties were in part resolved by the creation of fictitious markets where speculation in asset values could take off unchecked by any regulatory apparatus. Where will all this investment go now?

Leaving aside the undisputable constraints in the relation to nature (with global warming of obvious paramount importance), the other potential barriers of effective demand in the market place, of technologies and of geographical/geopolitical distributions are likely to be profound, even supposing – which is unlikely – that no serious active oppositions to continuous capital accumulation and further consolidation of class power materialise. What spaces are left in the global economy for new spatial fixes for capital surplus absorption? China and the ex-Soviet bloc have already been integrated. South and south-east Asia are filling up fast. Africa is not yet fully integrated, but there is nowhere else with the capacity to absorb all this surplus capital. What new lines of production can be opened up to absorb growth? There may be no effective long-term capitalist solutions (apart from reversion to fictitious capital manipulations) to this crisis of capitalism. At some point quantitative changes lead to qualitative shifts and we need to take seriously the idea that we may be at exactly such an inflexion point in the history of capitalism. Questioning the future of capitalism itself as an adequate social system ought, therefore, to be in the forefront of current debate.

Yet there appears to be little appetite for such discussion, even as conventional mantras regarding the perfectibility of humanity with the help of free markets and free trade, private property and personal responsibility and low taxes and minimalist state involvement in social provision sound increasingly hollow. A crisis of legitimacy looms. But legitimation crises typically unfold at a different pace and rhythm to stock market crises. It took, for example, three or four years for the stock market crash of 1929 to produce the massive social movements (both progressive and fascistic) that emerged after 1932 or so. The intensity of the current pursuit by political power of ways to exit the present crisis measures the political fear of looming illegitimacy.

The existence of cracks in the ideological edifice does not mean it is utterly broken. Nor does it follow that because something is clearly hollow, people will immediately recognise it as such. As of now, faith in the underlying presumptions of free market ideology have not eroded too much. There is no indication that people in the advanced capitalist countries (apart from the usual malcontents) are looking for radical changes of lifestyle, although many recognise that they may have to economise here or save more there. Those foreclosed upon in the United States (so preliminary surveys tell us) typically blame themselves for their failure (sometimes through bad luck) to live up to the personal responsibilities of homeownership. While there is anger at bankers' duplicity and populist outrage over their bonuses, there seems to be no movement in North America or Europe to embrace radical and far-reaching changes. In the global south, Latin America in particular, the story is rather different. How the politics will play out in China and the rest of Asia, where growth continues and politics turns on different axes, is uncertain. The problem there is that growth is continuing, though at a lower rate.

The idea that the crisis had systemic origins is scarcely mooted in the mainstream media. Most of the governmental moves so far in North America and Europe amount to the perpetuation of business as usual, which translates into support for the capitalist class. The 'moral hazard' that was the immediate trigger for the financial failures is being taken to new heights in the bank bail-outs. The actual practices of neoliberalism (as opposed to its utopian theory) always entailed blatant support for finance capital and capitalist élites (usually on the grounds that financial institutions must be protected at all costs and that it is the duty of state power to create a good business climate for solid profiteering). This has not fundamentally changed. Such practices are justified by appeal to the dubious proposition that a 'rising tide' of capitalist endeavour will 'lift all boats', or that the benefits of compound growth will magically 'trickle down' (which it never does except in the form of a few crumbs from the rich folks' table).

Throughout much of the capitalist world, we have lived through an astonishing period in which politics has been depoliticised and commodified. Only now, as the state steps in to bail out the financiers, has it become clear to all that state and capital are more tightly intertwined than ever, both institutionally and personally. The ruling class, rather than the political class that acts as its surrogate, is now actually seen to rule.

So how will the capitalist class exit the current crisis and how swift will that exit be? The rebound in stock market values from Shanghai and Tokyo to Frankfurt, London and New York is a good sign, we are told, even as unemployment pretty much everywhere continues to rise. But notice the class bias in that measure. We are enjoined to rejoice in the rebound in stock values for the capitalists because it always precedes, it is said, a rebound in the 'real economy' where jobs for the workers are created and incomes earned. The fact that the last stock rebound in the United States after 2002 turned out to be a 'jobless recovery' appears to have been forgotten already. The Anglo-Saxon public in particular appears to be seriously afflicted with amnesia. It too easily forgets and forgives the transgressions of the capitalist class and the periodic disasters its actions precipitate. The capitalist media are happy to promote such amnesia.

Meanwhile the young financial sharks have taken their bonuses of yesteryear, and collectively started boutique financial institutions to circle Wall Street and the City of London, sifting through the detritus of yesterday's financial giants to snaffle up the juicy bits and start all over again. The investment banks that remain in the US – Goldman Sachs and J. P. Morgan – though reincarnated as bank holding companies have gained exemption (thanks to the Federal Reserve) from regulatory requirements and are making huge profits (and setting aside moneys for huge bonuses to match) out of speculating dangerously using taxpayers' money in unregulated and still booming derivative markets. The leveraging that got us into the crisis has resumed big time as if nothing has happened. Innovations in finance are on the march as new ways to package and sell fictitious capital debts are being pioneered and offered to institutions such as pension funds, desperate to find new outlets for surplus capital. The fictions are back!

Consortia are buying up foreclosed properties, either waiting for the market to turn before making a killing or banking high-value land for a future moment of active redevelopment. Wealthy individuals, corporations and state-backed entities (in the case of China) are buying up vast tracts of land at an astonishing rate throughout Africa and Latin America as they seek to consolidate their power and guarantee their future security. Or is this yet another speculative frontier that will sooner or later end in tears? The regular banks are stashing away cash, much of it garnered from the public coffers, also with an eye to resuming bonus payments consistent with a former lifestyle, while a whole host of entrepreneurs hover in the wings waiting to seize this moment of creative destruction backed by a flood of public moneys.

Meanwhile raw money power wielded by the few undermines all semblances of democratic governance. The pharmaceutical, health insurance and hospital lobbies, for example, spent more than $133 million in the first three months of 2009 to make sure they got their way on health care reform in the United States. Max Baucus, head of the key Senate finance committee that shaped the Health Care Bill, received $1.5 million for a bill that delivers a vast number of new clients to the insurance companies without any protections against ruthless exploitation and profiteering (Wall Street is delighted). Another electoral cycle, legally corrupted by immense money power, will soon be upon us. In the United States, the parties of 'K Street' and of Wall Street will be duly re-elected as working Americans are exhorted to work their way out of the mess that the ruling class has created. We have been in such dire straits before, we are reminded, and each time working Americans have rolled up their sleeves, tightened their belts, and saved the system from some mysterious mechanics of autodestruction for which the ruling class denies all responsibility. Personal responsibility is, after all, for the workers and not for the capitalists.

The capitalist class has to convince us, however, that capitalism is not only good for them but good for all of us. It will point to 250 years of continuous growth (with occasional moments like now of creative destruction) and that there is no reason why all of that should come to an end. Its endless innovations have, after all, laid the basis for wondrous new technologies like Velcro and Maclaren pushchairs that can benefit the whole of humanity and there are research frontiers yet to be conquered, capable of spawning the new product lines and the new markets so necessary to continuous expansion. Green technologies and new 'cap and trade' markets in pollution rights will help save planet earth. An even more likely candidate for the next innovation wave lies in biomedical and genetic engineering. Here lies an ethical field (however dubious) promising us eternal life and chemically and biologically supported life forms, with states (if the US model now emerging is anything to go on) guaranteeing huge profits to the medical, pharmaceutical and health care industrial complex. This is the field that the most affluent foundations like Gates and Soros have been assiduously cultivating by their donations. The rents on intellectual property rights and patents will guarantee returns long into the future to those who hold them. (Imagine what will happen when life itself is patented!)

Increasing cross-border monopolisation (both state and corporate) will make the economic system less vulnerable to 'ruinous competition'. The effective demand problem will be better controlled (it is hoped) by state-sponsored markets, funded by printing money, in fields other than the customary military defence, policing and surveillance. Better public support for private provision in fields like health care, housing and education can also conveniently be portrayed as a proliferation of civil and democratic rights for the mass of the population even as it fills the coffers of private corporations.

And if there are difficulties in this place, then why not export them (move the crisis around geographically) in the hope that their re-export back to you can somehow be warded off? Either that, or move the crisis tendencies around slickly from one barrier to another. We have an effective demand problem now, so why not solve it by chucking so much money at it that an inflation problem will erupt five years later (conveniently beyond the range of the electoral cycle)? The response to an inflation crisis will be, of course, to take back any meagre gains which working people achieved during the profligate years of deficit financing, while still leaving the bankers and financiers rolling in clover. It is as if the capitalists are collectively engaged upon a steeplechase race, leaping one hurdle after another with such consummate grace and ease as to create the illusion that we are always in (or about to be in) the promised land of endless capital accumulation. If this is the outline of the exit strategy, then almost certainly we will be in another mess within five years. Indeed, there are troubling signs that the crisis has yet to run its course. Dubai World suddenly announces it cannot meet its payments in November 2009 and global stock markets swoon until oil-rich Abu Dhabi steps in to offer its support. The Greek sovereign debt is called into question shortly thereafter (as happened earlier to Latvia) and some analysts begin to worry that Ireland, Spain and even the United Kingdom may be next. Will the European Union rally to support its parts or will it actually disintegrate under the financial stress? Meanwhile the Chinese economy roars on at an 8 per cent rate of growth, based on a huge infrastructural investment programme and the creation of new productive capacity without regard for what might happen to the old. But, as always happens in booms of this sort, the creation of surplus productive capacity, fuelled by a huge speculative lending binge by the Chinese banks as mandated by the Central Government, may not become evident until much later. But what else can the Chinese do, faced with such huge reserves of restive surplus labour? Meanwhile the resultant vibrancy of the Chinese internal market fires up local effective demand to counter to some degree the loss of export markets. India likewise rediscovers growth, given its huge internal market and weak dependency on foreign exports except in the realm of services which have been less affected by the crisis than other sectors. But the benefits are badly distributed. The number of

Indian billionaires increased (according to *Forbes* magazine) from twenty-seven to fifty-two in the midst of the crisis of 2008. Is this yet another case of assets returning to their supposedly rightful owners in the midst of a crisis? Plainly, the uneven geographical development of both crisis and recovery continues apace.

The faster we come out of this crisis and the less excess capital is destroyed now, the less room there will be for the revival of long-term active growth. The loss of asset values at the time of writing (mid-2009) is, we are told by the IMF, at least $55 trillion, which is equivalent to almost exactly one year's global output of goods and services. Already we are back to the output levels of 1989. We may be looking at losses of $400 trillion or more before we are through. Indeed, in a recent startling calculation, it was suggested that the US state alone was on the hook to guarantee more than $200 trillion in asset values. The likelihood that all of those assets will go bad is minimal, but the thought that many of them could is sobering in the extreme. Just to take a concrete example: Fannie Mae and Freddie Mac, now taken over by the US government, own or guarantee more than $5 trillion in home loans, many of which are in deep trouble (losses of more than $150 billion were recorded in 2008 alone). So what, then, are the alternatives?

———

It has long been the dream of many that an alternative to capitalist (ir)rationality can be defined and rationally arrived at through the mobilisation of human passions in the collective search for a better life for all. These alternatives – historically called socialism or communism – have been tried in various times and places. In the 1930s, the vision of one or other of them operated as a beacon of hope. But recently they have both lost their lustre and been dismissed, not only because of the failure of historical experiments with communism to make good on promises and the penchant for communist regimes to cover over their mistakes by repression, but also because of their supposedly flawed presuppositions concerning human nature and the potential perfectibility of the human personality and of human institutions.

The difference between socialism and communism is worth noting. Socialism aims to democratically manage and regulate capitalism in ways that calm its excesses and redistribute its benefits for the common good. It is about spreading the wealth around through progressive taxation arrangements while basic needs – such as education, health care and even housing – are provided by the state out of reach of market forces. Many of the key achievements of distributive socialism in the period after 1945, in Europe and beyond, have become so socially embedded as to be immune from neoliberal assault. Even in the United States, social security and Medicare are extremely popular programmes that right-wing forces find almost impossible to dislodge. The Thatcherites in Britain could not touch national health care except at the margins. Social provision in Scandinavia and most of western Europe seems to be an unshakable bedrock of the social order.

Under socialism, the production of the surplus is typically managed either through active interventions in the market or through the nationalisation of the so-called 'commanding heights' (energy, transport, steel, even automobiles) of the economy. The geography of capital flow is controlled by state interventions, even as international trade quietly flourishes through trade agreements. The rights of labour in the workplace as well as in the market place are reinforced. These elements of socialism have been rolled back since the 1980s almost everywhere. In effect, the neoliberal revolution succeeded in privatising the production of the surplus. It liberated capitalist producers from constraints – including geographical constraints – and in the process undermined the progressive redistributive character of state functions. This produced the rapid increase in social inequality.

Communism, on the other hand, seeks to displace capitalism by creating an entirely different mode of both the production and distribution of goods and services. In the history of actually existing communism, social control over production, exchange and distribution meant state control and systematic state planning. In the long run though this proved to be unsuccessful, for reasons that cannot be elaborated upon here, its conversion in China (and its earlier adoption in places like Singapore) has proven far more successful than the pure neoliberal model in generating growth. Contemporary attempts to revive the communist hypothesis typically abjure state control and look to other forms of collective social organisation to displace market forces and capital accumulation as the basis for organising production and distribution. Horizontally networked, as opposed to hierarchically commanded, systems of coordination between autonomously organised and self-governing collectives of producers and consumers are envisaged as lying at the core of a new form of communism. Contemporary technologies of communication make such systems seem feasible. All manner of small-scale experiments around the world can be found in which such economic and political forms are being constructed. In this there is a convergence of some sort between the Marxist and anarchist traditions that harks back to the broadly collaborative situation between them in the 1860s in Europe before their break-up into warring camps after the Paris Commune in 1871 and the blow-up between Karl Marx and one of the leading radicals of the time, the anarchist Michael Bakunin, in 1872.

While nothing is certain, it could be that where we are at now is only the beginning of a prolonged shake-out in which the question of grand and far-reaching alternatives will gradually bubble up to the surface in one part of the world or another. The longer the uncertainty and the misery are prolonged, the more the legitimacy of the existing way of doing business will be questioned and the more the demand to build something different will escalate. Radical as opposed to band-aid reforms to patch up the financial system may seem more necessary.

If, for example, we are now witnessing a return of a repressed 'Keynesian moment', but one that is oriented to bailing out the upper classes, then why not redirect it to the working classes that Keynes originally targeted (not, it should be remembered, out of political but economic necessity)? Ironically, the more such a political turn is taken the more likely the economy will regain some semblance of at least temporary stability. The capitalist fear is, however, that any move in this direction will ignite a sense of re-empowerment for the deprived, the discontented and the dispossessed that will encourage them to take matters further (as they did towards the end of the 1960s). Give them an inch, it is said, and they will take a mile. It will in any case require that the capitalists willingly give up some of their individual wealth and power to save capitalism from itself. Historically they have always fiercely resisted doing that.

The uneven development of capitalist practices throughout the world has produced, however, anti-capitalist movements all over the place. The state-centric economies of much of east Asia generate different discontents compared to the churning anti-neoliberal struggles occurring throughout much of Latin America, where the Bolivarian revolutionary movement of popular power exists in a peculiar relationship to capitalist class interests that have yet to be truly confronted. Differences over tactics and policies in response to the crisis among the states that make up the European Union are increasing even as a second attempt to come up with a unified EU constitution is underway. Revolutionary and resolutely anti-capitalist movements, though not all are of a progressive sort, are also to be found in many of the marginal zones of capitalism. Spaces have been opened up within which something radically different in terms of dominant social relations, ways of life, productive capacities and mental conceptions of the world can flourish. This applies as much to the Taliban and to communist rule in Nepal as to the Zapatistas in Chiapas and indigenous movements in Bolivia or the Maoist movements in rural India, even as they are worlds apart in objectives, strategies and tactics.

The central problem is that in aggregate there is no resolute and sufficiently unified anti-capitalist movement that can adequately challenge the reproduction of the capitalist class and the perpetuation of its power on the world stage. Neither is there any obvious way to attack the bastions of privilege for capitalist élites or to curb their inordinate money power and military might. There is, however, a vague sense that not only is another world possible – as the alternative globalisation movement began to proclaim in the 1990s (loudly after what became known as the battle of Seattle in 1999, when the meetings of the World Trade Organization were thoroughly disrupted by street action) – but that with the collapse of the Soviet empire another communism might also be possible. While openings exist towards some alternative social order, no one really knows where or what it is. But just because there is no political force capable of articulating, let alone mounting, such a programme, this is no reason to hold back on outlining alternatives.

Lenin's famous question 'What is to be done?' cannot be answered, to be sure, without some sense of who might do it and where. But a global anti-capitalist movement is unlikely to emerge without some animating vision of what is to be done and why. A double blockage exists: the lack of an alternative vision prevents the formation of an oppositional movement, while the absence of such a movement precludes the articulation of an alternative. How, then, can this blockage be transcended? The relation between the vision of what is to be done and why, and the formation of a political movement across particular places to do it, has to be turned into a spiral. Each has to reinforce the other if anything is actually to get done. Otherwise potential opposition will be for ever locked down into a closed circle that frustrates all prospects for constructive change, leaving us vulnerable to perpetual future crises of capitalism, with increasingly deadly results.

———

The central problem to be addressed is clear enough. Compound growth for ever is not possible and the troubles that have beset the world these last thirty years signal that a limit is looming to continuous capital accumulation that cannot be transcended except by creating fictions that cannot last. Add to this the facts that so many people in the world live in conditions of abject poverty, that environmental degradations are spiralling out of control, that human dignities are everywhere being offended even as the rich are piling up more and more wealth under their command, and that the levers of political, institutional, judicial, military and media power are under such tight but dogmatic political control as to be incapable of doing much more than perpetuating the status quo.

A revolutionary politics that can grasp the nettle of endless compound capital accumulation and eventually shut it down as the prime motor of human history requires a sophisticated understanding of how social change occurs. The failings of past endeavours to build socialism and communism are to be avoided and lessons from that immensely complicated history plainly must be learned. Yet the absolute necessity for a coherent anti-capitalist revolutionary movement must also be recognised. The fundamental aim of that movement has to be to assume social command over both the production and distribution of surpluses.

Let's take another look at the theory of co-evolution laid out in chapter 5. Can this form the basis for a co-revolutionary theory? A political movement can start anywhere (in labour processes, around mental conceptions, in the relation to nature, in social relations, in the design of revolutionary technologies and organisational forms, out of daily life or through attempts to reform institutional and administrative structures including the reconfiguration of state powers). The trick is to keep the political movement moving from one sphere of activity to another in mutually reinforcing ways. This was how capitalism arose out of feudalism and this is how something radically different – call it communism, socialism or whatever – must arise out of capitalism. Previous attempts to create a communist or socialist alternative fatally failed to keep the dialectic between the different activity spheres in motion and also failed to embrace the unpredictabilities and uncertainties in the dialectical movement between the spheres. Capitalism has survived precisely by keeping that dialectical movement going and by embracing the inevitable tensions, including crises, that result.

Imagine, then, some territory within which a population wakes up to the probability that endless capital accumulation is neither possible nor desirable and that it therefore collectively believes another world not only is but must be possible. How should that collectivity begin upon its quest to construct alternatives?

Change arises out of an existing state of affairs and it has to harness the possibilities immanent within an existing situation. Since the existing situation varies enormously from Nepal, to the Pacific regions of Bolivia, to the deindustrialising cities of Michigan and the still booming cities of Mumbai and Shanghai and the damaged but by no means destroyed financial centres of New York and London, so all manner of experiments in social change in different places and at different geographical scales are both likely and potentially illuminating as ways to make (or not make) another world possible. And in each instance it may seem as if one or other aspect of the existing situation holds the key to a different political future. But the first rule for an anti-capitalist movement is: never rely on the unfolding dynamics of one moment without carefully calibrating how relations with all the others are adapting and reverberating.

Feasible future possibilities arise out of the existing state of relations between the different spheres. Strategic political interventions within and across the spheres can gradually move the social order on to a different developmental path. This is what wise leaders and forward-looking institutions do all the time in local situations, so there is no reason to think there is anything particularly fantastic or utopian about acting in this way.

It must first be clearly recognised, however, that development is not the same as growth. It is possible to develop differently on the terrains, for example, of social relations, daily life and the relation to nature, without necessarily resuming growth or favouring capital.

It is false to maintain that growth is a precondition for poverty and inequality reduction or that more respectful environmental policies are, like organic foods, a luxury for the rich.

Secondly, transformations within each sphere will require a deep understanding of both the internal dynamics of, for example, institutional arrangements and technological change in relation to all the other spheres of action. Alliances will have to be built between and across those working in the distinctive spheres. This means that an anti-capitalist movement has to be far broader than groups mobilising around social relations or over questions of daily life in themselves. Traditional hostilities between, for example, those with technical, scientific and administrative expertise and those animating social movements on the ground have to be addressed and overcome.

Thirdly, it will also be necessary to confront the impacts and feedbacks (including political hostilities) coming from other spaces in the global economy. Different places may develop in different ways given their history, culture, location and political-economic condition. Some developments elsewhere can be supportive or complementary, while others might be deleterious or even antagonistic. Some inter-territorial competition is inevitable but not all bad. It depends on what the competition is about – indices of economic growth or the liveability of daily life? Berlin, for example, is a very liveable city but all the usual capitalist-inspired indices of economic success depict it as a backward place. Land values and property prices are lamentably low, which means that people of little means can easily find not bad places in which to live. Developers are miserable. If only New York or London were more like Berlin in that regard!

There have to be, finally, some loosely agreed upon common objectives. Some general guiding norms can be set down. These might include respect for nature, radical egalitarianism in social relations, institutional arrangements based in some sense of common interests, democratic administrative procedures (as opposed to the monetised shams that now exist), labour processes organised by the direct producers, daily life as the free exploration of new kinds of social relations and living arrangements, mental conceptions that focus on self-realisation in service to others and technological and organisational innovations oriented to the pursuit of the common good rather than to supporting militarised power and corporate greed. These could be the co-revolutionary points around which social action could converge and rotate. Of course this is utopian! But so what! We cannot afford not to be.

Suppose the preferred form of social relations is that of radical egalitarianism, between both individuals and self-defined social groups. The case for this presumption arises out of centuries of political struggle in which the principle of equality has animated political action and revolutionary movements, from the Bastille to Tiananmen Square. Radical egalitarianism also grounds an immense literature and the idea seems to transcend many geographical and cultural differences. In the United States, polls show a deep attachment to the principle of equality as the proper foundation for political life and as the bedrock for organising social relations between both individuals and social groups. The extension of civil and political rights to former slaves, to women, to gays, to the handicapped may have taken 200 years, but the claim for progress on these fronts is undeniable, as is the continuing quest for equality not only between individuals but also between social groups. Conversely, the way in which contempt for élites in the US is politically mobilised (and often perverted) derives from this egalitarianism.

While the principle of radical egalitarianism may appear unassailable in itself, problems arise out of the way in which it gets articulated with other spheres of action. The definition of social groups is always contested, for example. While multiculturalism can accommodate the ideal of equality between most self-identified social groups, the one persistent divide that creates the greatest difficulty is that of class. This is so because class is the foundational inequality necessary to the reproduction of capitalism. So the answer of existing political power is either to deny that class exists, or to say that the category is so confusing and complicated (as if the other categories like race and gender are not) as to be analytically useless. In this way, the question of class gets evaded, denied or ignored, whether it be so in hegemonic intellectual constructions of the world (in, say, the field of economics) or in practical politics. Class consciousness, unlike political subjectivities given by race, gender, ethnicity, religion, sexual preference, age, consumer choices and social preferences, is the least discussed and the most actively denied except as some quaint residual from former political times and places (like 'old' Europe).

Clearly, class identities, like racial identities, are multiple and overlapping. I work as a labourer but have a pension fund that invests in the stock market and I own a house that I am improving with sweat equity and which I intend to sell for speculative gain. Does this make the concept of class incoherent? Class is a role, not a label that attaches to persons. We play multiple roles all the time. But we do not say because most of us play the roles of both car drivers and pedestrians that it is impossible to plan a decent city around an analysis of relations between drivers and pedestrians. The role of the capitalist is to use money to command the labour or the assets of others and to use that command to make a profit, to accumulate capital and thereby augment personal command over wealth and power. The relation between the roles of capital and labour need to be confronted and regulated even within capitalism. A revolutionary agenda entails rendering the relation truly redundant as opposed to hidden and opaque. Designing a society without capital accumulation is no different in principle to designing a city without cars. Why can't we all just work alongside each other without any class distinction?

The way radical egalitarianism articulates with other spheres in the co-evolutionary process therefore complicates matters at the same time as it illuminates how capitalism works. When the individual liberty and freedom it promises is mediated through the institutional arrangements of private property and the market, as it is in both liberal theory and practice, then huge inequalities result. As Marx long ago pointed out, the liberal theory of individual rights that originated with John Locke, writing in the seventeenth century, underpins surging inequalities between an emergent class of owners and another class made up of those who have to sell their labour power in order to live. In the neoliberal theory of the Austrian philosopher/economist Friedrich Hayek, writing in the 1940s, this connectivity is tightly coupled: the only way, he argues, to protect radical egalitarianism and individual rights in the face of state violence (that is, fascism and communism) is to install inviolable private property rights at the heart of the social order. This deeply entrenched view has to be challenged head on if capital accumulation and the reproduction of class power are to be effectively challenged. In the field of institutional arrangements, therefore, a wholly new conception of property – of common rather than private property rights – will be required to make radical egalitarianism work in a radically egalitarian way. The struggle over institutional arrangements, then, has to move to the centre of political concerns.

This is so because the radical egalitarianism to which capitalism subscribes in the market place breaks down when we move inside of what Marx called 'the hidden abode' of production. It disappears on the building sites, down the mines, in the fields and in the factories, offices and retail stores. The autonomista movement is quite correct to insist, therefore, that the achievement of radical egalitarianism within the labour process is of paramount importance to the construction of any anti-capitalist alternative. Schemes of autogestion and worker self-management here fit the bill, particularly when interwoven with the other spheres in democratic ways. The same applies when we try to connect principles of radical egalitarianism to the conduct of daily life. When mediated through private property and market arrangements, radical egalitarianism produces homelessness for the poor and gated communities of MacMansions for the rich. That, surely, is not what radical egalitarianism in daily life should mean.

A critique of labour processes and of everyday life shows how the noble principle of radical egalitarianism is impoverished and debased under capitalism by the institutional arrangements with which it is articulated. This finding should not be surprising. Private property and a state dedicated to preserving and protecting that institutional form are crucial pillars to the sustenance of capitalism, even as capitalism depends upon a radical entrepreneurial egalitarianism to survive. The UN Declaration of Human Rights does not protect against unequal outcomes, turning the distinction between civil and political rights on the one hand and economic rights on the other into a minefield of contested claims. 'Between equal rights,' Karl Marx once famously wrote, 'force decides.' Like it or not, class struggle becomes central to the politics of radical egalitarianism.

Ways must be found to cut the link between radical egalitarianism and private property. Bridges must be built with institutions based, say, in the development of common property rights and democratic governance. The emphasis must shift from radical egalitarianism to the institutional sphere. One of the aims of the right to the city movement, to take one example, is to create a new urban commons to displace the excessive privatisations and exclusions (associated as much with state ownership as with private property) that put much of the city off limits to most of the people most of the time.

In like fashion, the connectivity between radical egalitarianism and the organisation of production and the functioning of labour processes has to be rethought along the lines advocated by workers' collectives, autonomista organisations, cooperatives and various other collective forms of social provisioning. The struggle for radical egalitarianism also requires a reconceptualisation of the relation to nature, such that nature is no longer viewed as 'one vast gasoline station', as the German philosopher Martin Heidegger complained in the 1950s, but as a teaming source of life forms to be preserved, nourished, respected and intrinsically valued. Our relation to nature should not be guided by rendering it a commodity like any other, by futures markets on raw materials, minerals, water, pollution credits and the like, nor by the maximisation of rental appropriations and land and resource values, but by the recognition that nature is the one great common to which we all have an equal right but for which we all also bear an immense equal responsibility.

What now seems pie in the sky can, however, take on an entirely different meaning once our mental conceptions and our institutional and administrative arrangements are opened up to transformative political possibilities. So can shifts in mental conceptions change the world?

———

When Her Majesty the Queen paid a visit to the London School of Economics in November 2008, she asked how was it that no economists had seen the financial crisis coming. Six months later, the economists in the British Academy sent her a somewhat apologetic letter. 'In summary, Your Majesty,' it concluded, 'the failure to foresee the timing, extent and severity of the crisis and to head it off, while it had many causes, was principally a failure of the collective imagination of many bright people, both in this country and internationally, to understand the risks to the system as a whole.' It is 'difficult to recall a greater example of wishful thinking combined with hubris,' they observed of the financiers, but went on to admit that everyone – presumably including themselves – had been caught up in a 'psychology of denial'. On the other side of the Atlantic, Robert Samuelson, a columnist for the *Washington Post*, wrote in a somewhat similar vein: 'Here we have the most spectacular economic and financial crisis in decades … and the one group that spends most of its waking hours analyzing the economy basically missed it.' Yet the country's 13,000 or so economists seemed singularly disinclined to engage in 'rigorous self-criticism to explain their lapses'. Samuelson's own conclusion was that the economic theorists were too interested in sophisticated forms of mathematical model-building to bother with the messiness of history and that this messiness had caught them out. The Nobel Prize-winning economist and columnist for *The New York Times* Paul Krugman agreed (sort of!). '[T]he economics profession went astray,' he wrote, 'because economists, as a group, mistook beauty, clad in impressive-looking mathematics, for truth.' The British economist Thomas Palley, in a follow-up open letter to the Queen, was even less generous: the profession of economics had become 'increasingly arrogant, narrow and closed minded', he wrote, and was completely unable 'to come to grips with its sociological failure which produced massive intellectual failure with huge costs for society'.

I do not cite these examples to single out the economists. First off, not all of them failed. Current chair of the White House's National Economic Council Larry Summers, in a telling analysis of the effects of government bail-outs on financial behaviour in the wake of the stock market crash of 1987, clearly saw where the problems of moral hazard might lead, but concluded that the effects of government not standing behind financial institutions would be far worse than the effects of always bailing them out. The policy problem was not to avoid but to constrain moral hazard. Unfortunately, when Treasury Secretary in the late 1990s he forgot his own analysis and promoted exactly the kind of unconstrained moral hazard that he had earlier shown might wreck the economy (a clear case of denial in action). Paul Volcker, past chair of the Federal Reserve, warned of a financial crash within five years back in 2004. But majority opinion sided with Ben Bernanke, before he became chair at the Fed, when he said in 2004 that 'improvements in monetary policy' had reduced 'the extent of economic uncertainty confronting households and firms', thus making recessions 'less frequent and less severe'. Such was the view of the Party (and what a party it was!) of Wall Street. But go tell that to the Indonesians or the Argentinians. It is devoutly to be wished that Bernanke's prognosis in August 2009 that the worst of the crisis is over turns out to be more reliable.

Ideas have consequences and false ideas can have devastating consequences. Policy failures based on erroneous economic thinking played a crucial role in both the run-up to the debacle of the 1930s and in the seeming inability to find an adequate way out. Though there is no universal view among historians and economists as to exactly which policies failed, it is agreed that the knowledge structure through which the crisis was understood needed to be revolutionised. Keynes and his colleagues accomplished that task. But by the mid-1970s it became clear that the Keynesian policy tools were no longer working, at least in the way they were being applied, and it was in this context that monetarism, supply-side theory and the (beautiful) mathematical modelling of micro-economic market behaviours supplanted broad-brush macro-economic Keynesian thinking. The monetarist and narrower neoliberal theoretical frame that dominated after 1980 is now in question.

We need new mental conceptions to understand the world. What might these be and who will produce them, given both the sociological and intellectual malaise that hangs over knowledge production more generally? The deeply entrenched mental conceptions associated with neoliberal theories and the neoliberalisation and corporatisation of the universities has played more than a trivial role in the production of the present crisis. For example, the whole question of what to do about the financial system, the banking sector, the state–finance nexus and the power of private property rights cannot be broached without going outside of the box of conventional thinking. For this to happen will require a revolution in thinking, in places as diverse as the universities, the media and government, as well as within the financial institutions themselves.

Karl Marx, while not in any way inclined to embrace philosophical idealism, also held that ideas are a material force in history. Mental conceptions constitute, after all, one of the seven spheres in his general theory of co-revolutionary change. Autonomous developments and inner conflicts over what mental conceptions shall become hegemonic therefore have an important historical role to play. It was for this reason that Marx wrote *The Communist Manifesto* (with Engels), *Capital* and innumerable other works. These works provide a systematic critique, albeit incomplete, of capitalism and its crisis tendencies. But as Marx also insisted, it was only when these critical ideas carried over into the fields of institutional arrangements, organisational forms, production systems, social relations, technologies and relations to nature that the world would truly change.

Since Marx's goal was to change the world and not merely to understand it, ideas had to be formulated with a certain revolutionary intent. This inevitably meant a conflict with modes of thought more convivial to and useful for the ruling class. The fact that Marx's oppositional ideas have been the targets, particularly in recent years, of repeated repressions and exclusions (to say nothing of bowdlerisations and misrepresentations galore) suggests that they may still be too dangerous for the ruling classes to tolerate. While Keynes repeatedly avowed that he had never read Marx, in the 1930s he was surrounded and influenced by many people like his economist colleague Joan Robinson who had. While many of them objected vociferously to Marx's foundational concepts and his dialectical mode of reasoning, they were acutely aware of and deeply affected by some of his more prescient conclusions. It is fair to say, I think, that the Keynesian theory revolution could not have been accomplished without the subversive presence of Marx lurking in the wings.

The trouble in these times is that most people have no idea who Keynes was and what he really stood for, while understanding of Marx is negligible. The repression of critical and radical currents of thought – or to be more exact the corralling of radicalism within the bounds of multiculturalism and cultural choice – creates a lamentable situation within the academy and beyond, no different in principle to having to ask the bankers who made the mess to clean it up with exactly the same tools as they used to get into it. Broad adhesion to postmodern and post-structuralist ideas which celebrate the particular at the expense of big picture thinking does not help. To be sure, the local and the particular are vitally important and theories that cannot embrace, for example, geographical difference are worse than useless (as I have earlier been at pains to emphasise). But when that fact is used to exclude anything larger than parish politics, then the betrayal of the intellectuals and abrogation of their traditional role become complete. Her Majesty the Queen would, I am sure, love to hear that a huge effort is underway to put the big picture into some sort of copious frame such that all can see it.

But the current crop of academicians, intellectuals and experts in the social sciences and humanities are by and large ill equipped to undertake such a collective task. Few seem predisposed to engage in that self-critical reflection that Robert Samuelson urged upon them. Universities continue to promote the same useless courses on neoclassical economic or rational choice political theory as if nothing has happened and the vaunted business schools simply add a course or two on business ethics or how to make money out of other people's bankruptcies. After all, the crisis arose out of human greed and there is nothing that can be done about that!

The current knowledge structure is clearly dysfunctional and equally clearly illegitimate. The only hope is that a new generation of perceptive students (in the broad sense of all those who seek to know the world) will clearly see that it is so and insist upon changing it. This happened in the 1960s. At various other critical points in history student-inspired movements, recognising the disjunction between what is happening in the world and what they are being taught and fed by the media, were prepared to do something about it. There are signs, from Tehran to Athens and on to many European university campuses of such a movement. How the new generation of students in China will act must surely be of deep concern in the corridors of political power in Beijing.

A youthful, student-led revolutionary movement, with all of its evident uncertainties and problems, is a necessary but not sufficient condition to produce that revolution in mental conceptions that can lead us to a more rational solution to the current problems of endless growth. The first lesson it must learn is that an ethical, non-exploitative and socially just capitalism that redounds to the benefit of all is impossible. It contradicts the very nature of what capital is about.

What would happen if an anti-capitalist movement were constituted out of a broad alliance of the discontented, the alienated, the deprived and the dispossessed? The image of all such people everywhere rising up and demanding and achieving their proper place in economic, social and political life is stirring indeed. It also helps focus on the question of what it is they might demand and what it is that needs to be done.

The discontented and the alienated are made up of all those who, for whatever reason, see the current path of capitalist development as leading to a dead end if not to a catastrophe for humanity. The reasons for thinking so are as varied as they are separately persuasive. Plenty of people, including many scientists, see the looming environmental constraints as insuperable. A steady state global economy and global population has for them to be the long-term aim. A new political economy of nature has to be constructed. This means radical recon-figurations in daily life, in urbanisation as well as in dominant social relations, production systems and in institutional arrangements. It would require great sensitivity to geographical differences. New environments and new geographies would have to be produced to replace the old. The trajectory of technological development would likewise have to change, away from the gargantuan and the militaristic into more 'small is beautiful' and 'less is more' consumerism. All of this would be deeply antagonistic to capitalist compound growth.

Others, nurturing political or moral objections to mass poverty and increasing inequalities, may forge alliances with those opposed to the authoritarian, anti-democratic, money-saturated and carcareal drift of capitalist state policies almost everywhere. There is, in addition, an immense amount of work to be done in the field of social relations, to rid ourselves of racialisation, sexual and gender discriminations and violence against those who are merely different in lifestyle, cultural values, beliefs and daily habits from ourselves. But it is hard to deal with these forms of violence without dealing with the social inequalities that arise in daily life, in labour markets and in labour processes. The class inequalities upon which capital accumulation rests are frequently defined by identities of race, gender, ethnicity, religion and geographical affiliations.

Many alienated intellectuals and cultural workers likewise protest the deadening weight of power relations in the media and in institutions of learning and cultural production that debase the languages of civil discourse, convert knowledge into ceaseless propaganda, politics into nothing more than competing big lies, discourses into special pleading and vehicles for peddling prejudice and hate, and social institutions that should protect the people into cesspools of corruption. These conditions cannot change without the professional intellectuals first getting their own house in order. The great betrayal of the intellectuals who became so complicitous with neoliberal politics from the 1980s onwards has first to be reversed before meaningful alliances can be constructed with the deprived and the dispossessed.

Armed with a theory of co-revolutionary politics, the intellectual wing of the alienated and discontented is in a critical position to deepen the ongoing debate on how to change the course of human development. It can set out the broad picture of the contexts in which the hows and whys of political revolutionary change must occur. The emphasis upon how to understand the dynamics of capitalism and the systemic problems that derive from compound growth can best be articulated from this perspective. Unravelling the enigma of capital, rendering transparent what political power always wants to keep opaque, is crucial to any revolutionary strategy.

But for this to be politically meaningful, the alienated and discontented must join with those whose conditions of labouring and living are most immediately affected by their insertion into the circulation and accumulation of capital only to be deprived and dispossessed of their command not only over their labour but over the material, cultural and natural relations of their own existence.

It is not the place of the alienated and discontented to instruct the deprived and dispossessed as to what they should or should not do. But what we, who constitute the alienated and discontented, can and must do is to identify the underlying roots of the problems that confront us all. Again and again, political movements have constructed alternative spaces in which something seemingly different happens, only to find their alternative quickly re-absorbed into the dominant practices of capitalist reproduction. (Look at the history of workers' cooperatives, participatory budgeting, or whatever.) The conclusion must surely then be that it is the dominant practices that have to be addressed. The clear exposure of how those dominant practices work must be the focus of radical theorising.

There are two broad wings of the deprived and the dispossessed. There are those who are dispossessed of the fruits of their creative powers in a labour process under the command of capital or of a capitalist state. Then there are those who have been deprived of their assets, their access to the means of life, of their history, culture and forms of sociality in order to make space (sometimes quite literally) for capital accumulation.

The first category conjures up the Marxist figure of proletarian subjects struggling mightily to liberate themselves from their chains, constituting themselves as a vanguard in the quest to create socialism or communism. The workers located in the factories and in the mines of industrial capitalism were the ones who really mattered. This was so because their conditions of exploitation were so dramatically obvious to themselves as well as to others as they entered the factory gates or went down the mine. Furthermore, their assembly into common spaces facilitated the rise in class consciousness and their organisation of collective action. They also had the collective power to stop capitalism in its tracks by withdrawing their labour.

This fixation on factory labour as the locus of 'true' class consciousness and revolutionary class struggle has always been too limited, if not misguided (leftists have erroneous ideas, too!). Those working in the forests and fields, in the 'informal sectors' of casual labour in the backstreet sweatshops, in the domestic services or in the service sector more generally, and the vast army of labourers employed in the production of space and of built environments or in the trenches (often literally) of urbanisation cannot be treated as secondary actors. They work under different conditions (often of low-wage, temporary and insecure labour in the case of construction and urbanisation). Their mobility, spatial dispersal and individualised conditions of employment may make it more difficult to construct class solidarities or set up collective forms of organisation. Their political presence is more often marked by spontaneous riots and voluntarist uprisings (such as those that occurred in the Paris *banlieues* in recent times or the *piqueteros* (demonstrators) who erupted into action in Argentina after the country's financial collapse of 2001) rather than persistent organisation. But they are fully conscious of their conditions of exploitation and are deeply alienated by their precarious existence and antagonistic to the often brutal policing of their daily lives by state power.

Now often referred to as 'the precariat' (to emphasise the floating and unstable character of their employment and lifestyles) these workers have always accounted for a large segment of the total labour force. In the advanced capitalist world they have become ever more prominent over the last thirty years because of changing labour relations imposed by neoliberal corporate restructuring and deindustrialisation.

It is wrong to ignore the struggles of all these other workers. Many of the revolutionary movements in capitalism's history have been broadly urban rather than narrowly factory based (the revolutions of 1848 throughout Europe, the Paris Commune of 1871, Leningrad in 1917, the Seattle general strike of 1918, the Tucuman uprising of 1969, as well as Paris, Mexico City and Bangkok in 1968, the Shanghai Commune of 1967, Prague in 1989, Buenos Aires in 2001–2 … the list goes on and on). Even when there were key movements in the factories (the Flint strike in Michigan of the 1930s or the Turin Workers Councils of the 1920s) the organised support in the neighbourhoods played a critical but usually uncelebrated role in the political action (the women's and unemployed support groups in Flint and the communal 'houses of the people' in Turin).

The conventional left has been plain wrong to ignore the social movements occurring outside of the factories and mines. Class consciousness is produced and articulated as much in the streets, bars, pubs, kitchens, chapels, community centres and back yards of working-class neighbourhoods as in the factories. The first two decrees of the Parisian communards in 1871 were, interestingly, the suspension of night work in the bakeries (a labour process question) and a moratorium on rental payments (an urban daily life question). The city is as much a locus of class movements as is the factory and we need to raise our sights to at least this level and scale of political organisation and political practice, in alliance with the wide range of rural and peasant movements, if some grand alliance for revolutionary change is to be constructed.

This brings us to the second grand category of the dispossessed, which is much more complicated in its composition and in its class character. It is largely formed by what I call 'accumulation by dispossession'. As usual, it takes a seemingly infinite variety of forms in different places and times. The list of the deprived and dispossessed is as imposing as it is long. It includes all those peasant and indigenous populations expelled from the land, deprived of access to their natural resources and ways of life by illegal and legal (that is, state-sanctioned), colonial, neo-colonial or imperialist means, and forcibly integrated into market exchange (as opposed to barter and other forms of customary exchange) by forced monetisation and taxation. The conversion of common rights of usage into private property rights in land completes the process. Land itself becomes a commodity. These forms of dispossession, still extant but most strongly represented in the early stages of capitalist development, have many modern equivalents. Capitalists open up spaces for urban redevelopment, for example, by dispossessing low-income populations from high-value spaces at the lowest cost possible. In places without secure private property rights, such as China or the squatter settlements of Asia and Latin America, violent expulsions of low-income populations by state authorities often lead the way with or without modest compensation arrangements. In countries with firmly established private property rights, seizure by eminent domain can be orchestrated by the state on behalf of private capital. By legal and illegal means financial pressures (that is, rising property taxes and rents) are brought to bear on vulnerable populations. It seems sometimes as if there is a systematic plan to expel low-income and unwanted populations from the face of the earth.

The credit system has now become, however, the major modern lever for the extraction of wealth by finance capital from the rest of the population. All manner of predatory practices as well as legal (usurious interest rates on credit cards, foreclosures on businesses by the denial of liquidity at key moments, and the like) can be used to pursue tactics of dispossession that advantage the already rich and powerful. The wave of financialisation that occurred after the mid-1970s has been spectacular for its predatory style. Stock promotions and market manipulations; Ponzi schemes and corporate fraud; asset stripping through mergers and acquisitions; the promotion of levels of debt incumbency that reduce whole populations, even in the advanced capitalist countries, to debt peonage; dispossession of assets (the raiding of pension funds and their decimation by stock and corporate collapses) – all these features are central to what contemporary capitalism is about.

Wholly new mechanisms of accumulation by dispossession have also opened up. The emphasis upon intellectual property rights in the World Trade Organization negotiations (the so-called TRIPS agreement) points to ways in which the patenting and licensing of genetic materials, seed plasmas, and all manner of other products, can now be used against whole populations whose practices have played a crucial role in the development of those materials. Biopiracy is rampant and the pillaging of the world's stockpile of genetic resources is well underway, to the benefit of the pharmaceutical companies. The transformation of cultures, histories and intellectual creativity into commodities for sale entails dispossession both past and present of human creativity. Pop music is notorious for the appropriation and exploitation of grassroots culture and creativity. The monetary losses for the creators involved are, unfortunately, by no means the end of the story. Disruptions of social networks and destruction of social solidarities can be every bit as serious. Loss of social relations is impossible to recompense with a money payment.

Finally we need to note the role of crises. A crisis, after all, is nothing less than a massive phase of dispossession of assets (cultural as well as tangible). To be sure, the rich as well as the poor suffer, as the cases of housing foreclosures and losses from investing with Bernie Madoff's crazy Ponzi scheme show. But this is how wealth and power get redistributed both within and between classes. Devalued capital assets left over from bankruptcies and collapses can be bought up at fire-sale prices by those blessed with liquidity and profitably recycled back into circulation. Surplus capital thus finds a new and fertile terrain for renewed accumulation.

Crises may be, for this reason, orchestrated, managed and controlled to rationalise the irrational system that is capitalism. This is what state-administered austerity programmes, making use of the key levers of interest rates and the credit system, are often all about. Limited crises may be imposed by external force upon one sector or upon a territory. This is what the International Monetary Fund is so expert at doing. The result is the periodic creation of a stock of devalued and, in many instances, undervalued assets in some part of the world, which can be put to profitable use by those with capital surpluses that lack opportunities elsewhere. This is what happened in east and south-east Asia in 1997–8, in Russia in 1998 and in Argentina in 2001–2. And this is what got out of hand in 2008–9.

Deliberate provocation of crises by state policies and collective corporate actions is a dangerous game. While there is no evidence of active and narrow conspiracies to create such crises, there are plenty of influential 'Chicago School' macro-economists and economic policy makers around the world, along with all sorts of entrepreneurial opportunists, who believe that a good bout of creative destruction is required now and again for capitalism to survive and for the capitalist class to be reformed. They hold that attempts by governments to ward off crises with stimulus packages and the like are profoundly misguided. Better by far, they say, to let a market-led 'structural adjustment' process (of the sort typically mandated by the IMF) do its work. Such medicine is necessary to keep capitalism economically healthy. The closer capitalism gets to death's door, the more painful the cure. The trick, of course, is not to let the patient die.

———

The political unification of diverse struggles within the labour movement and among those whose cultural as well as political-economic assets have been dispossessed appears to be crucial for any movement to change the course of human history. The dream would be a grand alliance of all the deprived and the dispossessed every-where. The aim would be to control the organisation, production and distribution of the surplus product for the long-term benefit of all.

There are two preliminary difficulties with this idea that must be confronted head on. Many dispossessions have little directly to do with capital accumulation. They do not necessarily lead to anti-capitalist politics. The ethnic cleansings in the former Yugoslavia, the religious cleansings during the Northern Ireland emergency or during the anti-Muslim riots in Mumbai in the early 1990s and the Israeli dispossession of Palestinian land and water rights are all examples of this. The colonisation of urban neighbourhoods by immigrants, by lesbians and gays or by people of a different colour often displaces older residents who fight against the dispossessions that may arise. While market forces and changing property values may play an instrumental or ancillary role, the political struggles that ensue are over who likes or dislikes who and who has the right to live where on our increasingly crowded planet. Questions of security, fear of others, social preferences and prejudices all play their part in the fluid conflicts between social groups over the control of space and over access to valued assets. Social groups and individuals establish a proprietary sense of ownership over and belonging to a particular space. The corollary is widespread fear of dispossession.

Not all insurgent movements against dispossession are anti-capitalist. An older generation of mainly white male workers in the US, for example, are incensed at what they consider to be the rising power of minorities, immigrants, gays and feminists, aided and abetted by arrogant intellectual ('coastal) élites and greedy and ungodly Wall Street bankers who are generally perceived (wrongly) to be Jewish. Radical right-wing and armed militia movements of the sort that nurtured Timothy McVeigh of Oklahoma bombing fame have revived since Obama's election. They would plainly not join some grand anti-capitalist struggle (even though they are express-ing antagonisms to bankers, corporations and élites and hatred for the Federal Reserve). They bear witness to a struggle on the part of those who feel alienated and dispossessed to repossess the country that they love by any means.

Such social tensions offer possibilities for capitalist exploitation. In US cities in the 1960s the practice of blockbusting neighbourhoods was widespread (it still persists). The idea was to introduce a black family into an all-white neighbourhood in the hope of stimulating white fear and white flight. Falling property values created oppor-tunities for speculators to purchase housing cheaply before selling dear to minority populations. The responses of the threatened white populations varied from violent resistance (such as the firebombing of the home of any black family who tried to move in) through to more moderate attempts (sometimes mandated by civil rights laws) to integrate as peacefully as possible.

The second big problem is that some dispossessions are either necessary or progressive. Any revolutionary movement has to come up with a way to dispossess capitalists of their property, wealth and powers. The whole historical geography of dispossessions under capitalism has been riddled with ambivalences and contradictions. While the class violence involved in the rise of capitalism may have been abhorrent, the positive side to the capitalist revolution was that it dispossessed arbitrary feudal institutions (such as the monarchy and the Church) and their powers, liberated creative energies, opened up new spaces and knitted the world closer together through exchange relations, opened up society to strong currents of technological and organisational change, overcame a world based on superstition and ignorance and replaced it with an enlightened science with the potentiality to liberate all of humanity from material want and need. None of this could have occurred without someone somewhere being dispossessed.

It achieved all of this at a huge social and environmental cost (made much of by critics in recent years). But it was nevertheless possible to view accumulation by dispossession (or what Marx called 'primitive accumulation') as a necessary though ugly stage through which the social order had to go in order to arrive at a state where both capitalism and some alternative called socialism or communism might be possible. Marx for one placed little if any value on the social forms destroyed by original accumulation and he did not argue, as some do now, for any restoration of pre-capitalist social relations or productive forms. It was for socialism and communism to build upon the progressive aspects of capitalist development. These progressive aspects included movements for land reform, the rise of democratic forms of government (always sullied by the role of money power), freedom of information (always contingent but nevertheless vital) and of information and of expression, and the creation of rights civil and legal.

While struggles against dispossession can form a seedbed of discontent for insurgent movements, the point of revolutionary politics is not to protect the ancient order but to attack directly the class relations and capitalist forms of state power.

Revolutionary transformations cannot be accomplished without at the very minimum our changing our ideas, abandoning our cherished beliefs and prejudices, giving up various daily comforts and rights, submitting to some new daily regimen, changing our social and political roles, reassigning our rights, duties and responsibilities, and altering our behaviours to better conform to collective needs and a common will. The world around us – our geographies – must be radically reshaped, as must our social relations, the relation to nature and all of the other spheres of action in the co-revolutionary process. It is understandable, to some degree, that many prefer a politics of denial to a politics of active confrontation with all of this.

It would also be comforting to think that all of this could be accomplished pacifically and voluntarily, that we would dispossess ourselves, strip ourselves bare, as it were, of all that we now possess that stands in the way of the creation of a more socially just, steady-state social order. But it would be disingenuous to imagine that this could be so, that no active struggle would be involved, including some degree of violence. Capitalism came into the world, as Marx once put it, bathed in blood and fire. Although it might be possible to do a better job of getting out from under it than getting into it, the odds are heavily against any purely pacific passage to the promised land.

The recognition that dispossession may be a necessary precursor to more positive changes raises the whole question of the politics of dispossession under socialism and communism. It was, within the Marxist/communist revolutionary tradition, often deemed necessary to organise dispossessions in order to implement programmes of modernisation in those countries that had not gone through the initiation into capitalist development. This sometimes entailed appalling violence, as with Stalin's forced collectivisation of agriculture in the Soviet Union (the elimination of the kulaks). These policies were hardly great success stories, precipitating great tragedies such as the grand famine caused by Mao's Great Leap Forward in China (which temporarily halted the otherwise rapid increase in life expectancies) and sparking political resistance that was in some instances ruthlessly crushed.

Insurgent movements against dispossession other than in the labour process have therefore in recent times generally taken an anti-communist path. This has sometimes been ideological but in other instances simply for pragmatic and organisational reasons, deriving from the very nature of what such struggles were and are about. The variety of struggles against the capitalist forms of dispossession was and is simply stunning. It is hard to even imagine connections between them. The struggles of the Ogoni people in the Niger delta against what they see as the degradation of their lands by Shell Oil; peasant movements against biopiracy and land grabbing; struggles against genetically modified foods and for the authenticity of local production systems; fights to preserve access for indigenous populations to forest reserves, while curbing the activities of timber companies; political struggles against privatisation; movements to procure labour rights or women's rights in developing countries; campaigns to protect biodiversity and to prevent habitat destruction; hundreds of protests against IMF-imposed austerity programmes and long-drawn-out struggles against World Bank-backed dam construction projects in India and Latin America: these have all been part of a volatile mix of protest movements that have swept the world and increasingly grabbed the headlines since the 1980s. These movements and revolts have been frequently crushed with ferocious violence, for the most part by state powers acting in the name of 'order and stability'. Client states, supported militarily or in some instances with special forces trained by the major military apparatuses (led by the US with Britain and France playing a minor role), took the lead in a system of repressions and liquidations to ruthlessly check activist movements challenging accumulation by dispossession.

———

Movements against dispossession of both sorts are widespread but inchoate, both geographically and in their organising principles and political objectives. They often exhibit internal contradictions, as, for example, when indigenous populations claim back rights in areas that environmental groups regard as crucial to protect biodiversity. And partly because of the distinctive geographical conditions that give rise to such movements, their political orientation and modes of organisation also differ markedly. The Zapatista rebels in Mexico, frustrated at the loss of control over their own lands and local resources and the lack of respect for their cultural history, did not seek to take over state power or accomplish a political revolution. They sought instead to work through the whole of civil society in a more open and fluid search for alternatives that would look to answer to their specific needs as a cultural formation and to restore their own sense of dignity and self-respect. The movement avoided avant-gardism and refused to take on the role of a political party. It preferred instead to remain a movement within the state, seeking to form a political power bloc in which indigenous cultures would be central rather than peripheral to political power arrangements. It sought thereby to accomplish something akin to a passive revolution within the territorial logic of power commanded by the Mexican state.

The general effect of such movements has been to shift the terrain of political organisation away from traditional political parties and labour organising in the factories (though that still goes on, of course) into what was bound to be in aggregate a less focused political dynamic of social action across the whole spectrum of civil society. What emerges is a very different organising model from that constructed historically around the labour movement. The two forms of dispossession thus spawn conflicting aspirations and organisational forms. What the broader movement across civil society loses in focus it gains in terms of relevance, precisely because it connects so directly to the politics of daily life in specific geographical contexts.

There are various broad fractious currents of thought on the left as to how to address the problems that now confront us. There is, first of all, the usual sectarianism stemming from the history of radical action and the articulations of left-wing political theory. Curiously, the one place where amnesia is not so prevalent is within the left itself (the splits between anarchists and Marxists that occurred back in the 1870s, between Trotskyists, Maoists and orthodox communists, between the centralisers who want to command the state and the anti-statist autonomists and anarchists). The arguments are so bitter and so fractious as to sometimes make one think that more amnesia might be a good thing. But beyond these traditional revolutionary sects and political factions, the whole field of political action has undergone a radical transformation since the mid-1970s. The terrain of political struggle and of political possibilities has shifted, both geographically and organisationally.

There are now vast numbers of non-governmental organisations which play a political role that was scarcely visible before the mid-1970s. Funded by both state and private interests, populated often by idealist thinkers and organisers (they constitute a vast employment programme), and for the most part dedicated to single-issue questions (environment, poverty, women's rights, anti-slavery and trafficking work, etc.), they refrain from straight anti-capitalist politics even as they espouse progressive ideas and causes. In some instances, however, they are actively neoliberal, engaging in privatisation of state welfare functions or fostering institutional reforms to facilitate market integration of marginalised populations (micro-credit and microfinance schemes for low income populations are a classic example of this).

While there are many radical and dedicated practitioners in this NGO world, their work is at best ameliorative. Collectively, they have a spotty record of progressive achievements, although in certain arenas such as women's rights, health care and environmental preservation they can reasonably claim to have made major contributions to human betterment. But revolutionary change by NGO is impossible. They are too constrained by the political and policy stances of their donors. So even though, in supporting local empowerment, they help open up spaces where anti-capitalist alternatives become possible, and even support experimentation with such alternatives, they do nothing to prevent the re-absorption of these alternatives into the dominant capitalist practice; they even encourage it. The collective power of NGOs in these times is reflected in the dominant role they play in the World Social Forum, where attempts to forge a global justice movement, a global alternative to neoliberalism, have been concentrated over the last ten years.

The second broad wing of opposition arises out of anarchist, autonomist and grassroots organisations (GROs) which refuse outside funding even as some of them do rely upon some alternative institutional base (such as the Catholic Church, with its 'base community' initiatives in Latin America or broader church sponsorship of political mobilisation in the inner cities of the United States). This group is far from homogeneous (indeed there are bitter disputes among them, pitting, for example, social anarchists against those they scathingly refer to as mere 'lifestyle' anarchists). There is, however, a common antipathy to negotiation with state power and an emphasis upon civil society as the sphere where change can be accomplished. The self-organizing powers of people in the daily situations in which they live has to be the basis for any anti-capitalist alternative. Horizontal networking is their preferred organising model; so-called 'solidarity economies' based on bartering, collectives and local production systems is their preferred political economic form. They typically oppose the idea that any central direction might be necessary and reject hierarchical social relations or hierarchical political power structures along with conventional political parties. Organisations of this sort can be found everywhere and in some places have achieved a high degree of political prominence. Some of them are radically anti-capitalist in their stance and espouse revolutionary objectives and in some instances are prepared to advocate sabotage and other forms of disruption (shades of the Red Brigade in Italy, the Baader-Meinhof Gang in Germany and the Weather Underground in the United States in the 1970s). But, leaving aside their more violent fringes, the effectiveness of all these movements is limited by their reluctance and inability to scale-up their activism into organisational forms capable of confronting global problems. The presumption that local action is the only meaningful level of change and that anything that smacks of hierarchy is anti-revolutionary is self-defeating when it comes to larger questions. Yet these movements are unquestionably providing a widespread base for experimentation with anti-capitalist politics.

The third broad trend is given by the transformation that has been occurring in traditional labour organising and left political parties, varying from social democratic traditions to more radical Trotskyist and communist forms of political party organisation. This trend is not hostile to the conquest of state power or hierarchical forms of organisation. Indeed, it regards the latter as necessary to the integration of political organisation across a variety of political scales. In the years when social democracy was hegemonic in Europe and even influential in the United States, state control over the distribution of the surplus became a crucial tool to diminish inequalities. The failure to take social control over the production of surpluses and thereby really challenge the power of the capitalist class was the Achilles heel of this political system. However, we should not forget the advances that it made, even if it is clear now that it is insufficient to go back to such a political model with its social welfarism and Keynesian economics.

Both organised labour and left political parties have taken some hard hits in the advanced capitalist world over the last thirty years. Both have either been convinced or coerced into broad support for neoliberalisation, albeit with a somewhat more human face. One way to look upon neoliberalism, as was earlier noted, is as a grand and quite revolutionary movement (led by that self-proclaimed revolutionary figure, Margaret Thatcher) to privatise the surpluses, or at least prevent their further socialisation.

While there are some signs of recovery of both labour organizing and left politics (as opposed to the 'third way' celebrated by New Labour in Britain under Tony Blair and disastrously copied by many social democratic parties in Europe), along with signs of the emergence of more radical political parties in different parts of the world, the exclusive reliance upon a vanguard of workers is now in question, as is the ability of those leftist parties that have gained some access to political power to have a substantive impact upon the development of capitalism and to cope with the troubled dynamics of crisis-prone accumulation. The performance of the German Green Party in power has hardly been stellar relative to their political stance out of power, while social democratic parties have lost their way entirely as a true political force. But left political parties and labour unions are significant still and their takeover of aspects of state power, as with the workers' party in Brazil or the Bolivarian movement in Venezuela, has had a clear impact on left thinking, not only in Latin America. The complicated problem of how to interpret the role of the Communist Party in China and what its future policies might be is not easily resolved either.

The co-revolutionary theory laid out earlier would suggest that there is no way that an anti-capitalist social order can be constructed without seizing state power, radically transforming it and reworking the constitutional and institutional framework that currently supports private property, the market system and endless capital accumulation. Inter-state competition and geoeconomic and geopolitical struggles over everything from trade and money to questions of hegemony are also either far too significant to be left to local social movements or cast aside as too big to contemplate. How the architecture of the state–finance nexus is to be reworked, along with the pressing question of the common measure of value given by money, cannot be ignored in the quest to construct alternatives to capitalist political economy. To ignore the state and the dynamics of the inter-state system is therefore a ridiculous idea for any anti-capitalist revolutionary movement to accept.

The fourth broad trend is constituted by all the social movements that are not so much guided by any particular political philosophy or leanings but by the pragmatic need to resist displacement and dispossession (through gentrification, industrial development, dam construction, water privatisation, the dismantling of social services and public educational opportunities, or whatever). In this instance the focus on daily life in the city, town, village or wherever provides a material base for political organising against the threats that state policies and capitalist interests invariably pose to vulnerable populations.

Again, there is a vast array of social movements of this sort, some of which can become radicalised over time as they come to realise more and more that the problems are systemic rather than particular and local. The bringing-together of such social movements into alliances on the land (like the landless movement in Brazil or peasants mobilising against land and resource grabs by capitalist corporations in India) or in urban contexts (the right to the city movements in Brazil and now the United States) suggest the way may be open to create broader alliances to discuss and confront the systemic forces that underpin the particularities of gentrification, dam construction, privatisation or whatever. Driven by pragmatism rather than by ideological preconceptions, these movements nevertheless can arrive at systemic understandings out of their own experience. To the degree that many of them exist in the same space, such as within the metropolis, they can (as supposedly happened with the factory workers in the early stages of the industrial revolution) make common cause and begin to forge, on the basis of their own experience, a consciousness of how capitalism works and what it is that might be done collectively. This is the terrain where the figure of the 'organic intellectual' leader, made so much of in the early twentieth-century Marxist writer Antonio Gramsci's work, the autodidact who comes to understand the world first hand through bitter experiences, but shapes his or her understanding of capitalism more generally, has a great deal to say. To listen to the peasant leaders of the MST in Brazil or the leaders of the anti-corporate land grab movement in India is a privileged education. In this instance the task of the educated discontented is to magnify the subaltern voice so that attention can be paid to the circumstances of exploitation and repression and the answers that can be shaped into an anti-capitalist programme.

The fifth epicentre for social change lies with the emancipatory movements around questions of identity – women, children, gays, racial, ethnic and religious minorities all demanding an equal place in the sun. The movements claiming emancipation on each of these issues are geographically uneven and often geographically divided in terms of needs and aspirations. But global conferences on women's rights (Nairobi in 1985, which led to the Beijing declaration of 1995) and anti-racism (the far more contentious conference in Durban in 2009) are attempting to find common ground and there is no question that social relations are changing along all of these dimensions, at least in some parts of the world. When cast in narrow essentialist terms, these movements can appear to be antagonistic to class struggle. Certainly within much of the academy they have taken priority of place at the expense of class analysis and political economy. But the feminisation of the global labour force, the feminisation of poverty almost everywhere and the use of gender disparities as a means of labour control make the emancipation and eventual liberation of women from their repressions a necessary condition for class struggle to sharpen its focus. The same observation applies to all the other identity forms where discrimination or outright repression can be found. Racism and the oppression of women and children were foundational in the rise of capitalism. But capitalism as currently constituted can in principle survive without these forms of discrimination and oppression, though its political ability to do so will be severely curtailed, if not mortally wounded, in the face of a more unified class force. The modest embrace of multiculturalism and women's rights within the corporate world, particularly in the United States, provides some evidence of capitalism's accommodation of these dimensions of social change, even as it re-emphasises the salience of class divisions as the principle dimension for political action.

These five broad tendencies are not mutually exclusive or exhaustive of organisational templates for political action. Some organisations neatly combine aspects of all five tendencies. But there is a lot of work to be done to coalesce these various tendencies around the underlying question: can the world change materially, socially, mentally and politically in such a way as to confront not only the dire state of social and natural relations in so many parts, but also the perpetuation of endless compound growth? This is the question that the discontented must insist upon asking, again and again, even as they learn from those who experience the pain directly and who are so adept at organising resistances to the dire consequences of compound growth on the ground.

———

Communists, Marx and Engels averred in their original conception laid out in *The Communist Manifesto*, have no political party. They simply constitute themselves at all times and in all places as those who understand the limits, failings and destructive tendencies of the capitalist order, as well as the innumerable ideological masks and false legitimations that capitalists and their apologists (particularly in the media) produce in order to perpetuate their singular class power. Communists are all those who work incessantly to produce a different future to that which capitalism portends. This is an interesting definition. While traditional institutionalised communism is as good as dead and buried, there are by this definition millions of *de facto* communists active among us, willing to act upon their understandings, ready to creatively pursue anti-capitalist imperatives. If, as the alternative globalisation movement of the late 1990s declared, 'another world is possible', then why not also say 'another communism is possible'? The current circumstances of capitalist development demand something of this sort, if fundamental change is to be achieved.

Communism is, unfortunately, such a loaded term as to be hard to re-introduce, as some now want to do, into political discourse. In the United States it would prove much more difficult than in, say, France, Italy, Brazil or even central Europe. But in a way the name does not matter. Perhaps we should just define the movement, our movement, as anti-capitalist or call ourselves the Party of Indignation, ready to fight and defeat the Party of Wall Street and its acolytes and apologists everywhere, and leave it at that. The struggle for survival with justice not only continues; it begins anew. As indignation and moral outrage build around the economy of dispossession that so redounds to the benefit of a seemingly all-powerful capitalist class, so disparate political movements necessarily begin to merge, transcending barriers of space and time.

To understand the political necessity of this requires first that the enigma of capital be unravelled. Once its mask is torn off and its mysteries have been laid bare, it is easier to see what has to be done and why, and how to set about doing it. Capitalism will never fall on its own. It will have to be pushed. The accumulation of capital will never cease. It will have to be stopped. The capitalist class will never willingly surrender its power. It will have to be dispossessed.

To do what has to be done will take tenacity and determination, patience and cunning, along with fierce political commitments born out of moral outrage at what exploitative compound growth is doing to all facets of life, human and otherwise, on planet earth. Political mobilisations sufficient to such a task have occurred in the past. They can and will surely come again. We are, I think, past due.

Afterword

There's class warfare, all right, but it's my class, the rich class, that's making war and we're winning.

Warren Buffett, 'The Sage of Omaha'

When policy makers and expert economists seem so blithely unaware of the crisis prone character of capitalism, when they so cheerfully ignore the warning signs building up all around them and dub the years of volatility and turmoil since the 1990s as 'the great moderation', then the folk on Main Street can be forgiven for having so little understanding of what has hit them when a crisis breaks, and so little trust in the expert explanations they are offered. Now that the economists have confessed to not understanding the 'systemic risks' inherent in free market capitalism, they still seem to have no idea what they are or what to do about them. A former chief economist of the International Monetary Fund says, 'We sort of know vaguely what systemic risk is and what factors might relate to it. But to argue that it is a well-developed science at this point is overstating the fact.' In a formal paper published in the summer of 2010, the IMF described the study of systemic risk as 'in its infancy'. In Marxian theory (as opposed to myopic neoclassical or financial economic theory), 'systemic risk' translates into the fundamental contradictions of capital accumulation. The IMF could save itself a lot of trouble by studying it. In this book I tried to illuminate, as clearly as I could, the reasons for the crisis-prone character of capitalism, the role of crises (such as the one we are still going through) in the reproduction of capitalism and the long-term systemic risks that capital poses to life on planet earth.

Capital, I concluded, never solves its crisis tendencies, it merely moves them around. It does so in a double sense, from one part of the world to another and from one kind of problem to another. Thus the crisis that broke out primarily in the housing markets of the south and the south-west of the United States (along with those of the United Kingdom, Ireland and Spain) impacted financial markets in New York City and London before 'going global' and threatening global trade almost everywhere (after passing through Icelandic banks, Dubai World, the Latvian bankruptcy, the Californian budgetary disaster and the Greek and then the Irish debt crises). While there are some national banking systems, such as those of Ireland, Portugal and Spain, that will or may require further bail-outs given the high volume of toxic assets left over from the fictitious property market booms that preceded the crisis, the global financial system appears to have been stabilised by a patchwork of government interventions. The effect has been to shift the brunt of the crisis from the banks to state debt. In North America and Europe the response to the swelling state debt has been to propose and then implement draconian austerity measures to reduce the debt by cutting state services and threatening public well-being.

In some parts of the world, however, the crisis has been long gone. Even in the United States the recession was declared statistically over in June 2009. Ask about 'the economic crisis' in Brazil, Argentina, India or Australia and the answer will be, 'What crisis? That's your problem, not ours.' Geographical myopia is, of course, common enough. While many in western Europe and North America gave generously to the victims of the tsunami that flashed across the Indian Ocean in December 2004, they paid no mind to the 15 million Indonesians who lost their jobs in the economic collapse of 1997–8 or the huge increase in unemployment that surged in Argentina in their crisis of 2001–2. Those were their economic crises and their fault, not ours.

At the time of writing (December 2010) there is a deep sense as well as plenty of tangible evidence that the crisis is still with us in the United States and much of Europe. Unemployment is the big problem. A joint discussion document issued by the IMF and the International Labour Organisation in September of 2010 estimated the net global loss of jobs during the recession of 2007–9 to be 30 million. Of the 20 million that could be documented through official statistics, three-quarters were located in the advanced economies, with the United States accounting for 7.5 million, Spain for 2.7 million and the United Kingdom for 0.9 million. Net job losses were much less marked in emerging market economies, with China reporting 3 million which, given the huge size of its labour market, has been serious but not catastrophic. Curiously, small job increases were recorded in some low-income countries (in part due to the movement of jobs out of China towards even cheaper labour in south and south-east Asia).

The financial crisis that began in 2007 has had few long-lasting effects in many parts of the world. The revival of growth in China (more than 10 per cent in 2010, having fallen briefly as low as 6 per cent in early 2009) and India (with growth rates that may well soon outpace China's) is paralleled by strong growth in all those areas of the world that are oriented to the China trade. Countries supplying raw materials to China, such as Australia and Chile, came through the crisis relatively unscathed. In other instances adjustments have occurred in trading patterns, such as the ten-fold increase in trade with China on the part of Brazil and Argentina since 2000. The result has been the vigorous resumption of economic growth in various parts of Latin America (close to 8 per cent in both Argentina and Brazil), albeit at the price of turning much of the land into one vast soy bean plantation, with potentially harmful environmental consequences. Those countries exporting high-tech equipment to China, Germany in particular, have also done rather well.

Unemployment and job losses are highly concentrated in the United States and unevenly throughout Europe. Official unemployment rates increased by 11 percentage points in Spain, 9 in Ireland,

5 in the United States and between 3 and 4 in Greece, Portugal, Spain, the United Kingdom, Sweden and Italy. But the unemployment rate has remained low in the Netherlands, actually dropped in Germany (in part because of their policy of reducing working hours rather than laying off workers when faced with slumping markets) and barely budged in South Korea and China (in spite of the 3 million job losses reported in 2008).

The lingering persistence of job losses in the United States mimics the way that the previous two recessions there (1990–92 and 2001–2) were followed by so-called 'jobless recoveries' – except that this one seems more like a 'joblessness-creating recovery'. Furthermore, the proportion of unemployed deemed 'long-term' (out of work for more than six months), which never exceeded a quarter in the past, now accounts for more than half the people out of work. When discouraged workers and workers in unsatisfactory temporary employment are added to the official unemployment rate of close to 10 per cent, then nearly one-fifth of the US population lacks adequate work. The existence of such a vast labour reserve of unemployed workers has put downward pressure on wage rates and working conditions for those who are employed. The negotiated bankruptcy of General Motors led to the creation of a two-tier labour system in which people joining the labour force agree to lower wages and benefits than those who are already employed. This two-tier system has now spread throughout much of the US. Profits have consequently revived at what is described in the business press as a 'breakneck pace' since their low point at the end of 2008, helping to spark also a recovery in the stock market as well as in the profligate lifestyles of the Wall Streeters. But all of this has been at the expense of a further deepening of the wage repression that began back in the late 1970s. The wage share in the national income has continued to decline even as the profit share soars to pre-crisis levels. A collateral effect of unemployment is that the housing foreclosures that triggered the crash in 2007 continue unabated and the toxicity of asset portfolios grows worse. The monthly rate of initiated foreclosure proceedings fell from a high of

142,000 in April 2009 to just over 100,000 in August 2010, but the number of actual repossessions reached an all-time high of 95,000 in that same month. The financial institutions assumed legal title to over a million dwellings in 2010. Small wonder that consumer confidence has been slow to recover and that the consumer market stays in the doldrums.

Is this state of affairs in the United States (paralleled throughout many parts of Europe) an economic necessity or a political choice? The answer is a bit of both. But the political side of it is now more blatant than it was last year. Throughout much of the advanced capitalist world, following an initial flirtation with a revival of Keynesianism, the sovereign debt crisis has become an excuse for the capitalist class to dismantle what is left of the welfare state through a politics of austerity. Capital has always had trouble internalising the costs of social reproduction (the care of the young, the ill, the maimed and the aged, the costs of social security, education and health care). During the 1950s and 1960s many of these social costs were internalised either directly (corporate health care plans and pensions) or indirectly (tax-financed services to the population at large). But the whole period of neoliberal capitalism after the mid-1970s, has been marked by a struggle by capital to shed itself of such burdens, leaving it to populations to find their own ways to procure and pay for these services. How we reproduce ourselves is, we have been told by powerful right-wing voices in politics and the media, a matter of personal responsibility, not state obligation.

Some major areas have yet to be privatised – social security and state old age pensions for starters (though Chile long ago privatised both). The current emphasis upon austerity is, therefore, a further step down this path towards the personalisation of the costs of social reproduction. The assault on the well-being of the population has put the state on a collision course not only with the last redoubts of trade union power in many countries, the public sector unions, but also with those populations most directly dependent upon state provision (such as students, from Athens to Paris, London and Berkeley). The assault has provoked stirrings of revolt such that even the IMF has tried to warn the more gung-ho right-wing governments that they risk provoking major social unrest. The burgeoning signs of unrest in Europe beginning in the autumn of 2010 suggest that the IMF might be right.

The economic case for austerity is murky at best and at worst clearly counter-productive. It is estimated by responsible analysts that the measures announced by the newly elected Conservative-led British government in October 2010 will throw around 1.6 million people out of work in the next three years – close to 500,000 in the public sector and the remaining million primarily in that part of the private sector that services government contracts. The idea that the private sector, unaided, will pick up the slack, when the best it has been able to do is to create jobs at around 300,000 per year in Britain, is wishful thinking, to put it mildly. The recent Republican victory in the House of Representatives in the US ensures that the so-called 'deficit hawks' will heavily influence all things except for the renewal of deficit-busting huge tax breaks for the richest sectors of the population. But even when the Democrats held all the reins of power they had no stomach to deny the deficit hawks in order to help the people. The 'Party of Wall Street', as I call it, is far too powerful for that, given that it finances the elections of both Democrats and Republicans. And as time goes on it is sadly all too clear that President Obama is of that party too.

What is being done to the United States today is in effect what has been done time and time again since the early 1980s, both at home and abroad. In 1982, for example, a debt crisis broke out in many developing countries, with Mexico as the poster child that had made the mistake of borrowing heavily from the New York invest-ment bankers. Defaulting on its debt would have destroyed the New York bankers, so the US Treasury and the IMF bailed out Mexico to pay off the bankers but in so doing administered austerity measures in the country so severe that they resulted in a 25 per cent decline in standards of living. Rescue the banks and sock it to the people has been the standard recipe ever since. This is what happened to Greece in early 2010 and Ireland in the autumn. In Greece's case it was the German and French banks which were at risk, while in Ireland the bank exposure was mainly British. The decline in the standard of living of the Greek population has been palpable and Ireland follows not far behind. Last year the banks were saved in the United States, so now it is time for the federal government to sock it to the people even more than is already being done in California, which, with the ninth largest public budget in the world, has been prevented from going the way of Greece and Ireland only by savage state-wide budget cuts and federal transfers of tax revenues to support social security, Medicare and the like. The rate at which investors began to withdraw from the tax-exempt bond market for local and state government debt in December of 2010 suggests, however, that this may be the locus for the next wave of the financial crisis in the United States. Whether or not there will be mass defaults of municipal and state governments will depend on the responses of the federal government and the Federal Reserve. But a crisis of this sort will be far harder to resolve, in part because of its depth and width and in part for political reasons, than was the case with the banking sector.

Almost certainly it would have been better for Greece and Ireland to default. Then the banks and the bond holders would have shared the pain with the people. The bond holders would have 'taken a hair cut', as the saying goes in financial circles. Argentina effectively defaulted in 2004. Dire consequence were threatened – 'You will never see international investors again', it was told – but within a couple of years foreign investors, desperate to find profitable markets for their surplus capital, were feeding an economic boom in the country that lasted with very few dents even through the rocky times of 2007–9. Austerity in both Greece and Ireland has blocked those countries' economic recovery, worsened their debt situation and pointed the way to a downward spiral of never-ending austerity. In the light of that experience, influential voices in the mainstream media (including a lead editorial in *The New York Times*) have finally begun to wonder whether default (politely known as 'restructuring') might not be a better option. Even Angela Merkel, the German chancellor, has signalled that bond holder 'hair cuts' are to be expected after 2013, when the European bail-out fund winds down. The effect would be to shift at least a part of the burden of the crisis back towards the banks, where in any case many members of the public believe it belongs, particularly given the penchant of the bankers to shamelessly pay themselves gargantuan bonuses. In the Greek case it would also shift the burden back geographically to the French and rather weak German banking systems and ultimately to the French and German governments, where many Greeks also think it belongs.

But socking it to the people for the benefit of big capital has been on the agenda from the right wing and the capitalist class all along. President Ronald Reagan ran up a huge deficit in the 1980s through an arms race with the Soviet Union. He also cut the tax rate on the highest earning Americans from 72 per cent to close to 30 per cent. As his budget director David Stockman later confessed, the plan was to run up the debt and then use that as an excuse to diminish or demolish social protections and social programmes. President George Bush the younger, another Republican with the backing of a Republican-controlled Congress, followed Reagan's example to the letter. He turned what had been a budget surplus in the late 1990s into a huge deficit between 2001 and 2009, by fighting two wars of choice, passing a Medicare drug package that was a gift to big pharma and delivering massive tax cuts to the wealthy. The tax cut, the Bush folk said, would pay for itself through accelerating investment. It did not (it mostly added to speculation). The wars, it was said, would also pay for themselves with Iraqi oil. When it was estimated back in 2003 that the war might cost $200 billion the estimators were savagely attacked as unpatriotic naysayers. Now the wars have cost 2 trillion dollars or more, but no one minded in the Bush years because, as Vice President Dick Cheney was fond of saying, 'Reagan taught us deficits do not matter!'

They do matter, of course, but the best way to reduce them is to stimulate growth. A significant portion of current deficits are due to revenue reductions consequent upon the recession and surging unemployment. Compared to that, the net cost of the bail-outs has not been that great. In some instances the bail-out money is being returned with interest. Revive the economy and solve the economic growth problem and you are well on the way to curing the deficit problem through rising revenues (as was proven by the boom years of the 1990s under Clinton). Austerity politics, as I have already argued, take the economy in the opposite direction. The present economic difficulties in both the US and Britain, as well as throughout Europe, are essentially being deepened for a political reason rather than out of economic necessity. That political reason is the desire to have done with capital's responsibility to cover costs of social reproduction.

The assault upon the social well-being of the masses derives from the incessant drive to preserve and enhance the wealth of the already well-to-do. This is what Warren Buffett clearly acknowledges. Income inequalities have soared in the United States since the 1970s to the point where the bottom 90 per cent of Americans now own just 29 per cent of the wealth, leaving 10 per cent to control the rest and the top 1 per cent owning 34 per cent of wealth and garnering 24 per cent of income (three times more than they had in 1970). All the signs are that, with some exceptions, the wealthiest have not been hurt too much by recent events. Leading hedge fund managers have actually augmented their power significantly (George Soros and John Paulson earned $3 billion each in 2008, for example). In the midst of an immense public clamour for austerity and cutting the deficit, the Republicans successfully fought to extend the Bush tax cuts. This will gift $370,000 a year each to the wealthiest 0.1 per cent of US tax payers and increase the deficit by $700 billion over the next ten years. Meanwhile, some municipalities have closed down their police and fire departments and in certain instances have even turned off street lighting for lack of funds. Imagine what mayhem would follow if such draconian budget-cutting policies were to come to the large cities with already restive populations. This is plutocracy politics at its worst.

The politics of protecting the already-advantaged applies also in the field of inter-state relations. Countries that have survived the recent disruptions reasonably well on the basis of their trading export surpluses – Germany and China, in particular – fiercely resist any measures that may reduce their competitive advantage. They continue to suck in wealth at the expense of consumerism in the rest of the world. The failure of the G-20 to come up with any coordinated global response to the current malaise is almost entirely due to differences over appropriate trade deficits and surpluses, currency rates and the like. Angela Merkel of Germany promotes the politics of austerity rather than of stimulus as a universal principle because it helps protect Germany's export advantage. Her finance minister called a recent US Federal Reserve attempt to stimulate economic activity and diminish unemployment 'clueless.' Both the Germans and the Republicans in the US want the US economy to stay in the doldrums until the next election. Our first priority, says Mitch McConnell, the Republican leader in the US Senate, is to ensure that Obama is not re-elected. The best way to do that was to pursue a ruthless politics of austerity that hinders economic revival in the name of fiscal rectitude. But the Party of Wall Street, having won its battle to preserve tax cuts for the most affluent, then came to its senses. It decided that two years of total austerity was too much to take. It persuaded an electorally victorious Republican Party to fund some broad deficit-financed stimulus measures in the hope of keeping the revival of corporate profits on track.

The austerity mantra is not, however, accepted and practised everywhere. The world is bifurcated between deficit paranoia in North America and Europe and a Keynesian expansionism in east Asia, led by China. There the politics are very different and the outcomes even more strikingly so. The rate of recovery of the China-centered universe, along with those of India and Latin America, has been remarkable. Neither past-president Ignacio Lula in Brazil nor President Christina Kirchner in Argentina, and certainly not President Hu-Jintao of China, talk austerity, though the last of these is perfectly happy to encourage the United States in its suicidal policies as a matter of simple real geopolitik.

Possessed of huge surpluses and an untroubled banking system easily manipulated by central government, China had the means to act in a more full-blooded Keynesian way. The crash of export-oriented industries and the threat of mass unemployment (remember the 3 million net loss of jobs) and unrest in early 2009 forced the government's hand. The stimulus package devised had two forks. Close to $600 billion were put largely into infrastructural projects – highway building on a scale that dwarfs that of the US interstate highway system of the 1960s, new airports, vast water projects, high-speed rail lines and even whole new cities. Secondly, the central government forced the banks (defying the central government is not an option for Chinese bankers) to loosen credit for local state and private projects.

The big question is whether these investments will increase national productivity. Given that the spatial integration of the Chinese economy (the interior in relation to the coastal regions in particular) is far from complete, there are reasons to believe it may do so. But whether the debts can be paid off when due or whether China will become the epicentre of yet another global crash is an open question. Negative effects include rising inflation (a frequent Achilles heel in the administration of Keynesian policies) and rising speculation in asset markets such as housing, with a doubling of property prices in Shanghai in 2009 and a national increase in property values of more than 10 per cent in that same year. There are other troubling signs of overcapacity in manufacturing and infrastructures – a whole city has even been built in central China that has yet to receive any residents – and many banks are rumoured to be overextended. The newly built cities in the interior of China are desperately seeking foreign investors, judging by the glossy ads in the US press designed to entice them to this new utopian frontier for international capitalism (with shades of the troubled history of Dubai World, where spectacular over-extension in real estate development ended in bankruptcy).

271

There is also evidence of the emergence of an unregulated 'shadow banking system', of over-the-counter trading in assets and loans, that is repeating some of the mistakes that occurred in the US banking system from the 1990s on. But the Chinese have dealt with non-performing loans before, as high as 40 per cent of assets in the late 1990s. They then used their foreign exchange reserves to erase them. Unlike with the Troubled Asset Relief Program in the US, which was passed by a reluctant Congress in 2008 under President Bush and which has since provoked much public resentment, the Chinese government can take immediate action to re-capitalise their banking system. Whether or not they can crack down on and control shadow banking behaviours appears to be a more open question. Worries about inflation seem to have escalated rapidly in recent months. Serious attempts, seem to be in train, such as curbing bank lending, to bring growth down below 10 per cent in order to tame inflation. Such policies of restraint send predictable shivers through global stock markets.

The Chinese eventually embraced other aspects of a Keynesian programme: the stimulation of the internal market by increasing the empowerment of labour and addressing social inequality. The central government suddenly became willing to tolerate (or unable to resist) spontaneous strikes not organised by the official unions controlled by the Communist Party, such as those at major producers like Toyota, Honda and FoxConn (where a spate of worker suicides created a scandal about wages and working conditions) in the early summer of 2010. These strikes resulted in significant wage increases (in the range of 20 or 30 per cent or so). The politics of wage repression were being reversed, though after inflation the gains were not so impressive. But as wages rise in China so capital is moving off shore to lower-wage locations in Bangladesh, Cambodia and other parts of south-east Asia.

The government increased investments in health care and social services (increasing the social wage) and has pushed hard on the development of environmental technologies to the point where

China is now a global leader. The fear of being called socialist or communist, which so bedevils political action in the United States, sounds comical to the Chinese. The American mantra that only private entrepreneurialism can be economically successful sounds hollow if not ridiculous when put up against the phenomenal state-managed growth in China, as well as in Singapore, Taiwan and South Korea.

China has clearly emerged from the crisis faster and more success-fully than anywhere else. The increase in internal effective demand has not only worked within China but has also entrained other economies, particularly those of its neighbours (from Singapore to South Korea) and raw material producers (Australia, for example). General Motors makes more cars and profits in China than anywhere else. China managed to stimulate a partial revival in international trade and demand for its own export goods. The export-oriented economies in general, particularly throughout much of east and south-east Asia as well as Latin America, have revived faster than others. China's investments in US debt have helped sustain effective demand for its low-cost products there, although there are signs that it is gradually diversifying its holdings. The effect has been to produce the beginnings of a hegemonic shift in economic power from West to East within the global economy. While obviously still a major player, the United States cannot, as became clear at the G20 meeting in Seoul in November 2010 at which Obama was shown to be isolated and relatively powerless, call the shots any more.

The Chinese thirst for raw materials has not only moved the terms of trade in favour of raw material producers (before 1990 these terms were generally negative) but it also underpins an intensify-ing long-term competition between states, corporations and wealthy individuals for control over land, natural resources and other crucial sources of rental income (such as intellectual property rights). The politics of dispossession that attach to what amounts to a vast global land grab engulfing much of the African continent as well as Latin America, central Asia and what remains of the empty regions of south-east Asia, has unquestionably been led by the Chinese as newcomers to this traditional scene of great power and corporate competition. But even internally within states, the dispossession of whole populations, as has been occurring in the mineral-rich regions of central and north-east India, has been proceeding apace in the face of fierce resistance from indigenous peoples. There are, it seems, many interests who are intent on securing treasure-laden arks to protect themselves against the threat of some future economic collapse.

The revival of the export-oriented economies has, interestingly, extended to Germany. But this brings us to the problem of the fractious responses to the crisis across the European Union. After an initial burst of stimulus politics, Germany took the lead, dragging a more reluctant France along with it, in directing the Eurozone towards a monetary policy of deficit reduction out of fear of sparking inflation. This policy is now echoed by the new Conservative-led coalition in Britain. The move coincided with a sudden deterioration in public finances elsewhere. The so-called PIGS (Portugal, Ireland, Greece and Spain) found themselves in dire financial straits, in part through their own mismanagement but even more significantly because their economies were particularly vulnerable to the credit collapse and the sudden decline in property markets and tourism (much of it financed by speculative northern European capital). Lacking the industrial base of countries like Germany, they could not respond adequately to the fiscal crisis that threatened to engulf them.

There is, evidently, a grand divide in political strategy emerging. Much of the West is pursuing the holy grail of deficit reduction (resulting in reductions in standards of living) through austerity, while the East, along with the emerging markets of the South, follows an expansionary Keynesian strategy. If global growth is to revive, then it will be because the Eastern path of Keynesian stimulus prevails.

But therein lies a problem. As I argue in this book, a minimum of 3 per cent compound growth for ever, which is both empirically and conventionally accepted as necessary to the satisfactory functioning of capitalism, is becoming less and less sustainable. We can draw little comfort from the way China is covering itself with highways and automobiles and engaging in suburbanisation and new city building at breakneck speed, or spreading its influence far and wide by participating in a vast global land grab for resources throughout Africa in particular, but also anywhere else it can find a foothold, such as Latin America. The environmental consequences of China's rise are huge, but not only in China. Rapidly rising Chinese demand for oil, coal, cement, soy beans and the like are transforming much of Africa, Latin America and central Asia along with countries like Australia into satellite producers without regard for land degradation and resource exhaustion. In this, of course, the east Asians are merely following in the footsteps of the West's troubled and often barbaric pathway to affluence and power. But if we did it that way, who are we to say they should cease and desist, particularly when we show so little willingness to curb our own lifestyles to respond to environmental concerns?

The purpose of Keynesian stimulus programmes is not to operate permanently but to cover over short-term recessions in order to recoup on the deficits when conditions improve. The problem back in the 1960s was that it was too politically difficult to recoup, or to recognise, as William McChesney Martin, one-time chairman of the Federal Reserve once put it, that the job of political power is 'to take away the punch bowl just when the party gets going'. And we are now suffering from Alan Greenspan, the supposedly Delphic chairman of the Federal Reserve during the halcyon years of the 1990s and early 2000s, having failed to do just that. Whether or not the Chinese can take away the punch bowl at the right moment is an open question.

It has long been evident to dispassionate observers that individual capitalists operating in their own self-interest are prone to behave in such a way as to collectively drive capitalism deeper into crisis. The same can be said of the various factional interests that periodically dominate political and economic power: the bonus-hungry bankers and financiers who now set so much of the agenda in Washington and London; the resurgent class of rentiers who extract rents not only from control over land, property and resources but also increasingly from intellectual property rights; and the merchant capitalists, like Wal-Mart and Ikea, who tightly bind producers to their scheduling and order books such that producers become mere pawns in their competitive games. Individuals and factions pursuing their own particular interests have almost always signally failed to produce a cogent and coherent political agenda to stabilise, let alone revive, an ailing capitalist system. The signs are everywhere in evidence, that this is so this time around. How else is it possible to explain the vast financial support given by the wealthiest individuals and powerful factions in finance and the media to the incoherent politics of the Tea Party movement in the United States?

Even more troublesome is inter-state competition for wealth and power, as well as competitive power-bloc formation, if only because states still claim – and to some degree maintain either individually or collectively (through alliances such as NATO) – a certain monopoly over the means of violence. The political-military world all too frequently magnifies rather than assuages the inner contradictions of capital accumulation to the detriment of all but the wealthiest and the most powerful. Such dangers have long been well understood. As the British political philosopher William Thompson noted in 1824: 'In comparison to the preservation of this actual distribution (of wealth), the ever recurring misery or happiness of the whole human race has been considered as unworthy of regard. To perpetuate the results of force, fraud and chance, has been called security; and to the support of this spurious security, have all the productive powers of the human race been unrelentingly sacrificed.' This is precisely what the spurious security of austerity as well as the spurious security of endless compound growth deliver.

What has held back such an incoherent capitalist politics in the past has been a vast panoply of struggles of the exploited and the dispossessed, of workers against capitalists, of citizens against rentiers and predatory merchants, of whole populations against the often violent extractions of colonialism and imperialism, along with vaguer but no less influential struggles for justice, rights and a more ethical and democratic social order. Over the last forty years the organised institutional frameworks of such resistance to capital's uncivilising mission have been shattered, leaving behind a strange mix of old and new institutions of the sort I described in the last chapter of *Enigma*, which have difficulty articulating a cohesive opposition or a coherent alternative programme. This is a situation that bodes just as ill for capital as it does for the people. It leads to a politics of *après moi le deluge*, in which the rich fantasise that they can float safely off in their well-armed and well-provisioned arks (is this what the global land grab signifies?) leaving the rest of us to cope with the deluge. But the rich cannot ever hope to float above the world that capital has made because there is now literally no place to hide.

It remains to be seen if another set of institutions can be sutured together in our times to save capital from itself and prevent the outcome that Thompson depicted. But even if such a politics and associated institutions can be created, they will not only have to look very different from those of the past. They will need to do far more than struggle to bring a more civilised capitalism into being. The quixotic quest to construct a capitalism that might be ethical and just will have to be abandoned. At the end of the day it matters not one wit, as Adam Smith pointed out in acknowledging the power of the market's hidden hand to regulate human behaviours, whether we are well-intentioned and ethically inclined or self-indulgently greedy and competitively destructive. The logic of endless capital accumulation and of endless growth is always with us. It internalises hidden imperatives, of which the invisible hand of the market is but one, to which we either willingly or mindlessly submit, no matter our ethical inclinations. This is the dominant praxis, with all its subtly implanted political subjectivities, against which we must constructively rebel if we are to change our world in any fundamental way. The problem of endless compound growth through endless capital accumulation will have to be confronted and overcome. That is the political necessity of our times.

From this long-run perspective, the drive to re-animate capitalist growth in east and south Asia as well as in other regions such as the wealthy Gulf States, by constructing an exaggerated version of the American ('drive to stay alive and shop until you drop') lifestyle is profoundly in error. The global land grab going on right now is surely evidence of this error in the making. And while it may seem perversely appropriate, in the light of long-run imperatives, to condemn North America and Europe to slow growth and endless austerity, this is only done in the name of defending the privileges of a plutocracy and goes nowhere when it come to substituting the endless possibilities for the development of human capacities and powers for the impossibility of endless compound growth. The short-run burst of capitalist growth in emerging market economies, from east and south Asia to Latin America, may help to re-equilibrate the global distribution of wealth and power and thereby create a healthier and more egalitarian basis for the achievement of a more rationally organised global economy. The short-run revival of growth, as opposed to proliferating distress, can also buy time for longer-term solutions to the transition to be worked out. But bought time is only useful if it is put to good use.

An alternative will have to be found. And it is here that the emergence of a global co-revolutionary movement becomes critical not only to stemming the tide of self-destructive capitalistic behaviours (which in itself would be a significant achievement) but also to our reorganising ourselves and beginning to build new collective organisational forms, knowledge banks and mental conceptions, new technologies and systems of production and consumption, all the while experimenting with new institutional arrangements, new forms of social and natural relations, and with the redesign of an increasingly urbanised daily life.

While capital has provided us with an abundance of means with which to approach the task of anti-capitalist transition, the capitalists and their hangers-on will do all in their power to prevent such a transition no matter how imperative the circumstances may be. But the task of transition lies with us, not with the plutocrats. As Shakespeare once advised: 'The fault ... is not in our stars, but in ourselves that we are underlings.' Right now, as Warren Buffett asserts, his class is winning. Our immediate task is to prove him wrong.

David Harvey
New York, January 2011

Appendix 1: Major Debt Crises and Bail-outs, 1973–2009

1973–75 *Property market crash in US and UK, fiscal crises of federal, state and local governments in the US (New York City's near bankruptcy), oil price hike and recession*

1979–82 *Inflationary surge and Volcker interest rate shock forces Reagan Recession, with unemployment rising above 10 per cent in the US and knock-on effects elsewhere*

1982–90 *Developing Countries Debt Crisis (Mexico, Brazil, Chile, Argentina, Poland, etc.) sparked by 'Volcker shock' of high interest rates. US investment bankers rescued by aid to indebted countries organised by the US Treasury and a revitalised IMF (purged of Keynesians and armed with 'structural adjustment' programmes)*

1984 *Continental Illinois Bank rescued by Fed, Treasury and FDIC*

1984–92 *Failures of US savings and loan institutions investing in real estate. Closure and FDIC rescue of 3,260 financial institutions. Recession in UK property market after 1987*

1987 *Hurricane in stock markets, October 1987, met with massive liquidity injections by the Fed and Bank of England*

1990–92 *Property market-led Nordic and Japanese bank crises. Bail-outs of City Bank and Bank of New England in the US*

1994–95 *Mexican peso rescue to protect US investors holding high-risk Mexican debt. Heavy losses in derivatives culminating in Orange County bankruptcy and serious losses for other municipal governments with similar high-risk investments*

1997–98 *Asian Currency Crisis (partly property based). Lack of liquidity forces massive bankruptcies and unemployment, providing opportunities for predatory institutions to make quick profits after punitive IMF bail-outs (South Korea, Indonesia, Thailand, etc.)*

1998 *Long Term Capital Management bail-out by the Fed in the US*

1998–2001 *Capital flight crises from Russia (which goes bankrupt in 1998), Brazil (1999), culminating in Argentina Debt Crisis (2000–2002), devaluation of peso, followed by mass unemployment and political unrest*

2001–02 *Dot-com bubble and stock market crashes, Enron and WorldCom bankruptcies. Fed cuts interest rates to prop up asset values (real estate bubble begins)*

2007–10 *Property-led crises in the US, UK, Ireland and Spain, followed by forced mergers, bankruptcies and nationalisations of financial institutions. Bail-outs worldwide of institutions that invested in CDOs, hedge funds, etc., followed by recession, unemployment and collapses in foreign trade met by various Keynesian-style stimulus packages and liquidity injections by central banks*

Appendix 2: Financial Innovations and the Rise of Derivative Markets in the US, 1973–2009

1970   *Mortgage-backed securities introduced*

1972   *Chicago Currency Futures Market opens*

1973   *Chicago Board Options Exchange; trading in equity futures begins*

1975   *Trading in Treasury Bill and mortgage-backed bonds futures*

1977   *Trading in Treasury bond futures*

1979   *Over-the-counter and unregulated trading, particularly in currency futures, becomes commonplace. The 'shadow banking system' emerges*

1980   *Currency swaps*

1981   *Portfolio insurance introduced; interest rate swaps; futures markets in Eurodollars, in Certificates of Deposit and in Treasury instruments*

1983   *Options markets on currency, equity values and Treasury instruments; collateralised mortgage obligation introduced*

1985   *Deepening and widening of options and futures markets; computerised trading and modelling of markets begins in earnest; statistical arbitrage strategies introduced*

1986   *Big Bang unification of global stock, options and currency trading markets*

1987–8   *Collateralised Debt Obligations (CDOs) introduced along with Collateralised Bond Obligations (CBOs) and Collateralised Mortgage Obligations (CMOs)*

1989   *Futures on interest rate swaps*

1990   *Credit default swaps introduced along with equity index swaps*

1991   *'Off balance sheet' vehicles known as special purpose entities or special investment vehicles sanctioned*

1992–2009   *Rapid evolution in volume of trading across all of these instruments. Volume of trading, insignificant in 1990, rose to more then $600 trillion annually by 2008*

Sources and Further Reading

I relied on news reports for much of the detailed information I cite throughout the text. *The New York Times*, supplemented by the *Guardian* and the *Financial Times*, were the primary sources. I also relied on other accounts of the crisis, particularly those written before the breakdown in the summer of 2008, for both theoretical insights and structural understandings. The idea of an alliance between the discontented and the dispossessed comes from Peter Marcuse and I am grateful to him for the formulation. I also want to thank Margit Mayer and the participants in my graduate seminars at the Graduate Center, City University of New York, and the Freie Universität in Berlin who commented on some early drafts of the text.

I found the following works particularly helpful as both theoretical guides and as sources for detailed information:

Arrighi, G., 1994, *The Long Twentieth Century: Money, Power, and the Origins of Our Times*, London and New York, Verso.

Arrighi, G. and Silver, B., 1999, *Chaos and Governance in the Modern World System*, Minneapolis, University of Minnesota Press.

Bellamy Foster, J. and Magdoff, F., 2009, *The Great Financial Crisis: Causes and Consequences*, New York, Monthly Review Press.

Bookstaber, R., 2007, *A Demon of Our Own Design: Markets, Hedge Funds, and the Perils of Financial Innovation*, Hoboken, NJ, John Wiley.

Brenner, R., 2002, *The Boom and the Bubble: The US in the World Economy*, New York, Verso.

Cohan, W., 2007, *The Last Tycoons: The Secret History of Lazard Frères & Co.*, New York, Doubleday.

Dicken, P., 2007, *Global Shift: Reshaping the Global Economic Map in the 21st Century*, fifth edition, New York, The Guilford Press. It is worth looking over the earlier editions, beginning in 1986, to get a sense of the immense geographical shifts that have occurred in the global economy over the past couple of decades.

Duménil, G. and Lévy, D., trans. D. Jeffers, 2004, *Capital Resurgent: Roots of the Neoliberal Revolution*, Cambridge, MA, Harvard University Press.

Eichengreen, B., Yung Chul Park and Wyplosz, C. (eds.), 2008, *China, Asia and the New World Economy*, Oxford and New York, Oxford University Press.

Galbraith, J. K., 2008, *The Predator State: How Conservatives Abandoned the Free Market and Why Liberals Should Too*, New York, Free Press.

Galbraith, J. K., 1975, *Money: Whence it Came, Where it Went*, Boston, Houghton.

Galbraith, J. K., 1993, *A Short History of Financial Euphoria*, Knoxville, TN, Whittle Direct Books.

Gautney, H., 2009, *Protest and Organization in the Alternative Globalization Era: NGOs, Social Movements, and Political Parties*, New York, Palgrave Macmillan.

Greider, W., 1989, *Secrets of the Temple: How the Federal Reserve Runs the Country*, New York, Simon and Schuster.

Harvey, D., 2005, *A Brief History of Neoliberalism*, Oxford, Oxford University Press.

Harvey, D., 2007 edition, *The Limits to Capital*, London, Verso.

Helleiner, E., 1994, *States and the Reemergence of Global Finance: From Bretton Woods to the 1990s*, Ithaca, NY, Cornell University Press.

Klein, N., 2007, *The Shock Doctrine: The Rise of Disaster Capitalism*, New York, Metropolitan Books.

Maddison, A., 1982, *Phases of Capitalist Development*, Oxford, Oxford University Press.

Maddison, A., 2007, *Contours of the World Economy, 1–2030 AD: Essays in Macro-Economic History*, Oxford, Oxford University Press.

Mertes, T. (ed.), 2004, *A Movement of Movements: Is Another World Really Possible?*, London, Verso.

Milanovic, B., 2005, *Worlds Apart: Measuring International and Global Inequality*, Princeton, NJ, Princeton University Press.

Panitch, L. and Konings, M. (eds.), 2008, *American Empire and the Political Economy of Global Finance*, New York, Palgrave Macmillan.

Partnoy, F., 2003, *Infectious Greed: How Deceit and Risk Corrupted Financial Markets*, New York, Henry Holt.

Peet, R. and Watts, M. (eds.), 2004 edition, *Liberation Ecologies*, New York, Routledge.

Phillips, K., 2006, *American Theocracy: The Peril and Politics of Radical Religion, Oil and Borrowed Money in the 21st Century*, New York, Viking.

Phillips, K., 2009, *Bad Money: Reckless Finance, Failed Politics, and the Global Crisis of American Capitalism*, New York, Viking.

Pollin, R., 2003, *Contours of Descent: US Economic Fractures and the Landscape of Global Austerity*, London, Verso.

Porter, P., Sheppard, E. et al., 2009 2nd edition, *A World of Difference: Encountering and Contesting Development*, New York, The Guilford Press.

Santos, B. de Sousa, 2006, *The Rise of Global Left: The World Social Forum and Beyond*, London, Zed Books.

Santos, B. de Sousa (ed.), 2006, *Another Production is Possible: Beyond the Capitalist Canon*, London, Verso.

Silver, B., 2003, *Forces of Labor: Workers' Movements and Globalization since 1870*, Cambridge, Cambridge University Press.

Smith, N., 2008 3rd edition, *Uneven Development: Nature, Capital, and the Production of Space*, Athens, GA, University of Georgia Press.

Turner, G., 2008, *The Credit Crunch: Housing Bubbles, Globalisation and the Worldwide Economic Crisis,* London, Pluto.

United Nations Development Program, 1989–2009, *Human Development Report* (annual issues), New York, Palgrave Macmillan.

Walker, R. and Storper, M., 1989, *The Capitalist Imperative: Territory, Technology and Industrial Growth,* Oxford, Wiley–Blackwell.

Wang Hui, 2003, *China's New Order: Society, Politics and Economy in Transition,* Cambridge, MA, Harvard University Press.

Wolf, M., 2008, *Fixing Global Finance,* Baltimore, MD, Johns Hopkins University Press.

Wolf, R., 2009, *Capitalism Hits the Fan: The Global Economic Meltdown and What to Do about It,* New York, Olive Branch Press.

The Worldwatch Institute, *State of the World 2009,* New York, Norton. (Previous twenty-five years of reports are interesting to compare.)

Useful websites

Tomas Piketty and Emmanuel Saez on shifting income and wealth inequality in the United States: http://elsa.berkeley.edu/~saez/

Realtytrac compiles local and national US data on the foreclosures: http://www.realtytrac.com

The Mortgage Bankers Association keeps tabs on US delinquencies and mortgage applications: www.mbaa.org/

For David Harvey on Marx's *Capital* and the urban origins of the crisis: http://DavidHarvey.org

International Monetary Fund global reports and data: http://www. imf.org

Bank of International Settlements working papers and reports, particularly on the differential geographical impact of the crisis: http://www.bis.org

World Bank comparable global data and reports: http://worldbank.
org/

Asian Development Bank is a mine of information and reports on
what is happening in the region: http://www.adb.org/Economics/

Brad DeLong's website, which while far from being as fair and
balanced as he claims, offers a lively debate from a conventional
economist's perspective on the crisis: http://delong.typepad.com/
main/

The New York Times article archive: http://www.nytimes.com/ref/
membercenter/nytarchive.html

Le Monde Diplomatique offers global coverage of what the
alternative globalisation movement is up to, along with critical
discussions of a wide range of social, political, environmental
and economic issues: http://www.monde.diplomatique.fr/

The Socialist Register over the years has thematically explored
many of the topics taken up here. The archive can be accessed
through http://socialistregister.com/index.php/srv/issue/archive

The *Monthly Review* keeps a lively flow of critical commentary
and contemporary information going. See http://www.
monthlyreview.org/mrzine/

The materials on Japanese land prices are adapted from G. Turner,
2008, *The Credit Crunch: Housing Bubbles, Globalisation and the
Worldwide Economic Crisis*, London, Pluto Press. The data on page
27 on growth of GDP: The World and Major Regions come from
A. Maddison, 2007, *Contours of the World Economy, 1–2030 AD:
Essays in Macro-Economic History*, Oxford, Oxford University Press.

Index